SATISFIED
by the
PROMISE
of the
SPIRIT

Books by Thomas R. Edgar
Miraculous Gifts
Satisfied by the Promise of the Spirit

SATISFIED *by the* PROMISE *of the* SPIRIT

*Affirming the Fullness of God's
Provision for Spiritual Living*

THOMAS R. EDGAR

Grand Rapids, MI 49501

Satisfied by the Promise of the Spirit
Copyright © 1996 by Thomas R. Edgar

Published by Kregel Resources, an imprint of Kregel, Inc., P.O. Box 2607, Grand Rapids, MI 49501. Kregel Publications provides trusted, biblical publications for Christian growth and service. Your comments and suggestions are valued.

All rights reserved. No part of this book may be reproduced, stored in a retrieval system, or transmitted in any form or by any means—electronic, mechanical, photocopy, recording, or otherwise—without written permission of the publisher, except for brief quotations in printed reviews.

Cover and book design: Alan G. Hartman

Library of Congress Cataloging-in-Publication Data
Edgar, Thomas R., 1933–
   Satisfied by the promise of the Spirit / Thomas R. Edgar.
     p.   cm.
   Includes bibliographical references.
    1. Pentecostalism—Controversial literature.
2. Pentecostal churches—Controversial literature. 3. Gifts, Spiritual. 4. Evangelicalism. I. Title.
BR1644.E34   1996   234'.13—dc20   95-7815
                                                                                                CIP

ISBN 0-8254-2510-7

Printed in the United States of America
  2 3 4 5 / 00

*To my son, Thomas Anthony Edgar,
and
my father, Thomas Irwin Edgar*

Contents

Introduction	9
1. Experience or Scripture?	11
2. Scripture: For Validity or Mere Credibility?	22
3. Biblical Information Regarding Spiritual Gifts	35
4. Edifying Gifts: Apostle and Prophet	52
5. The Gift of Miracles and the Gift of Healing	89
6. Tongues: The Nature of the Gift	120
7. Tongues: The Purpose for the Gift	165
8. The Gifts in History	201
9. Cessation of Gifts: Are Some Gifts Temporary?	231
10. Conclusion	250
Bibliography	265
Scripture Index	275
Subject Index	281

Introduction

THIS BOOK IS WRITTEN in order to discuss whether certain of today's spiritual gifts are identical to those in the Bible. Therefore, the Bible, and especially the New Testament, is the authoritative source for a study of the phenomena in the apostolic church that the New Testament authors describe as healing, miracles, and speaking in tongues. Most charismatic adherents have assumed that today's phenomena are the same as the New Testament gifts. Others who are not specifically interested in the Bible but are interested in studying these phenomena, particularly tongues, have also assumed this position. If they are not the same, then we have on the present scene a phenomenon of significance in several fields, in which a group by mistaken identification with biblical concepts has encouraged practices that they would not otherwise promote.

While many people of various persuasions promote the charismatic movement, many people disagree with its claims. Many pastors and laypersons, as well as theological students, are perplexed when confronted with all of its publicity and discussion. Often they do not agree with the charismatic movement, yet they are uncertain as to how to respond to it. While many Christians are not involved in the present charismatic movement and are not interested in personally experiencing the phenomena associated with the movement, they are nevertheless interested in the subject of spiritual gifts and their place in the Christian life.

As Christians we need to understand all spiritual gifts, for we believe that they are all God-given. In this book we will narrow our definition of "miraculous" by using it to refer to those gifts that are overtly miraculous and cannot be duplicated by human effort. We include among these the gifts of apostle, prophet, miracles, healings, and speaking in tongues. Such gifts are connected either with the performance of miracles or with a more overt function of the Holy Spirit.

The basic issue and disagreement today is in regard to these specific gifts. The consideration of these gifts gives rise to numerous questions, questions that need answers. Consequently, we will direct our attention toward resolving such questions.

Sound, Bible-teaching churches have always offered teaching regarding the proper use of spiritual gifts. Given the present emphasis today upon these miraculous gifts by various charismatic groups, we need to examine the questions raised by such practices and provide answers to these queries. The express purpose of this work, therefore, is to look for as many biblical answers as possible to the many questions about these miraculous gifts.

✶ ✶ ✶

Biblical quotations are, in most cases, my own translation; otherwise they are from the *King James Version* of the Bible (KJV). In some instances, the KJV is modified for clarity.

CHAPTER 1

Experience or Scripture?

CHRISTIANS OFTEN WONDER, How can I live the Christian life to its fullest? Every person who believes in Jesus Christ has their sins forgiven and is immediately justified. The Holy Spirit indwells every believer immediately upon salvation. Every believer has access to God in prayer and has other believers available for fellowship, edification, and counsel. Every Christian has all of this immediately upon justification. Is my justification sufficient so that by faith, with the Scriptures and its promises to guide me and motivate me, I can live the Christian life as God intended? Can I be satisfied with that which God has provided for me in Christ?

For many the answer is, No. A large number of Christians, called "charismatics," say that we need more. What all believers received when they believed in Jesus Christ is not enough. Every believer needs more in the sense of supernatural evidence, including miracles, healings, exorcisms, and power. They look for personal, self-oriented miracles as evidence of God's presence and power. The desire for these miracles is caused by a basic lack of satisfaction with a life of faith. This sense of lack is a consistent testimony from those who turn to the charismatic position. For example, John Wimber was not satisfied with the results of his ministry and sought more "power."[1] Jack Deere was not satisfied and longed for more "passion for God."[2] For these believers the answer to their need is not found in Scripture but in the overt, visible evidence of God's presence. This outlook regards the miracles of the New Testament as being valuable evidence for that time, but today more is needed. The idea that the New Testament age was unique and provided the historical and evidential foundation for the church is neglected. Instead, the stress among charismatics today is on miraculous experiences, experiences that serve mainly to confirm and strengthen the individual believer and to make one's ministry effective. Such experiences primarily meet the individual believer's personal needs.

Accordingly, we must ask the question, Has God provided all that we need in Christ or is Christ's work lacking? Is Christ's work effectively limited to the area of salvation, and now the Spirit must provide ongoing evidence for the believer's spiritual life? Only Scripture can provide answers to these questions.

Background

The charismatic elements of the church have come a long way since 1901 when modern-day "speaking in tongues" occurred at Parham's Bethel Bible School in Topeka, Kansas. Although the "tongues movement" did not gain momentum until it was coupled with belief in divine healing, it gradually grew into a significant movement within the church. This group known as Pentecostals kept themselves separate from the mainline denominations and traditional evangelical groups. To qualify as a Pentecostal, a person not only has to believe many of the orthodox Christian doctrines, but also in a postconversion "baptism of the Spirit," evidenced by speaking in tongues, and in divine healing.[3] The various groups differed in many specific practices and doctrines. Due to its strong emphasis on speaking in tongues, this movement is often described as the tongues movement. In general, they believe that all of the spiritual gifts described in the book of Acts, including the overtly miraculous gifts, should be operative in the church today. Their basic opinion is that the church today should experience miracles and healings and tongues; that is, all of the power of the church in Acts.

Although tongues received great stress, in some cases healing was the primary emphasis. This occurred in the "deliverance" ministries of healing revivalists like Oral Roberts and Kathryn Kuhlman. Pentecostals often believe that the doctrine of the atonement includes healing; that is, Christ's sacrifice healed us physically as well as spiritually. Thus we are healed, and any sickness is directly due to sin. Many of these groups believe that the gifts of the apostolic age continued but were squelched by the organized church due to a lack of belief in the miraculous. Others hold to a "latter-day rain" theory; that is, the gifts stopped until the end times and are now recurring in order to prepare for the Lord's coming. Although large in number, this "first wave" of the charismatic movement did not make a great impact on the traditional church. The traditional Protestant church believed that the overtly miraculous gifts and events described in the book of Acts were basically limited to the apostolic period. Although the edifying gifts, such as teacher and evangelist, continued, the more miraculous gifts, such as miracles, healing, tongues, prophecy, and apostle, ceased with the apostolic age.

In 1960 the Pentecostal movement began to expand into mainline denominations. Dennis Bennett, who introduced these practices into the Episcopal church, is usually credited with beginning this "second wave," or neo-Pentecostal movement. It has now spread and penetrated most of the mainline denominations and many more independent groups. Since this movement now includes both Pentecostals and neo-Pentecostals, this second wave is referred to more broadly as the "charismatic movement." Even though some Pentecostals are not in agreement with the neo-Pentecostals, both groups embrace the belief that the gifts and power demonstrated in the book of Acts are available today and should be in effect today. In contrast to this are those people who hold to the more traditional belief that the overtly miraculous gifts described in the New Testament ceased during the first century and are no longer available today. People who believe this are often referred to as "cessationists."

The success of this movement of charismatic or Pentecostal ideas into non-Pentecostal churches has resulted in a continuing worldwide expansion of charismatic ideas and practices. A wide range of practices has been the result, including the "Word of Faith" movement of Kenneth Copeland and Kenneth Hagin, whose teachings promise not only physical healing but material prosperity. Movements such as "shepherding" and a variety of "restoration" groups have developed, some of which have serious doctrinal aberrations. Although they continue Pentecostal practices, they increasingly stress practices such as healing, miracles, exorcisms, revelations, and visions. Much stress is placed upon the sensational and the concept of "power for service."

Another recent movement, often referred to as the "signs and wonders" movement, is sometimes called the "third wave" of Pentecostalism. Often identified with John Wimber's Vineyard Fellowship, this is apparently only part of the group. C. Peter Wagner of Fuller Seminary and Wimber are two of the most prominent representatives. Sarles describes it as "a blending of evangelical commitments and charismatic practices. Those associated with this recent trend affirm the continuation of all the miraculous gifts mentioned in the New Testament...."[4] They believe that *all* Christians should experience this power. Believers need this power to live spiritual lives.[5]

Although they do not like to be classified as charismatic, without question they belong under this label. They are not necessarily Pentecostal, unless they stress postconversion "baptism of the Spirit" and tongues speaking as its initial evidence, but they definitely believe that the full range of the charismatic gifts is available and should be sought today. Accordingly, they oppose the cessationist's position. Many of those involved in this movement are evangelicals who have avoided doctrinal aberrations, particularly those affecting the doctrines of the Trinity and the person of Christ. Hopefully this will continue.

The basic difference between those in the signs and wonders camp and the traditional evangelical groups concerns the issue of the miraculous gifts. The controversy concerns cessationist versus noncessationist (i.e., charismatic) viewpoints on the availability of the gifts today. The entire charismatic movement has become established on the basis of its claim that the experiences of charismatics today are the same experiences and the same gifts as evidenced by the apostles and the early church, particularly as described in the book of Acts.[6] This claim garnered them credence and acceptance in the church at large. Admittedly, the charismatic movement includes a large number of persons from different theological perspectives. As Lederle states, "The largest contingent of charismatic theologians comes from the Roman Catholic Church," and "Roman Catholic scholars have led the way."[7] While Lederle regards "Spirit baptism" as the central experience for charismatics,[8] this is not the main issue between traditional evangelicals and evangelicals who are charismatic. For them the issue is cessationism or noncessationism.

The Charismatic Movement: Experience-Oriented Christianity

Due to his background and training, Jack Deere has become one of the main apologists within the evangelical camp for the "signs and wonders" movement and thus, in effect, for the entire charismatic movement. He has recently published a second book, which according to pre-publication advertising also promotes these concepts.⁹ Since Deere originally began from the noncharismatic or cessationist perspective (he graduated from and taught at Dallas Theological Seminary, a leading seminary in the cessationist camp), his testimony is seemingly a strong argument for the charismatic, "signs and wonders" view. The fact that he was a former Dallas Seminary professor is stressed on the cover and title page of his first book, as well as in the advertising. Since this school emphasizes the study of the biblical text, we would expect to see some new, particularly biblical, arguments in Deere's work. In actuality, he gives no new arguments but generally appeals to those commonly used. Although he does emphasize the idea of a category of gifts that are not on the same qualitative level as those of the apostles, a seemingly new idea, such a notion is actually implied in much charismatic thinking and has been previously expressed by other writers.¹⁰ This is the keystone to his entire argument.

Several scholars and others have stated that Deere's book must be read and must receive a response from cessationists, which suggests that his book is significant in presenting the charismatic perspective. Deere's arguments and perspective will give us a fairly accurate idea of the arguments commonly used by charismatics as well as the latest charismatic thinking on this issue. What Deere's basic arguments are will be presented and discussed before we discuss specific scriptural evidence.

Experience Is Central

Without question Deere's main argument is the same basic argument used by other charismatics, whether scholars or laypersons. That argument is that personal experience (which I interpret to be from the Holy Spirit) validates the charismatic's position and invalidates any arguments against it. This is not only my analysis of Deere's argument but that of others who critique it as well. For example, Mitchell, in a book review generally friendly to Deere, analyzes Deere's book with the following statements:

> . . . and his personal experiences punctuate each chapter. Indeed, there is almost a sense in which the book affirms that the power of the Spirit is real primarily because Deere experienced and saw it. He comes perilously close to using experience as a form of expanded translation of the biblical text.¹¹

Mitchell concludes with the statement that Deere "unfortunately leaves the reader with the impression that it is the religious experience itself that validates what he argues."[12] Mitchell may not realize that this is exactly what most charismatics, including Deere, are arguing.[13] The description of Deere's second book indicates that this is the same basic argument that he uses for prophecies, dreams, visions, and other revelations. Deere's book is highly touted because it presents the primary argument of all charismatic argumentation, whether by those academically trained or by laypersons with no theological training. It is the argument based on personal experience, namely, "It happened to me." For many charismatics it is their only argument.

In his book Deere relates that he graduated from Dallas Theological Seminary where he also taught for ten years. He also pastored a noncharismatic Bible church in Fort Worth, Texas, for seven years. Originally he believed that God did not give the miraculous gifts today and taught this idea dogmatically. He says that he believed this because that is what he was taught and because everyone in his circles accepted it as true. He makes it clear that although he was a professor and "loved to teach and preach the Word of God," he never made any attempt to verify the cessationist position from the Bible.[14] However, when a man named John White told him that he had actually seen miracles from God and described two of them, Deere's thinking began to change on the basis of this testimony. After seeing a few unusual incidents he became convinced they were miracles from God. He then studied the Scripture from this perspective to see if the Bible allowed for this. Deere states that after an intensive study of Scripture he came to the conclusion that the Bible did not support a cessationist view but rather the noncessationist, charismatic view. Now he teaches that anyone who will believe in the gifts and seek them will also have the same experience. He insists that the only reason anyone is a cessationist is because they have not had this experience.[15] While this is an argument from experience as it occurred in the life of one man, it is the same basic argument used by charismatics worldwide: "It happened to me!"

Is Scripture a Servant to Experience?

The place of Scripture as an authority or control also reveals the experience-centered nature of charismatic thinking. The issue seems to be whether our experience is interpreted and controlled by Scripture, or whether Scripture is interpreted in the light of our experience.

Although Deere declares that his position was based on "a patient and intense study of the Scriptures," his own testimony shows the opposite. On the basis of one telephone conversation with John White, Deere reports,

> I was convinced that he was telling me the truth. I was convinced that God had healed the two people he talked about. But I was also still convinced that God was not giving the gifts of the Spirit any longer and that there must be another explanation for the healings.[16]

Notice that Deere was convinced that God had healed two people through John White's ministry. The fact that Deere was still not convinced regarding the validity of miraculous gifts is inconsequential, since he argues for them on the basis of such general experiences. He makes no consistent distinction between such occurrences and gifts.[17] Nor do most charismatics. Deere was convinced of the reality of his present position before he studied Scripture. He was convinced that these were miracles from God through a man, John White. Thus, his study was not so much to see if Scripture implied or promoted his position but if it allowed for or could be reconciled with that about which he was already convinced. From the beginning, experience rather than Scripture controlled his thinking. The place of Scripture in his thinking is disclosed in his statement that "I had also begun to believe that God could speak apart from the Scriptures, though never in contradiction to the Scriptures."[18]

Notice that he believes, as do most charismatics, that the Scripture is only one source of information; miraculous experiences, especially prophecies, visions, dreams, and words of knowledge also demonstrate the voice of God. The only control is that they must not contradict Scripture. This sounds reasonable. However, contradiction is a relative term. For many charismatics, contradiction is a very flexible idea. A revelation of the meaning of "not contradict" is indicated by Deere's approval of John White's argument that the frequent failure of healings in charismatic circles is not "contradictory" to the biblical evidence. This is so, White argues, because the Bible does not say that the apostles did not fail in some of their healings; therefore, the apostles could have failed, and this fact was simply not recorded in the Bible.[19] Thus the failure of charismatic healers today is not regarded as contrary to Scripture. In other words the "miraculous experiences" and "revelations" of the charismatics do not in their thinking contradict Scripture unless there is an explicit statement that they cannot be true. When we analyze charismatic interpretation of what appear to be explicit statements of Scripture contradictory to their view and their interaction with those biblical passages supporting cessationism, we realize that even explicitly contradictory statements can be interpreted with unlikely interpretation or simply ignored.[20] Scripture has only token control and is at the mercy of charismatic experience.

The centrality of experience rather than Scripture is obvious also in the fact that the charismatics come from almost every branch of the Christian spectrum, including many whose doctrine is not even evangelical. Hollenweger describes the worldwide Pentecostal movement as "a movement whose main characteristic is not verbal agreement but correspondence of sentiments."[21] This experience-oriented thinking is revealed in Kydd's highly regarded charismatic analysis of church history. He states in his preface that he tried very hard to compensate for his prejudices.[22] Kydd discusses evidence of spiritual gifts from "heresy and superstition" and refers to the Gnostics, a group about which Scripture issues warnings to Christians. Yet, due to their possible interest in prophecies, healings, and signs, Kydd believes that there are hints of a deep spirituality within these groups.[23] From the remainder of his discussion it seems clear that Kydd would not see any such hints in the normal or traditional church, since they apparently did not promote these items.

Experience-Oriented View Regarding Cessationism

Deere repeatedly asserts that the only real basis for the cessationists' position is their lack of experience. He states rather dogmatically, "There is one basic reason why Bible-believing Christians do not believe in the miraculous gifts of the Spirit today. It is simply this: *They have not seen them.*"[24] He repeats,

> Christians do not disbelieve in the miraculous gifts of the Spirit because the Scriptures teach these gifts have passed away. Rather they disbelieve in the miraculous gifts of the Spirit because they have not experienced them.[25]

According to this, the sole reason one is a charismatic or a cessationist is whether one has had the experience. Deere refuses to acknowledge even the possibility that one could experience these miracles and on the basis of Scripture still remain a cessationist. The evidence of the miracles is so overwhelming in his mind and the minds of other charismatics that no matter what someone believes the Scriptures say, they assert that if that person has the experience they will change their thinking and reinterpret Scripture in light of the experience. Despite numerous protestations to the contrary, Deere realizes that his position is based solely on experience. Otherwise he could not argue that solely on the basis of experience every believer will become charismatic and solely on the lack of experience people are cessationists.

Rejection of Cessationism Not Based on Scripture

Some charismatics, in contradiction to others, claim that their position is not experience-oriented but rather scripturally supported. Despite his previous statements, Deere states this very explicitly when he insists, "This shift in my thinking was not the result of an experience with any sort of supernatural phenomena. *It was the result of a patient and intense study of the Scriptures.*"[26] As White describes it,

> As for the relevance of Bible study in his pilgrimage from cessationism to noncessationism, Deere rarely misses an opportunity to remind his readers of the open-mindedness, patience and/or intensity with which he has studied the Bible's statements on the Spirit's work.[27]

Deere insists that the initial change in his thinking was the result of a careful, thorough study of Scripture. Further he maintains that he holds his present position on that same scriptural basis. Do the facts bear this out?

As late as 1990 Deere apparently admitted that he had not studied 1 Corinthians 13:10, Ephesians 2:20, or Hebrews 2:3-4, some of the most crucial passages in the debate.[28] This refutes his claim that his position is a result of careful study of Scripture. I agree completely with White's analysis,

> that Deere's discussion of key texts bearing on the duration of the gifts ... have a decidedly perfunctory and well worn quality about them. ... But if we ask him for the necessary details on the texts that ostensibly create the most obvious or serious problems for him ... he asks us to wait for his next book or else buries his ever-so-brief discussion of these texts in appendices and footnotes.[29]

The evidence gives the definite impression that Deere's position results not from the study of Scripture but rather from his experience. Thus we see that despite the fact that he is a theologian trained in the Scriptures, Deere's primary argument both for his change in thinking as well as his present position is the argument of personal experience. Lederle made it very clear that this is the foundation for the charismatic perspective when he said, "The charismatic renewal movement is unashamedly experiential in its nature. It is this 'experience' of Spirit-Baptism that usually takes people by surprise."[30]

Since experience is the primary argument of charismatics, it was necessary to demonstrate the centrality of it to the charismatic perspective. For many it is their only argument. In addition, it determines the approach of their theologians and laypersons to Scripture and their response to cessationist arguments.

※ ※ ※

1. Ken L. Sarles, "An Appraisal of the Signs and Wonders Movement," *Bibliotheca Sacra* (January–March 1988): 59–60.
2. Jack Deere, *Surprised by the Power of the Spirit* (Grand Rapids: Zondervan, 1993), 182–83
3. John Thomas Nichol, *Pentecostalism* (New York: Harper and Row, 1966), 8–17; Henry I. Lederle, *Treasures Old and New: Interpretations of "Spirit-Baptism" in the Charismatic Renewal Movement* (Peabody, Mass.: Hendrickson, 1988), 21–23; Gary B. McGee, ed., *Initial Evidence: Historical and Biblical Perspectives on the Pentecostal Doctrine of Spirit Baptism* (Peabody, Mass.: Hendrickson, 1991), 96–97.
4. Sarles, 57.
5. Tim Stafford, "Testing the Wine From John Wimber's Vineyard," *Christianity Today* 8 Aug. 1986, 17–18.
6. McGee, xiv–xv.
7. Lederle, xix, 37.
8. Ibid., 37.
9. Deere, *Surprised.*
10. See, e.g., Wayne Grudem, *The Gift of Prophecy in the New Testament and Today* (Westchester, Ill.: Crossway, 1988), 109–12.
11. Kurt Mitchell, "Dispensing with Scofield," *Christianity Today* 10 Jan. 1994, 57.
12. Ibid.
13. Lederle, 37. Also, consider George Mallone's statement, "What we were seeing in our own experience suggested that these gifts were

available today," in his *Those Controversial Gifts* (Downers Grove, Ill.: InterVarsity, 1983), 11.
14. Deere, 13–19.
15. Ibid., 55.
16. Ibid., 20.
17. This is not to say that Deere does not claim to make this distinction. His arguments reveal that he does not do so. Charismatics commonly tend to view all allegedly supernatural events as evidence for gifts. For an example of this, see Ronald A. Kydd, *Charismatic Gifts in the Early Church* (Peabody, Mass.: Hendrickson, 1984), who seemingly regards any mention of the Spirit by early church figures as a reference to gifts.
18. Deere, 23.
19. Ibid., 18–19.
20. See the discussion of various passages throughout this book.
21. Walter J. Hollenweger, *The Pentecostals* (Minneapolis: Augsburg, 1972), xviii.
22. Kydd, ix.
23. Ibid., 49.
24. Deere, 55.
25. Ibid.
26. Ibid., 23.
27. R. Fowler White, "For the Sparrow in the Hurricane: A Review of Jack Deere's *Surprised by the Power of the Spirit*," (Paper delivered at the Annual Meeting of the Evangelical Theological Society, Eastern Region, Philadelphia, 1994), 7.
28. Ibid., 8.
29. Ibid.
30. Lederle, 37.

CHAPTER 2

Scripture: For Validity or Mere Credibility?

THE CESSATIONIST, rather than making an assumption based on experience, studies the Scripture to see if the charismatic experiences are truly the gifts described in the New Testament. The cessationist argument is based on the direct statements of Scripture. It also uses Scripture indirectly to determine the existence of a historical link between the charismatic gifts and New Testament times. Ultimately, Scripture is the standard. Either it must validate the charismatic gifts or it must validate the cessationist argument.

The Charismatic Argument: Scripture Provides Credibility for Experience

The significance of the experience-centered focus of the charismatic is often missed. Part of the problem that underlies the controversy is that cessationists assume that solid scriptural discussion will be the basis for determining the validity of the cessationist or charismatic viewpoint. Cessationists are often amazed at the limited goal and focus of the charismatic argument. One gets the impression that their goal seems merely to disprove cessationism. Charismatics do very little to demonstrate that their position is taught in the Scriptures; they just assume it. They take continuation of the miraculous gifts for granted despite the fact that the tenor of the New Testament signifies that the events of that time were unique.

Cessationists often do not really understand the charismatic mindset. The experience of the charismatic is interpreted experientially as from God. It is assumed to be true and has no need to be validated by Scripture. Therefore, scriptural argument will seldom convince charismatics that their interpretation of the experience is wrong. This perspective also explains the severely limited focus of the entire charismatic argument. The charismatic defense of their position has basically been to show that cessationism cannot be proven with certainty from Scripture. Most have really attempted to do little more than that. The argument runs something like the following: "If cessationism cannot be proven with certainty from Scripture, then my experience is a miracle from God." Even if cessationism could not be proven with certainty, this would establish none of the other assumptions necessary to conclude that an individual's personal experience is a miracle from God. The charismatic argument is not to establish the validity of its position, since this is assumed; rather it simply aims to remove an obstacle to its credibility by discrediting cessationism. Thus the basic charismatic argument is self-validating experience.

Personal Experience: An Unreliable Guide

Perhaps a definition of *experience* will help. *Webster's Ninth New Collegiate Dictionary* lists the following as one of the meanings for experience: "something personally encountered, undergone, or lived through."[1] In fact, all of the other meanings stress personal involvement in the sense of actually participating in, living through, or observing something as it occurs. The use of the term *experience* in the cessationist-charismatic controversy is consistent with this. The basic problem is that experience is not the same as fact. Fact is actuality. It does not depend on interpretation. Experience must be interpreted. The interpretations can vary, depending upon the interpreter; therefore, an objective control is needed to establish the validity of the interpretation.

The Problem of Nonobjective Interpretations by Charismatics

After hearing a charismatic's testimony, many people have committed a logical error by thinking that the person testifying must be telling the truth since the person does not seem to be lying. However, they have neglected the fact that the allegations that it was a miracle and that it was from God depend entirely on the interpretation of the person testifying. For example, we note that Deere responded in this manner when he heard John White's report of two healings from God. Deere thought,

> There are only two options. Dr. White is either telling me the truth, or he is lying to me. But he is not deceived. He is a medical doctor. . . . He knows the difference between organic illness and psychosomatic illness. He is not deceived. He is either telling me the truth or he is intentionally deceiving me.[2]

In the end Deere believed that Dr. White was not intentionally deceiving him, so he accepted White's entire testimony, including the testimony that these were miracles from God.

Let us assume, however, that White was not lying and that he would not be deceived regarding illness. This does not leave only the option that his entire testimony was true. Deere neglected some very significant facts. The fact that White was a doctor did not qualify him to determine whether this was indeed a miracle or that it was from God. After all, the Bible makes it clear that God is not the only source for miracles. So how did White know it was from God? Another fact overlooked by Deere was that White was not only a doctor, but he was a charismatic who was a doctor. Thus we are compelled to ask the question, Did he interpret this healing as a scientist or as a charismatic?

In addition, suppose everything in White's testimony was exactly the same except that he claimed these healings were from the Devil? Based on his own assumptions, that White would not lie and that he could not be deceived, Deere would be required to believe that these very same healings were from the Devil. There is no difference in the healings. The only difference would be to whom White gives credit for the miracles. Therefore, the healings and experiences themselves have nothing to do with the interpretation regarding the source. The source is purely whatever the interpreter assumes it to be. Thus an experience cannot validate itself; it cannot be self-validating. It must be interpreted, and the only way to interpret accurately is to have a standard other than experience. The only accurate standard for determining whether an experience is from God is the Scripture.

Personal Experience Requires Interpretation

Our analysis of our own individual experience is not necessarily accurate. When a person becomes a Christian, their testimony of that event is accurate only because the Bible defines the nature of salvation, not because of someone's personal experience of it. The testimony of a charismatic is often focused expressly on the experience, and as a result may give a distorted picture since it does not take into account all the facts.

Since Deere's testimony is typical for charismatics and since he also relates numerous details about himself, this will provide a good example. He testifies that he was a typical cessationist. However, after he heard John White's testimony about the healings and then studied the subject in the Bible, he became a convinced charismatic. Is his testimony an objective analysis that can now serve as a guide for others? We believe that on the basis of evidence that Deere himself supplies, his experience can be interpreted differently. If we include the additional details that Deere mentions and look at his testimony as a whole, we arrive at a far different interpretation.

We may also wonder why Deere was so insistent to have White, a charismatic, speak in his church. Most cessationist pastors would not do so. Why would Deere read fifteen books by White?[3] Perhaps Deere was interested in White's perspective long before this conversation. An extremely significant testimony is his statement that even before he entered seminary he felt that he did not have a biblical passion for God.[4] A feeling of such a lack is not uncommon among those who turn to the charismatic position. Perhaps the most telling statement is his comment that he chose a cessationist system so that he would have an excuse for not having a passion for God.[5] In other words, before seminary he had already felt a lack and also believed that cessationism was an "excuse."

Like many charismatics, Deere stresses the experience that changed his thinking. Someone else might place as much stress on the entire process leading to and resulting in Deere's particular interpretation of that experience. The experience by itself apart from this process was not necessarily the convincing factor. They would then conclude that Deere is an individual who was always seeking what charismatics claim to have. For some reason he was a cessationist by profession but always longing to be convinced to step out and become a charismatic. The experience was merely the catalyst that provided a reason to take this step.

Rather than a typical cessationist, Deere's own testimony reveals that he was always a charismatic "waiting to happen." Thus his experience did not really interpret itself so that it could not be interpreted some other way. Instead, Deere's prior inclination and thinking caused him to interpret his experience as he did. His experience is, therefore, not a reliable guide for others since it is interpreted in the light of an inclination that Deere had before his experience, an inclination that others may not have. Charismatic experiences are often interpreted mainly on the basis of a tendency toward a charismatic perspective that focuses on the experience itself and neglects other factors or possibilities. For many who become charismatic, the real cause is not the experience. The real cause is a dissatisfaction, a feeling of some lack. This is a consistent item in charismatic testimonies.[6]

Since experience can be interpreted differently, there must be some way to determine which interpretation is correct. The experience is not a reliable guide. In things concerning God, as this issue does, the only reliable standard of measurement by which to interpret the experience is the Bible.

Deere has explained his change from cessationist to charismatic as an argument to convince others to do the same. On the other hand, many others have changed from the charismatic to the cessationist position and can argue that their example should be followed. Thus, experience cannot be a guide since we cannot know which of these two opposite experiences to follow. The testimony of charismatics cannot be a reliable guide since it is offset by the testimonies of many who have left the charismatic camp. Furthermore, the testimony may be from a charismatic bias. Therefore, the only reliable and objective guide is Scripture.

The Cessationist Argument

The church as a whole throughout history has not held the charismatic view. The entire tenor of the New Testament, particularly the Gospels and the book of Acts, points to that time as a unique period with many unique events. Through the ages the church has always held that the apostolic age was different. Even those in the early postapostolic church who claimed to see miracles carefully differentiated these from those of the apostles.[7] Many charismatics concede that what we see today is not the same as in the book of Acts. The limited occurrence of any miraculous gifts in the history of the church supports cessationism. Thus the burden of proof should be on the charismatic to prove their position.

Cessationists point out biblical passages that either teach or imply cessationism. They also build biblical arguments inductively by putting together various biblical facts regarding the gifts, noting that no verse teaches that gifts will continue. They have also studied the biblical descriptions of the gifts and demonstrated that the present-day miraculous gifts do not agree with the description of the gifts in the New Testament. In addition, they show that there is no historical link between the charismatic gifts of today and those in the New Testament age. Therefore, the Scripture supports cessationism, the so-called miraculous gifts of today do not agree with the scriptural description of gifts, and there is no historical connection between today's gifts and the scriptural gifts. The cessationist position is validated by Scripture.

The Cessationist Emphasis on Scripture

Some are confused regarding the difference between fact and experience. They think that an argument based on the facts of history is arguing from experience. However, by definition experience refers to something in which the individual is involved as it occurs. They must be present. It may also include the individual's reaction or the effect on them. As it is used in the charismatic-cessationist debate, it includes all of these ideas. No one would regard the history of the church as "their experience." But a fact is different. It refers to something that has actually happened; it does not require personal involvement, nor does it depend on one's interpretation.[8] A fact is the same even if no one is present to experience it. History is properly a record of facts, a record of events rather than experiences. If I argue that we have no record of anyone in the history of the church performing miracles like the apostles, then this is an argument based on historical fact, not experience. If I state that today in my class no one was raised from the dead, this is an argument based on fact, not experience.

Thus, it is not a proper use of the term *experience* to accuse cessationists of also arguing from experience when they refer to history, either past or present.[9] This charge is intended to neutralize the fact that the charismatic argument is experience-oriented. In addition, it is using the term *experience* in a different way than is commonly used in discussing this issue. To use an accepted term inaccurately only serves to confuse. To use it differently in order to give the impression that cessationists are using the same kind of argument as charismatics is inappropriate. Regardless of the term used, arguing on the basis of historical fact is not the same as arguing on the basis of a purely subjective assumption that some event is a miracle from God. Even if history were described as experience, it would need to be modified by some terms like *factual* or *historical* experience to differentiate it from the subjective interpretation of events at which the individual must actually be present. An argument from history is an argument from fact, not from experience.

Regardless of what cessationists may think they are doing, Deere dogmatically asserts that no one is a cessationist because of the teaching of Scripture, but because they have not seen the gifts; they have not experienced them.[10] By this he means the charismatic gifts of today. This charge is blatantly untrue. Many have seen the alleged gifts of today, experienced all the charismatic experiences, been very deeply involved in the charismatic movement, and are now cessationists due to the study of Scripture. Often these people were more deeply involved and sincere than the average charismatic. But they changed due to study of the Bible, not because they were uninvolved in the movement. Many more have seen the gifts of today, have heard the testimonies of charismatics, and have been exposed in various ways to today's gifts, and yet they remain cessationists due to the study of Scripture. Deere's charge is contrary to the facts.

The charge that people are cessationists only because they have not seen the gifts contradicts one of the main arguments that charismatics use to explain the disappearance of the miraculous gifts from the church. They argue that the early church, particularly in the West, stopped believing in the miraculous gifts and so they did not receive them.[11] Notice the order of events: (a) the Christians stopped believing; and (b) as a result, the gifts were not given to them. This argument maintains that while the gifts were being exercised and while the church was involved in the full exercise of the miraculous gifts, the Christians stopped believing in them and became cessationists. The idea that the church as a whole saw the miraculous gifts in full bloom and still became cessationists is completely contradictory to Deere's charge that people are cessationists only because they have not seen the gifts. Which one of these two contradictory arguments does he actually believe? Are people cessationists because they have not experienced the gifts? Or did the church experience the gifts, then stop believing in them, and ultimately become cessationists? He cannot have it both ways. Either one of these arguments is wrong or both are wrong; but both cannot be right.

We have seen that an argument from history is not an argument from experience as the term is used in this discussion. However, someone may still attempt to discredit it by asserting that using the facts of history or comparing today's gifts with those in the Bible is not an argument based on Scripture.[12] In the first place, the fact that an argument is not based on Scripture does not mean it is an invalid argument in a discussion regarding biblical issues. To argue from history apart from Scripture that prophecy was fulfilled since Jerusalem was destroyed in A.D. 70 does not invalidate the argument. However, these are arguments founded on Scripture. If we compare someone's doctrine with Scripture and conclude that it does not agree with Scripture, this is a scriptural argument. To use the biblical requirements for elders to determine if certain individuals meet these requirements, and conclude that they do not qualify, is not an experiential or historical argument. It is scriptural; it is an argument founded on Scripture.

To use the New Testament description of the gifts to see if today's charismatic gifts meet these qualifications is a scriptural argument. The historical argument is also founded on Scripture. For example, someone could point to a twentieth-century building in Jerusalem and claim that it is the temple from Jesus' day. We could show that the building does not correspond to the temple or the buildings of that time, and that no temple building such as the one in the New Testament has been seen in Jerusalem since New Testament times. This is not an argument divorced from Scripture; rather it is history correlated with Scripture.

In a curious attempt to discredit the cessationist argument, Deere claims that none of it is based on Scripture.[13] Since cessationists do clearly use Scripture, he cannot prove his point by showing a lack of scriptural argumentation. Therefore, he uses philosophical reasoning. He argues that real objectivity is not possible since people who think they are objective interpreters hold different interpretations of Scripture. He seems to assume that if pure objectivity is not possible, then no one can really build an argument on Scripture. That people hold different interpretations does not mean that none are objective; it only means that some are not. The example he uses of amillennial (no future literal kingdom for Israel) versus premillennial (a future literal kingdom for Israel) interpretation is a poor choice for his argument since one of these must be true and therefore based on objective interpretation. He also argues that if a new Christian were locked in a room with only a Bible to study, he would never come out as a cessationist. How does he know this? He knows it by his own experience.[14] Of course, this is not true because Deere was never locked in a room as a new Christian and never had this experience. It is very improbable that a believer locked in a room would come out expecting anything like the present charismatic movement and "gifts."

Modern Charismatics: An Altered Position

When someone compares the gifts in the New Testament with those practiced by the charismatic movement, the comparison falls apart. Although modern charismatics claim that all of the gifts and power exhibited in the book of Acts and by the apostles are still available today, their gifts fall far short. For example, Jesus and the apostles never failed in their miraculous works, which contrasts greatly with the practices of charismatics today. The fact that history shows no continuance of gifts such as the apostles exhibited, nor any "power" in the church such as one can observe in the book of Acts is another huge obstacle to the charismatic position. Consequently, these factors have forced many modern charismatics to alter their claims regarding miracles, healings, and revelatory gifts. Many charismatic leaders explain the lack of conformity between their gifts and those in the New Testament by stating that they do not claim to have the same gifts as those described in the book of Acts and exercised by the apostles. For instance, they do not claim to have the gift of infallible prophecy as described in the Bible. Rather they claim to possess a gift of fallible prophecy given by the Holy Spirit. In regard to this, Grudem complains that cessationists are often

> . . . arguing against a view of prophecy which no responsible charismatic holds. . . . It would seem more productive (if one wishes to bring responsible criticism against the charismatic movement) to argue against the continuation of the *lesser* kind of prophecy which most responsible charismatic spokesmen are claiming does exist and function today.[15]

Grudem also states that

> there is almost uniform testimony from all sections of the charismatic movement that prophecy is imperfect and impure, and will contain elements which are not to be obeyed or trusted.[16]

Responsible charismatics are not claiming to have prophecy in the sense it is normally understood, as an infallible gift, but one which is of a lesser kind, one with no more authority than any teaching or preaching. Modern charismatics also no longer argue for the gifts that were exhibited in the book of Acts by the apostles. They do maintain, however, that the Holy Spirit distributed gifts among believers of the early church, but these gifts were not on the same qualitative level as those of the apostles. They were the same as the charismatic gifts of today, such as gifts of healing that often fail. Deere spends much time arguing that charismatics do not claim to have gifts like the apostles. They claim to have fallible or lesser gifts. He states that he does not see anyone performing miracles such as those in the apostles' ministry.[17] In other words, "responsible" charismatics are conceding that the apostolic gifts and the power exhibited in the book of Acts did cease with the apostolic age and are not seen today. They have conceded the basic cessationist argument. The lack of conformity between charismatic tongues and those in the New Testament has been defended for years by alleging a distinction between the "sign," as in the book of Acts, and the "gift," as in 1 Corinthians.

Most cessationists are unaware that charismatics have, in effect, conceded these cessationist arguments. Many charismatics probably do not realize what these "responsible" charismatics are actually doing to their beliefs. Grudem complains that cessationists are arguing against apostolic-quality gifts (such as infallible prophecy), which no responsible charismatic believes are available today. But his complaint is valid only in part. Charismatic leaders have stated that the charismatic gifts are of lesser quality. Although they have conceded the original cessationist points, they have never admitted that cessationists are correct. Instead they have continued to argue against the original cessationist arguments, which refer to apostolic-quality gifts. All of this has made it more difficult for others to realize that they have altered their original position. For instance, they protest that Warfield's arguments do not disprove their claims.[18] But they have already conceded his points and changed what they claim to have to a kind of gift that Warfield and other cessationists did not specifically address. They have confused the issue by not publicly admitting that they are changing what they claim to possess.

Another obstacle to the charismatic view has been the historical fact that gifts such as those in Acts did cease. Although some have tried to show the occurrence of miracles in history, it is generally recognized that gifts such as those in Acts have not occurred since the early years of the church. Even the evidence for the existence of lesser gifts such as those in the charismatic movement occurs at best in only sporadic and scattered instances. Because charismatics commonly recognize this problem, they try to explain it in two ways. First, they maintain that the gifts ceased in the church due to the church's unbelief in gifts. In other words, God gives gifts only to those who have faith in gifts. Second, some charismatics argue that God caused these gifts to cease but is now giving them back again in these "latter-days." This is the so-called latter-day rain. The theory of lesser quality or defective gifts not only serves to explain why the charismatic gifts of today do not meet the standards of those in the New Testament, but it also helps to overcome the historical problem. Clearly, the gifts mentioned in the book of Acts did not continue; however, there is more possibility for them to claim that defective gifts such as those in the charismatic movement do occur in history.

The charismatic movement gained credence and initial acceptance by claiming their gifts were the same as those in Acts. For most people this is why they are credible today. Yet now one of their primary defenses is the claim that they are not the same. Faced with the facts, they have had to revoke the very foundation of their original reason for existence.

Cessationists often do not understand what has taken place. Some changes in emphasis have occurred. For instance, charismatics do not emphasize tongues as much as they once were stressed in Pentecostal circles. Instead the emphasis is on miracles and signs. But a more significant change is in regard to the issue being discussed. Charismatics originally argued that all of the gifts and power displayed in Acts and by the apostles were throughout the New Testament church and are available today. The cessationists argued that those gifts functioned during the apostolic age and ceased with the close of it. Many knowledgeable charismatics admit that gifts such as the apostle's gifts do not exist today and that they have not existed since the apostolic age. No longer do they argue for gifts like the apostle's but for an inferior type of gift corresponding to the charismatic gifts. Since they cannot show that their experiences conform to Scripture, they try to show that Scripture conforms to their experiences.[19] Rather than showing that their prophecies are like the infallible prophecies of Scripture, they try to show that their fallible prophecies are in Scripture.[20]

The Need for Validity, Not Credibility

Assuming we are seeking the truth, merely neutralizing opposing arguments does not prove one's position. Charismatics need to demonstrate that their position is biblical, not merely assume it and attempt only to neutralize cessationist arguments. To determine the validity of the cessationist argument we must see if the Bible confirms it. We must also examine the nature of the New Testament gifts and determine if they are the same as the charismatic gifts of today. We must also see if there is any real evidence that the Spirit gives a lesser or defective type of gift comparable to those of today. In addition we must examine history to see if there is any historical link or continuity between the gifts in the New Testament and those gifts championed by contemporary charismatics.

※ ※ ※

1. *Webster's Ninth New Collegiate Dictionary*, s.v. "experience."
2. Deere, 20–22.
3. Ibid., 16.
4. Ibid., 182–83.
5. Ibid., 183.
6. Ibid. See also Ken Sarles, who describes Wimber's frustration ("An Appraisal of the Signs and Wonders Movement," *Bibliotheca Sacra* [January–March 1988]: 59–60).
7. See, e.g., Tertullian, *Against Marcion* 5:8. See also Clement of Rome, *Epistle to the Ephesians* 5:3–7; 42:1–5; and Ignatius, *To the Philadelphians* 5:1; 9:1.
8. *Webster's Ninth New Collegiate Dictionary*, s.v. "fact."
9. Deere, 55. It is absurd to argue, as Deere does, that arguing from history and comparing charismatic gifts with the biblical gifts is an argument from personal experience. Deere is also illogical when he claims that a lack of experience is experience. How can a lack of something be that same thing? Is a lack of intelligence to be equated with intelligence? Deere tries to disguise these factual arguments that certain events did not happen and that there is no comparison between the gifts of the New Testament and the charismatic gifts by stating that the fact that some events did not happen is not a fact but a lack of experience. However, an event that did not occur is not lack of experience. It is nothing.
10. Ibid.
11. Steve Durasoff, *Bright Wind of the Spirit: Pentecostalism Today* (Englewood Cliffs, N.J.: Prentice-Hall, 1972) 34; Ronald A. Kydd, *Charismatic Gifts in the Early Church* (Peabody, Mass.: Hendrickson, 1984), 56–57, 74, 85–87; Deere, 58, 73.

12. Deere, 56, 72–73.
13. Ibid., 45–56.
14. Ibid., 54.
15. Wayne Grudem, *The Gift of Prophecy in the New Testament and Today* (Westchester, Ill.: Crossway, 1988), 111–12.
16. Ibid., 110.
17. Deere, 67–68.
18. Ibid., 74.
19. Ibid., 57–71.
20. Grudem, 109–112.

CHAPTER 3

Biblical Information Regarding Spiritual Gifts

THE NEW TESTAMENT provides us with relatively little detailed information regarding any specific spiritual gift. In fact, in the case of several of the gifts we know only their names. Thus part of the controversy surrounding spiritual gifts is related to the fact that we lack detailed information about them.

New Testament Evidence for Spiritual Gifts

Although the Gospels describe many miracles or signs performed by the Lord Jesus Christ, Mark 16:17–20 is the only passage in the four Gospels that mentions spiritual gifts given to the church.[1] The gifts are not described except by the term "signs." The book of Acts relates numerous instances in which the miraculous gifts were exercised, but only a few of the gifts are described. Thus Acts provides us with little detail regarding spiritual gifts.

The only New Testament passages that actually list or name spiritual gifts occur in the letters of Paul and Peter. Gifts are discussed in Romans 12:6–8, 1 Corinthians 12–14, Ephesians 4:11, and 1 Peter 4:10–11. Apart from the gift of tongues, little information is given regarding the use of any other specific gift. Generally speaking we can deduce something about the nature of certain gifts only from the actual names of those gifts, since descriptions of them are simply lacking.

The main passage that discusses the proper use of a number of spiritual gifts is 1 Corinthians 12–14. These three chapters were written by Paul to the believers at Corinth to address the use of spiritual gifts and more specifically, the misuse of tongues in the Corinthian assembly. Casting out demons, speaking with tongues, taking up serpents, drinking deadly things, and healing the sick are listed in Mark 16:17–20. Mark stated that they were signs that were to accompany the preaching of the gospel; that is, they will confirm the gospel message to the unbeliever.

The gifts mentioned in Romans 12:6–8 include prophecy, ministry, teaching, exhorting, giving, ruling, and showing mercy. Those discussed in 1 Corinthians 12–14 are described under the general Greek term *pneumatikon*, "spiritual things" (see 12:1).[2] In 12:8–10 the gifts mentioned by Paul include the word of wisdom, the word of knowledge, faith, healing, the working of miracles, prophecy, discerning of spirits, tongues, and the interpretation of tongues. In 12:28–30 Paul includes apostles, prophets, teachers, miracles, healings, helps, governments, and tongues. Ephesians 4:11 refers to apostles, prophets, evangelists, pastors, and teachers, who are themselves gifts given by Christ to the church. First Peter 4:10–11 indicates that each believer receives a gift and that gifts are given to serve others.

Although 1 Corinthians 12 connects the giving of gifts with the Holy Spirit, the other passages make no mention of the Holy Spirit in connection with gifts. Ephesians 4:11 specifically connects the giving of gifts with Jesus Christ. Different Greek terms are used to designate these gifts, such as *pneumatikon*, "spiritual things" (1 Cor. 12:1); *charisma*, "gifts" (Rom. 12:6; 1 Cor. 12:4, 9, 28, 30–31; 1 Pet. 4:10); *doma*, "gifts" (Eph. 4:8); and *diakonia*, "ministries" (Rom. 12:7).

Definition of a Spiritual Gift

The New Testament clearly teaches that individuals themselves, such as apostles and prophets, are gifts given by Christ to the church. However, we normally think of gifts as something given to an individual. An apostle may be considered as one who has been given the gift or ability necessary for him to function as an apostle. A spiritual gift is an ability given to an individual supernaturally by God through the Holy Spirit so that the recipient may utilize that ability to minister to the needs of the church, the body of Christ. God supernaturally gives the believer special ability for service. This definition is important.

The issue under discussion is whether certain spiritual gifts from New Testament times are available today. Both charismatics and cessationists are discussing the same thing since the discussions concern apostles, prophets, miracles, and healing. However, in arguing for their position, charismatics often use arguments based on supernatural events in general rather than on scriptural references that specifically concern spiritual gifts. Thus the tendency is to confuse spiritual gifts with God's miraculous works.

In his own account of an interview with a student, Deere recounts how he asked this student about miraculous gifts.[3] The student responded that miracles were common in only three periods. Now, it is clear that the student is answering Deere's question about gifts, so that by "miracles" he obviously means miraculous gifts. In his answer he refers to Moses and Joshua, Elijah and Elisha, and Christ and the apostles, that is, to people who performed miracles. Thus, the answer referred to miraculous gifts. Deere also says that this student was using Warfield's argument, an argument that refers to gifts. In addition, Deere uses the same approach in Appendix C of his book, which was written to defend charismatic gifts.[4] Therefore, it is clear that the student in his argument was using the term *miracles* to refer to gifts.

Yet Deere argues that the idea of only three periods of miracles is inaccurate since God performed many miraculous works outside of these three periods, including works such as the creation of the world, the creation of human beings, the Flood, the confusion of languages at Babel, and many other miracles. But none of these occurrences are gifts, nor do they have any relevance whatever to the issue being discussed. Deere knows very well that cessationists do not claim that God acted only during three periods, nor do they claim that God ceased working at the end of the apostolic age. Deere's approach is to argue from general supernatural events as evidence for gifts, but this approach is completely invalid and irrelevant since it does not concern gifts. We must base our opinions about gifts on passages that refer to gifts, not on general supernatural events or works of God such as creation. In the instance described, the student was clearly right and Deere the one in error.

The same critique applies to Deere's discussion in Appendix C of his book where he includes a table of general supernatural events to demonstrate the continuance of the miraculous gifts. Deere also argues that Daniel and Jeremiah ministered at times outside of the three periods of miracles.[5] But this approach misrepresents the position of Warfield and other cessationists, since they do not deny special instances of prophets sent by God.

Deere says that Daniel's ministry was "filled with signs and wonders."⁶ In reality, however, Daniel simply passed on information he received from God in answer to prayer. He did not perform signs and wonders, nor did Jeremiah. We can see that Deere has confused the discussion. Deere's whole argument is vitiated by this lack of precision in attempting to build a case for miraculous gifts among believers today by arguing from the general supernatural events and occasional special occurrences of the past. The number of periods of miracles performed by men is not the real issue. The real issue is that signs and wonders performed by gifted people on other than special occasions has not occurred in history. Unfortunate for the charismatic position is the fact that there is no proof for the general performance of miracles continually throughout biblical history.

Recipients of Spiritual Gifts

The following passages indicate that all believers receive at least one spiritual gift.

1 Corinthians 12:7, 11—"But the manifestation of the Spirit is given to every man to profit withal. . . . But all these worketh that one and the selfsame Spirit, dividing to every man severally as he will."

Ephesians 4:16—"From whom the whole body fitly joined together and compacted by that which every joint supplieth, according to the effectual working in the measure of every part, maketh increase of the body unto the edifying of itself in love."

1 Peter 4:10—"As every man hath received the gift, even so minister the same one to another, as good stewards of the manifold grace of God."

The time of reception of spiritual gifts by the individual is not directly stated and can only be derived by implication from the New Testament. It seems that all believers have a gift, and therefore must receive it upon salvation.

People often hold to opinions regarding certain aspects of gifts without attempting to substantiate their opinions. The answers to some questions cannot be taken for granted, however. For example, should all believers seek the gift of tongues? This really involves two general questions. Can a Christian obtain a gift by seeking it? Should all Christians have or seek the same gift?

Biblical Information Regarding Spiritual Gifts 39

These questions need to be discussed before we consider the specific gifts.

Purpose of Spiritual Gifts

Why did God give gifts to his people? The gifts mentioned in Mark 16:17–20 are signs that accompany preaching of the gospel to the world. Romans 12:6–8 discusses the gifts as ministries to be exercised. First Corinthians 14:22 specifically states that tongues are given for the purpose of a sign to unbelievers: "Wherefore tongues are for a sign, not to them that believe, but to them that believe not."[7] First Corinthians 12:7 states that "the manifestation of the Spirit is given to every man to profit withal." The construction here and in 14:22 (*eis* with the accusative) indicates the desired end or purpose for giving the gifts. The purpose is for profit. It is evident from the remainder of the chapter that this profit is to be profit for *others*. First Corinthians 13 stresses that gifts are to be used for the good of *others*. They are to be used in love, otherwise the user is merely a noise, is merely "nothing." Naturally, this does not mean that the user is to love himself. Gifts are to be used in love; that is, for the benefit of *others*.

With its stress on the need to edify, 1 Corinthians 14 assumes that gifts are given to minister to others. For example, 14:14 says, "Even so ye, forasmuch as ye are zealous of spiritual gifts, seek that ye may excel to the edifying of the church," and 14:26 says, "How is it, then, brethren? when ye come together, every one of you hath a psalm, hath a doctrine, hath a tongue, hath a revelation, hath an interpretation. Let all things be done unto edifying" (see also 14:3, 6). Ephesians 4:11–12 states that people with their God-given gifts are to minister to the church in order to build it to maturity:

> And he gave some, apostles; and some, prophets; and some, evangelists; and some, pastors and teachers; for the perfecting of the saints, for the work of the ministry, for the edifying of the body of Christ.

First Peter 4:10 specifically states that "as every man hath received the gift, even so minister the same one to another, as good stewards of the manifold grace of God." This is a specific plea to use the gift to minister to others. To be good stewards of the gift, it must be used to help others as God intended when he gave them to us.

The entire New Testament describes spiritual gifts as being

used to minister to others. In no instance does it state that gifts were to be used for personal benefit. The nature of the gifts themselves indicates that they are given to enable the recipient to minister to others. For example, the gift of *teacher* is given to teach others, and the gift of helps is given to help others. Spiritual gifts are given by God in order to enable the one who has the gift to minister to others. Some gifts focus on ministry to unbelievers, while other gifts focus on ministry to believers. God did not give any gift merely to benefit the recipient of the gift.[8]

Diversity of Gifts

One of the basic and clear teachings of the New Testament is that God gives different gifts to believers. Not only does the very number of different gifts listed imply a diversity of gifts, but the biblical text explicitly states that all believers do not have the same spiritual gift. For example, Romans 12:4–5 says, "for as we have many members in one body, and all members have not the same function: so we, being many, are one body in Christ." This indicates that within the body of Christ are many different members having different functions. This is followed by the statement "having then gifts differing according to the grace that is given to us" (v. 6). This passage mentions a variety of gifts, and states that all do not have the same gift.

First Corinthians 12 also clearly indicates the diversity of gifts. Note the following statements:

Now there are diversities of gifts (v. 4);
For to one is given by the Spirit the word of wisdom; to another the word of knowledge by the same Spirit (v.8)
To another the working of miracles; to another prophecy (v. 10).

In fact the entire discussion of verses 12–30 is devoted to this subject. Not only does this passage state that all do not have the same gift, but it states that all *cannot* have the same gift (vv. 17–22). The statement, "If the whole body were an eye, where were the hearing?" (v. 17) indicates that there must be different gifts. Verse 22 reiterates this idea: "Nay, much more those members of the body, which seem to be more feeble, are necessary." Paul uses these figures of speech to demonstrate that all believers cannot have the same gift and that each one's gift is important.

God as the Giver of Spiritual Gifts

Another fundamental factor that is true of all spiritual gifts is that gifts are given sovereignly by God according to his will, not according to human desires. First Corinthians 12:11 expressly states this: "But all these worketh that one and the selfsame Spirit, dividing to every man severally as he will." This may be translated in more modern terms as "distributing to each single person just as He pleases." This entire section assumes that the individual did not select his own spiritual gift (1 Cor. 12:12–30). Individuals cannot acquire any gift by their own will. Otherwise why would Paul show so carefully that each gift is important and that the individual must be satisfied with it? Without doubt the "foot" cannot become a "hand" and therefore must be satisfied as a "foot."

With an emphasis on humility and the use of gifts, Romans 12:3–8 assumes that gifts are given by God's choice, not the desires of people. Verse 3 exhorts believers to think realistically regarding their importance in the body of Christ rather than exalting their importance in their own thinking. The word "for" (Gk. *gar*) connects the verses 3 and 4, demonstrating that this tendency to exalt one's own importance is related to the gift that one has in comparison to the gifts that others have. This situation would not arise nor would Paul's reasoning stand if believers could obtain specific gifts by seeking them.

Some will object, "But what about the passages which refer to seeking gifts? Don't these passages prove that a believer may obtain certain gifts if he so desires?" Before these passages are discussed specifically, notice that no passage in the New Testament indicates that anyone received a gift by seeking it. The only instance in which someone sought what may have been a gift is the incident described in Acts 8:18–24, "And when Simon [the sorcerer] saw that through laying on of the apostles' hands the Holy Ghost was given, he offered them money, saying, Give me also this power, that on whomsoever I lay hands, he may receive the Holy Ghost." Simon saw the spectacular nature of this gift that the apostles Peter and John used. He desired to have this power also and tried to buy it. We are not told of his motives for desiring the gift, but Peter states that Simon's act and intention was wicked (Acts 8:22).

The statements in 1 Corinthians 12:31; 14:1, 12, and 39 are often cited as evidence that a Christian should seek specific gifts and can obtain them. For example, Deere refers to these verses and criticizes MacArthur for saying that the Bible does not exhort believers to seek the miraculous gifts.[9] The verses need to be examined in light of this claim. They appear in the King James version as follows:

> But covet earnestly the best gifts: and yet shew I unto you a more excellent way. (1 Cor. 12:31)
>
> Follow after charity, and desire spiritual gifts, but rather that ye may prophesy. (1 Cor. 14:1)
>
> Even so ye, forasmuch as ye are zealous of spiritual gifts, seek that ye may excel to the edifying of the church. (1 Cor. 14:12)
>
> Wherefore, brethren, covet to prophesy, and forbid not to speak with tongues. (1 Cor. 14:39)

Other English versions translate these verses in essentially the same way.

The Greek word *zeteo*, "seek," in 1 Corinthians 14:12 does not refer to seeking a gift. Rather the church at Corinth was told to seek the edification of one another. First Corinthians 14:12, therefore, lends no support to the idea of seeking a spiritual gift.

Zeloo is the Greek work translated "covet" or "desire" in 1 Corinthians 12:31; 14:1, 39. Although *zeloo* is sometimes translated as "covet" or "desire," a thorough study of *zeloo* indicates that it means "to be zealous."[10] Zeal for something may imply "desire," but this meaning is derived from the context rather than the word *zeloo* itself. Biblical usage, including the twelve occurrences in the New Testament, indicates that "zeal" (or, negatively, "to be jealous") is the best translation for *zeloo* rather than the more interpretive meaning "covet" or "desire." In any case *zeloo* expresses attitude (zeal) rather than action (to seek).[11]

All of the verses in question occur in a passage addressed to the Corinthian church as a whole. The church is to restrict the way in which certain individuals can act during the assembly. The entire section (1 Cor. 12–14) stresses the priority of the edifying gifts (apostle, prophet, and teacher) over the more spectacular gift of tongues, which was apparently receiving undue emphasis at Corinth.[12] The instructions in 1 Corinthians 14 require action by the entire group. The church as a group is to exercise control over the use of gifts in the assembly, insuring that the proper emphasis is placed on edification in the assembly and that the appropriate rules are followed by the speakers. The normal meaning for *zeloo*, "be zealous or enthusiastic," fits perfectly in this verse and context as an exhortation to the entire assembly to be enthusiastic for the edifying gift of prophecy rather than for the more "showy" gift of tongues. As a church the Corinthians are to "be zealous for [emphasize] the greater gifts," which are clearly those that edify. Thus, regardless of the meaning given to *zeloo*, in this context it refers to the church as a whole and says nothing to indicate that individuals are to seek and expect to get any specific gift.

"Zeal" is an excellent translation for *zeloo* in 1 Corinthians 12:31, and several arguments weigh against translating it as "seek." The context of the passage is decidedly against it. Chapter 12 itself emphasizes the need to be content with the gift that God has given. Verse 15 states that the foot cannot become a hand, illustrating that a member of the body of Christ cannot become a member (gift) that they would prefer. "Seek" disagrees with this emphasis. Verse 11 of the same chapter stresses that the Spirit gives gifts as he pleases. To seek a gift disagrees with the explicit emphasis of this verse. This idea is repeated in verse 18, where the stress is once again on the fact that God gave gifts as he pleased.

The Greek language has words that definitely mean "to seek" (e.g., *zeteo, orego*) and "to desire" (e.g., *thelo, epithumeo,* and *boulomai*), but they are not used here. Paul is not against using these explicit words, since he does so in other verses. He uses *zeteo* frequently (nineteen times). He uses *orego* to describe the act of seeking to obtain or striving after the office of a bishop (1 Tim. 3:1), but he does not use it anywhere regarding spiritual gifts. The various words for desire also occur many times in Paul's Epistles (*thelo*, sixty times; *boulomai*, eight times; *epithumeo*, five times), yet he does not use any of them in this verse.

The interpreter has no reason to interpret *zeloo* in this passage as "seek." The context is decidedly against it. The word has in view one's attitude and cannot, therefore, mean to seek something. It is also doubtful if the meaning "covet" or "desire" is ever the best meaning. Thus, in this context it is definitely improper to interpret it this way. Even with this meaning it would not refer to individuals in this passage but to the church's attitude as a whole. The meaning of 1 Corinthians 12:31 is clear in its context. The church (as a group) is to be zealous (enthusiastic) for the greater gifts that edify, such as apostle, prophet, and teacher, rather than for such gifts as healing and tongues.

First Corinthians 14:1 and 14:39 use the same word and are very similar in their meaning and context; therefore, they should be interpreted in the same way. After an interlude in which he discusses the value of love (1 Cor. 13), Paul says, "Be zealous for spiritual things, but much more that you prophesy" (1 Cor. 14:1, author's translation).[13] The argument beginning in this verse and continuing through verse 25 has nothing to do with an individual seeking certain gifts, but concerns the priority or preference that the church as a group should give to the edifying gifts in the assembly.[14] As already stated, 1 Corinthians 14:39 is similar. The entire church is to be zealous for prophecy.

Each of these verses expresses the concept that the Corinthian church, and the individuals within it, should have a zeal for edifying the assembly (by prophesying) rather than being zealous (as they were) for speaking in tongues. The idea of individuals seeking certain gifts is not in view. Even if some insist, contrary to the evidence, on translating *zeloo* as "seek," it is clear that it is the church as a whole and not individuals who are to do this.

No statements in the New Testament or in the entire Bible, therefore, indicate that a person should seek specific gifts. Nor is there any indication that anyone did so or that a gift may be obtained by seeking it. On the contrary, 1 Corinthians 12 states that gifts are given according to God's plan and that each believer should be content with the gift he or she has received. In spite of the facts, if some still insist on seeking to acquire specific spiritual gifts, one concept is clear according to 1 Corinthians 14: they should seek edifying gifts rather than miraculous ones.

Control of Spiritual Gifts

I have known people who have said, "I was carried away in the Spirit and began to speak in tongues." Statements like this imply that the people who made them were not really in control of their gift but that their gifts took control of them. Let us examine the Bible to see if people maintain control of their own gifts or if the Holy Spirit supernaturally overpowers them so that they no longer have control of themselves. Thankfully, in this case Scripture provides us with a direct statement on the subject.

First Corinthians 14:26–35 assumes that individuals maintain control of their spiritual gifts and are not overpowered or carried away in the Spirit. In verses 27–28, Paul states that a person may speak in tongues in the assembly only if an interpreter is present.

This means that a person speaking in tongues must not speak unless certain conditions are met. In other words, people must control their gifts. Also, Paul says that people with the gift of tongues must speak one at a time, and a total of only two are to speak (three in some cases). If the Corinthians were not able to control their gift of tongues, then Paul could not instruct them in this way. The same instructions apply to prophecy (vv. 29–31). Paul also discusses the situation in which a prophet receives a direct revelation at the same time another prophet is speaking. The other is to allow him to speak. The fact of control is still apparent. The prophet who is speaking is to control his gift and let the one with the immediate revelation speak. Likewise, the one with the immediate revelation may speak when the other allows him to speak. These instructions could not be given unless the users were able to control the exercise of their respective spiritual gifts. However, the explicit statement regarding the control of gifts is yet to come. Perhaps Paul was anticipating that someone might say, "But I am carried away by the power of the Holy Spirit when I prophesy, and therefore I cannot stop and allow this other person to speak," for in verse 32 he says, "And the spirits of the prophets are subject to the prophets." The word *subject* means "to be in subjection," or, in this case, under the prophet's control. Paul states that the prophets can control their gift and are, therefore, responsible to exercise them in the assembly just as he has instructed them to do. Verse 33 gives the reason why the spirits of the prophets are in subjection to the prophets: "For God is not a God of disorder, but of peace." If believers could not control their spiritual gifts, the assembly would be one of disorder rather than peace.

In practice we all accept without question that people have control of their gift when gifts such as teaching or administration are considered. Of what use is a teacher who cannot control his gift? It would be impossible to have scheduled classes in Sunday school if the teachers could not start teaching at the proper time or, once started, could not stop. Most of us would have little patience with a teacher who claimed to be under the influence of the Spirit and began teaching the assembly during the pastor's sermon. The same applies to all gifts. In practice, modern tongues speakers do control their gift since they tend to speak only in surroundings where the practice is acceptable. How many attempt to speak in tongues in their place of work or in the shopping mall? First Corinthians directly states that speaking in tongues and prophesying are under the control of the speaker and are to be exercised only when it is proper to do so. All spiritual gifts are exercised under the control of the gifted individual. The claim that a believer can be carried away beyond his control is not true of gifts given by the Holy Spirit.

Significance of Spiritual Gifts to the Individual

As one would expect, opinions vary in regard to the importance of spiritual gifts. While some groups place much emphasis upon spiritual gifts, the concept is almost unknown among other groups. In the early church, certain gifts were important because they confirmed or validated the preaching of the gospel (see Mark 16:20; Rom. 15:19).

Ephesians 4:11–14 is very helpful in revealing the significance of gifts. Here it is stated that certain gifts are given to the church in order to train and perfect the saints. This training results in spiritual maturity, unity, stability in doctrine, knowledge of the Son of God, and the potential for every Christian to serve Christ.

Gifts are important to individual believers because they are the recipients of ministries performed by other gifted believers. For example, I benefit when someone uses their gift of teaching to instruct me regarding some truth about Jesus Christ. While there is no question that spiritual gifts benefit those who receive the ministry of that gift, this does not seem to be the emphasis in many circles today. In most charismatic groups, for example, the emphasis is often upon the importance of the gift to the one who possesses the gift; the importance for the recipients of the ministry performed by the gifted person is secondary. Rather than emphasizing the importance of a given gift for ministry, the attention is placed on the experiential or existential aspects of the gift to the one who has the gift. While some may possibly argue that the gift of tongues is an exception to this principle of gifts being given for ministry to others, according to Scripture tongues are also given for the purpose of ministry to others. Therefore, the principle mentioned above has no exceptions.

An examination of passages dealing with the spiritual life reveals that the possession of a spiritual gift has little or no part to play in the spiritual life and growth of the one possessing the gift. The Gospels give no indication that believers are to expect spiritual gifts in order to enhance their own spiritual growth. The Lord's final remarks in Mark 16:14–20 state that the signs that will accompany the early preachers are to confirm the Gospel to others, but it gives no mention of gifts relative to the possessor. The same is true of Luke 24:44–53. The verses that mention the Holy Spirit (24:48–49) refer to being witnesses and remaining in Jerusalem until the disciples are clothed with power, which occurs in the context of ministry to others. In John 21:16–17 Jesus tells Peter to "feed my sheep," but he makes no mention of spiritual gifts. In fact the final instructions in each of the four Gospels make statements regarding ministry to others but say nothing about personal benefit from possessing spiritual gifts.

The book of Acts provides numerous examples where spiritual gifts are exercised in ministry for the benefit of others. However, there is not the slightest indication that spiritual gifts were used to enhance the spiritual life and growth of the one using the gift. The emphasis of ministry for the benefit of others is clear in Acts 1:4–5, 8. Note that Acts 1:8 explicitly states that the power that the disciples were to receive from the Holy Spirit was to be for ministry to others—specifically Jerusalem, Judaea, Samaria, and the rest of the world.

The Epistles continually exhort believers to love the brethren, to do good works, to be holy, faithful, and sound in doctrine. However, there is no exhortation to utilize spiritual gifts to enhance one's own spiritual life. Gifts are mentioned in only a few passages (Rom. 12:6–8; 1 Cor. 12–14; Eph. 4:11; 1 Pet. 4:10–11) and in each instance the stress is solely on ministry to others. No one is told to seek a gift in order to enhance his own spirituality. First Corinthians 12:31, 14:1, and 14:39 are not admonitions for an individual to seek specific gifts. But even if someone insists that they refer to seeking, these verses still demonstrate that the seeking must be in order to minister to others.

Romans 12–16, a long section that deals with the spiritual life, mentions gifts only in 12:4–8. The stress of this brief section is on using one's gift to minister to others and to avoid being proud of one's gift. This passage does not imply that possession of a spiritual gift will help one to live according to the standards set forth in these chapters, and no where in this section is one's spiritual gift connected with any admonitions for spirituality. Gifts did not make the Corinthians spiritual. Despite the numerous erroneous practices and problems at Corinth that Paul attempted to resolve in his two letters to the Corinthians, he never intimated that spiritual gifts would solve any of them. Rather he stressed love, holiness, sincerity, and sound doctrine.

Ephesians 1:3–14 mentions the believer's spiritual blessings in Christ. This section begins with "Blessed be the God and Father of our Lord Jesus Christ, who has blessed us with every spiritual blessing in heavenly places in Christ" (v. 3); then it lists numerous blessings that we have in Christ, including election, predestination, redemption, forgiveness, knowledge of God's purposes, our inheritance in Christ, and our eternal security. However, no mention is made of spiritual gifts. In Ephesians 1:17–19 Paul prayed the following prayer:

> That the God of our Lord Jesus Christ, the Father of glory, may give unto you the spirit of wisdom and revelation in the knowledge of him: the eyes of your understanding being enlightened; that ye may know what is the hope of his calling, and what the riches of the glory of his inheritance in the saints, and what is the exceeding greatness of his power to usward who believe, according to the working of his mighty power.

He did not pray, however, that the Ephesians might have spiritual gifts. In fact the passage that discusses the "filling of the Spirit" (Eph. 5:18) makes no mention of spiritual gifts. Instead all believers must live according to the commands of Ephesians 5:15–19, regardless of one's gifts.

The famous passage in Ephesians 6 that deals with the necessity of putting on the whole armor of God in our battle against Satan also makes no mention of spiritual gifts as part of that armor. Instead truth, righteousness, the gospel, faith, salvation, the Word of God, and prayer are stated as the necessary items for spiritual warfare. Spiritual gifts are not part of the armor that the individual needs to stand against Satan and his wiles. Although Paul's letters to the Philippians and Colossians contain numerous admonitions regarding love and spirituality, they do not mention spiritual gifts. The same emphasis holds true throughout the New Testament, in the pastoral epistles, and the book of Hebrews.

The book of James says nothing regarding spiritual gifts. First Peter, which is written to believers undergoing trials, has much to say regarding the Christian life, but the only mention of gifts concerns ministry to others (1 Pet. 4:10–11). Second Peter 1:4 says, "Whereby are given unto us exceeding great and precious promises: that by these ye might be partakers of the divine nature, having escaped the corruption that is in the world through lust." God's promises revealed to us in the Bible are the means by which we can escape the world's corruption and become godly. But no reference is made to gifts. God's Word helps the Christian to become godly, but the value of possessing a gift for the purpose of godliness is not even implied.

The above discussion should be sufficient to show that the proper goal for the individual believer is a godly life and spiritual maturity. This is the end toward which all believers should be moving. The Bible does not suggest that the possession of a spiritual gift, regardless of which one, helps a believer toward this spiritual goal. The ministry of other gifted individuals may help the believer or the use of one's own gift in ministry to others may help others. In short, gifts are not for our own use or benefit but are to be used in service to others.

The Corinthian church is a perfect example of this. They had numerous gifts; even Paul said to them, "You do not lack [fall short] in any gift" (1 Cor. 1:7). It is evident from 1 Corinthians 12–14 that the Corinthians were very zealous and excited about certain spiritual gifts, especially the gift of tongues. But this did not produce spiritual believers. The Corinthian church apparently had more problems than any other church addressed in the New Testament. In fact the believers at Corinth were described as carnal and unable to receive more than the basics of Christian truth (1 Cor. 3:1–3). Yet, it is the only church in the New Testament that placed a special emphasis on spiritual gifts. Did the spiritual gifts make them carnal? No! But they did not use their gifts for ministry to others. The Corinthian church demonstrates that the possession of gifts, such as the gift of tongues, does not enhance the spirituality of the person possessing the gift. Gifts were not given for this purpose.

The main emphasis in the New Testament is on the godliness and spiritual maturity of believers. Christians are continually exhorted to demonstrate, among other things, faith, hope, and love. God has given spiritual gifts to Christians so that they may minister to one another and help one another reach the goal of maturity. Spiritual gifts are a means to that end. The mere possession of a gift does not enhance spirituality. Spiritual gifts are not given to build up the possessor, nor is there any indication that they will do so.[15] Gifts are given to perform a function within the whole body of Christ so that believers may minister to others.

The emphasis today is often wrong. While some churches or groups do stress the use of spiritual gifts for ministry, many place the stress entirely on the benefit for the individual who possesses the gift. As a result the correct concept that the gift is for ministry to others is lost. This personal-benefit concept of spiritual gifts, so common to the charismatic movement, is contrary to the New Testament. The fact that possession of specific spiritual gifts is not mentioned as a criterion for selecting elders, bishops, and deacons, indicates that gifts have no relationship to the spirituality of the one possessing them. The spiritual life of the individual is the criterion for selecting men for certain offices.

The Bible offers no instruction on how to recognize one's own spiritual gift. Instead the gift becomes obvious through its exercise, that is, when it is used in ministry. If possession of specific spiritual gifts were important in itself, the Bible would certainly give some information on how to recognize one's gift.

Spiritual gifts are very important to the church, since gifted individuals are necessary to minister to the body of Christ, the church. The concern over the exercise of gifts in ministry is proper. The emphasis on gifts as a mark of spirituality or as existing for the benefit or prestige of the one possessing the gift is false. Thus churches today need to be careful as to how they emphasize the use of gifts. If Christians are zealous to use their gifts to serve the Lord by ministering to other people, then they have the correct outlook.

※ ※ ※

1. This is to be expected, since spiritual gifts were not given to individuals prior to Pentecost. Mark 16:17–20 is prophetic in aspect, looking forward to the post-Pentecost period.
2. Discussions of the precise meaning of *pneumatikon* do not affect the findings herein. For example, see D. W. B. Robinson, "Charismata Versus Pneumatika," *Reformed Theological Review* 31 (May–August 1972): 49–55.
3. Deere, *Surprised by the Spirit* (Grand Rapids: Zondervan, 1993), 49–52.
4. Ibid., 253–62.
5. Ibid.
6. Ibid., 292.
7. This construction, including Grudem's unusual interpretation, will be discussed later in the section on tongues.
8. Passages such as 1 Cor. 14:4, which are often used to support the devotional use (i.e., personal-benefit use) of the gift of tongues, are discussed in Chapter 7, "The Purpose for the Gift of Tongues."
9. Deere ridicules MacArthur for saying that the Bible does not exhort believers to seek gifts. Furthermore, he states that MacArthur does not seriously interact with 1 Cor. 12:31; 14:1, 39, which according to Deere teach that one should seek specific gifts (*Surprised by the Spirit*, 281). Even though Deere seems to be aware of my book, *Miraculous Gifts*, he does not seem to have interacted with its arguments,

specifically, that neither the use of the Greek word in question, nor the context of the passage, nor even the specific situation allow the meaning of "seek" (see my *Miraculous Gifts* [Neptune, N.J.: Loizeaux, 1983], 22–30, 315–18). Nor does it seem that he has interacted with the biblical text, since he could not have studied these texts and made the assertions he has made. Since Deere has apparently not studied these texts and has ignored the arguments of those who have studied them, it is particularly inappropriate for Deere to accuse MacArthur, who has studied the passages, of not interacting with them.

10. A study of classical and koine Greek reveals that this word has the meaning "zeal" (or, negatively, "jealousy") in every instance. Any idea of seeking is derived only from this basic concept of zeal or enthusiasm in a specific context and is rarely the better translation.

11. Common versions of the Bible, such as the KJV, ASV, and NIV, do not translate *zeloo* in these verses as "seek."

12. Nothing in the New Testament indicates that all of the gifts are of equal importance to the assembly. First Cor. 12–14 shows that the edifying gifts have priority. Since all believers do not have the same gift, priorities must be recognized for the church to function effectively and avoid strife. The priority is to go to the edifying gifts of apostle, prophet, and teacher rather than to such gifts as healing and tongues.

13. The term *gifts* is not used in 14:1. The Greek word *pneumatika*, also used in 12:1, is the word translated "spiritual things." It probably refers to gifts in this context, but could possibly also include the manifestations and ministries as well (see also 12:4–6, referring to manifestations, in the same context as 12:1).

14. That 1 Cor. 14 refers to priority of activity in the assembly rather than to the priority of individual desires is obvious, but must be kept in mind in order to understand the verses involved. Therefore, it is the priority given by the church *as a group* to the ministration of gifts in the assembly that is discussed. First Cor. 14:1 says, "Be zealous [enthusiastic] for spiritual gifts, but especially that you prophesy." The phrase "that you prophesy" definitely refers to the *attitude* of the church as a whole, since the context of 1 Cor. 14 is decidedly against every individual prophesying. Paul has already stated that all are not prophets. The concept that everyone is to prophesy would also invalidate the entire emphasis of chap. 12, viz., that all members do not have the same function. Therefore, 1 Cor. 14:1 must refer to the attitude of the church as a whole.

15. First Cor. 13:1–3 implies that a gift will profit the user if it is exercised in love. This profit, however, is not directly from the gift itself. It is the profit that any believer experiences from serving the Lord in ministry to others.

CHAPTER 4

Edifying Gifts: Apostle and Prophet

NEXT TO JESUS CHRIST, the most important person in the early church was the apostle. Apostles were foundational and recognized as the authority. As a whole the church has always considered the gift of apostle as a first-century gift. Early Christian writers consistently testify that the apostles existed only at the inception of the church. Interestingly, many charismatics agree that apostles are not present today. However, other charismatics claim that apostles are for today. Ultimately, the Scriptures will help us to clarify the gift of apostle, will help us determine whether apostles are present today, and will give us a better understanding of God's provision for the church.

What Is an Apostle?

The word *apostle* is a translation of the Greek word *apostolos*. Secular Greek literature uses this word with various meanings, including "representative, ambassador, commander of a naval expedition."[1] *Apostolos* occurs once in the Septuagint, the Greek translation of the Old Testament, in 1 Kings 14:6 (IV Kings 14:6 LXX) where it translates the Hebrew word *shalach*, "send."[2] In this passage the wife of Jeroboam, king of Israel, went to Ahijah the prophet, who said, "I am an apostle *(apostolos)* to you." In this instance Ahijah did not travel; instead the woman came to him. Thus the idea of "sent" in the sense of a *representative* is more prominent than any idea of physical travel. Ahijah is a representative of God. It is precarious to equate a missionary with an apostle merely upon the basis of the idea of *sending forth* in the verb from the same root, *apostello*. The word *apostle* means "a sent one" only in the sense of a representative of God sent to people.

Apostle in the New Testament

In the Gospels

The Gospels demonstrate very clearly that the Twelve were *the* apostles. They were with Jesus and were sent out occasionally to preach and perform miracles (see Matt. 10:2; Luke 6:13; 9:1–10; 17:5).

In the Book of Acts

Several points are clear from the book of Acts. The Twelve were *the* apostles (see Acts 1–2). Also, the number of apostles remained twelve by choosing to replace Judas with a man who had witnessed the resurrection of Jesus Christ (Acts 1:21–26).

Wherefore of these men which have companied with us all the time that the Lord Jesus went in and out among us, beginning from the baptism of John, unto that same day that he was taken up from us, must one be ordained to be a witness with us of his resurrection. (Acts 1:21–22)

Matthias, the man chosen, was numbered along with *the eleven apostles*. Notice also that the apostles accompanied Jesus during his earthly ministry and were appointed to be witnesses of Jesus' resurrection (Acts 1:22; see also 4:33). An apostle was a witness of the resurrection. This is explicitly stated regarding the Twelve.

Other passages in the book of Acts state that the apostles were witnesses of the resurrection (e.g., Acts 1:1–14). The apostles whom Jesus chose were given indisputable proof of Jesus' resurrection (vv. 2–3) and were assigned to be witnesses of Jesus (v. 8). The apostles' sermons also show that the witness was primarily to his resurrection. In Acts 5:17–32 the apostles who were questioned by the authorities (v. 18) answered that they were witnesses of Jesus' resurrection and exaltation (vv. 29–32). In Acts 10:41–42 Peter stated that the resurrected Christ appeared "not to all the people, but unto witnesses chosen before of God, even to us, who did eat and drink with him after he rose from the dead. And he commanded us to preach unto the people, and to testify...."

The book of Acts teaches several additional concepts regarding the apostles. The apostles taught (2:42), performed miracles (5:12), and as the direct representatives of Christ they were characterized as the authority for the church (2:42; 4:35-37; 5:1-11; 6:2-6; 9:27). Paul and Barnabas are also called apostles in the book of Acts (14:4,14). However, it is not conclusive that Luke uses the term *apostle* in the precise sense as the Gospels. He may use it here in a broader sense, but this cannot be demonstrated. Except for Barnabas and Paul, the apostles were not characterized by missionary activity. On the contrary, the apostles remained in Jerusalem while others went forth with the message (see Acts 5:2, 18; 6:2-6; 8:1; 9:27; 15:2; Gal. 1:17-2:10). Acts 8:1 especially makes this clear, since the apostles remained in Jerusalem after the rest of the church was scattered and even years after this event (see Acts 11:1; 15:2; Gal. 1:18; 2:1). The initial outward thrust of Christianity was carried by Philip the evangelist (Acts 8:5-40) rather than by an apostle.

In the Epistles

The Gospels use the term *apostles* for the Twelve but provide little additional detail. The book of Acts reports actual historical situations in which apostles are involved rather than providing any doctrinal teaching regarding apostles. The Epistles, however, teach several principles concerning apostles.

The Epistles generally use the term *apostle* to refer to one of the Twelve or to Paul. Some claim that the Epistles indicate that the term *apostle* was applied to a group broader than the Twelve plus Paul and perhaps Barnabas. One of the passages usually referred to in support of this is Romans 16:7, which says, "Salute Andronicus and Junias, my kinsmen, and my fellow prisoners, who are of note among the apostles, who also were in Christ before me." The expression "of note among the apostles" is as inconclusive in Greek as it is in English. This may mean either that Andronicus and Junias were actually apostles or that the apostles recognized them as notable. Initially the expression "of note among the apostles" (Gk. *episemoi en tois apostolois*) seems to imply that Andronicus and Junias were in the circle referred to as apostles, but this notion raises numerous questions. For example, if "notable apostles" was Paul's intended meaning, why didn't he say this? If Andronicus and Junias were "notable apostles," why doesn't either Scripture or history ascribe such notoriety to them? This verse indicates that they were Jews and were saved even before Paul himself, yet the Gospels make no mention of these "notable apostles" and church history knows of no apostles at Rome other than Paul and possibly Peter. If they were apostles, why are they sandwiched in the middle of a list of salutations rather than in a more prominent position? In his salutation Paul asserted his apostleship and addressed the saints at Rome (Rom. 1:1, 7), yet he overlooked these "notable apostles" in the opening of the epistle and gave no special attention to them in Romans 16. Why did Paul need to write this letter to Rome if two apostles, who had the knowledge and authority of apostles, were already in Rome, especially if they were "notable apostles"? Also, Paul stated that he did not build on another's foundation (Rom. 15:20). Why did he state this and then indicate that he desired to minister to the church at Rome if two apostles were already there? If that were true, then he would very definitely be building on the foundation of others.

Once one considers these questions, it seems clear that Paul was referring to Andronicus and Junias as believers who were well known and respected by the apostles, but not apostles themselves. They were probably in Jerusalem at the very beginning of Jesus' ministry, since they were saved before Paul and were well known to the apostles.[3]

The salutation of certain Epistles is also used as an argument that those included along with Paul in his salutation have authority like him and are, therefore, apostles. For example, this argument states that Sosthenes must be an apostle since 1 Corinthians 1:1 lists him together with Paul (see also Timothy, in 2 Cor. 1:1; 1 Thess. 1:1; 2 Thess. 1:1). However, the very opposite is indicated, for Paul simply says, "Paul, called to be an apostle of Jesus Christ through the will of God, and Sosthenes our brother" (1 Cor. 1:1). If Sosthenes were an apostle, why not say, "Paul and Sosthenes, apostles of Christ"? Paul called himself an apostle but did not include Sosthenes under this title. Sosthenes (1 Cor. 1:1), Timothy (2 Cor. 1:1; Col. 1:1), and other believers (Gal. 1:1–2) were carefully excluded from the designation *apostle*. Notice that when others are directly included with Paul in the address without any intervening terms or connectives, the word *apostle* is not used (see Phil. 1:1; 1 Thess. 1:1; 2 Thess. 1:1). The salutation of the various Epistles indicates that the others mentioned with Paul were not considered apostles.

Second Corinthians 8:23 refers to "messengers" (KJV and NASB; NIV has "representatives"; lit. "apostles") of the churches which actually means "representatives from local assemblies of believers." The term *apostle* was commonly used in the culture of that day.

This verse shows that it did not necessarily refer to the spiritual gift or to an individual. Philippians 2:25 similarly describes Epaphroditus as a "messenger" (Gk. *apostolos*).

According to Galatians 2:7–9, those in Jerusalem did not take lightly the idea of apostleship. Recognition of Paul's apostleship was not granted easily by the early church but was carefully examined. Although Paul's apostleship was recognized, Barnabas was not included. Paul says, "when they saw that I had been entrusted with the gospel," and "He that worked in Peter to the apostleship of the circumcision, worked also in me toward the Gentiles" (v. 8). When Paul says, "and when [they] . . . perceived the grace that was given unto me" (v. 9), he uses only the first person pronoun "I, me" and excludes Barnabas. Thus it is probable that the use of *apostle* in Acts 14:4 and 14 does not mean that Luke views Barnabas as having the gift of apostle but merely that he is Paul's companion. Therefore, Galatians 2:7–9 causes us to question Barnabas' status as an apostle in the full sense of an "apostle of Christ" or as one of the Twelve.

Galatians 1:19 may suggest that James was an apostle, although this passage is often disputed. Its indirect nature leaves this open to question. First Thessalonians 2:7 is also used to include others in the category of apostle since Paul uses the phrase "apostles of Christ" with apparent reference to himself, Silvanus, and Timothy (see 1 Thess. 1:1). Conceivably, the use of "apostles" in the plural could include all of these individuals listed in the address of the letter, but this is highly improbable due to the statements of the letter itself. This appears to be an editorial use of the plural which is often used today. The statements in 1 Thessalonians 2 could apply to all three men, but they apply only to Paul in any precise sense. For example, in 1 Thessalonians 2:18 Paul states, "*We* would have come unto you, even *I Paul*, once and again" (italics added). This directly equates "we" with Paul alone. The same is true in the next few verses: "Wherefore when *we* could no longer forbear, *we* thought it good to be left at Athens *alone*; and sent Timotheus our brother, . . . to establish you" (1 Thess. 3:1–2). A comparison with Acts 17:14–15 and the use of the word "alone" in this passage indicates that neither Timothy nor Silvanus was with Paul in Athens, which precludes them from being included in the "we" of this passage (see 1 Thess. 3:5). Therefore, it is very doubtful that Paul is indicating that Silvanus and Timothy are apostles in 1 Thessalonians 2:7. Instead he uses "we apostles" to apply to himself specifically, and includes the others in only a very general sense.

The Epistles indicate that an apostle was a direct witness of the resurrection. In 1 Corinthians 9:1–2 Paul gives evidence for his apostleship: "Am I not an apostle? am I not free? have I not seen Jesus Christ our Lord?" Since Paul considered the fact that he had seen the resurrected Lord to be evidence of his apostleship, it is evident that to be an apostle one must have seen the resurrected Lord. An apostle saw the resurrected Lord in a real physical manifestation.

According to 1 Corinthians 15:5–8, Peter (Cephas), the twelve apostles, James, and Paul all saw the resurrected Lord. They are listed in this passage along with the five hundred fellow believers who were also witnesses of the resurrected Lord. Verse 9 begins with the word "for" *(gar)*, connecting the appearance of the resurrected Lord to Paul with Paul's apostleship.

In order to be an apostle one must have actually seen Jesus Christ in one of his resurrection appearances. Even if we were to include James, Barnabas, Andronicus, and Junias in the category of apostles, this principle holds true. We know that the Twelve, Paul, and James were witnesses of the resurrected Christ. Andronicus and Junias were in Christ before Paul and were very likely included among the five hundred believers who saw the resurrected Lord (1 Cor. 15:6). Barnabas was in Jerusalem at the very beginning of the church (Acts 4:36–37), and, unless he had just arrived, was there during the time of the resurrection appearances. Therefore, it is very likely that he also was a witness to the resurrection.

The Epistles indicate that an apostle was able to perform miracles. In 2 Corinthians 12:11 Paul states that he did not fall short of the very chief apostles in anything. Then he says, "Truly, the signs *(semeia)* of an apostle were wrought among you in all patience, in signs *(semeiois)*, and wonders *(terasin)*, and mighty deeds *(dunamesin)*" (v. 12). The article occurs with "apostle," marking it out as the specific apostolic gift. Paul clearly states that miracles are signs or proofs that he was an apostle. If these are proof, then it is clear that one must be able to perform miracles, wonders, and signs, if he is truly an apostle. This is one of the proofs of his apostleship.[4]

Some have interpreted the signs of an apostle to be characteristics such as the exercise of grace, the ability to plant churches, and other aspects rather than miracles.[5] One argument states that the terms *signs*, *wonders*, and *miracles* would be in the nominative case in the Greek rather than the instrumental (dative) case used here if it meant that the signs and wonders were the "sign" of apostleship.[6]

This is misleading since it is not true. The instrumental case used here conveys the customary interpretation of this verse. There is no reason why Paul would use the nominative when the case he uses is the normal case with this particular verb to convey the idea that the signs of an apostle consisted of miracles, signs, and wonders. It is extremely improbable that this verse means, as some claim, that the signs and wonders accompanied the signs of an apostle.[7]

The signs of an apostle must be something restricted essentially to the apostles and not something that any Christian can do, such as exercise grace and plant churches. What could the apostles do as a sign that other Christians could not do? We know that the apostles were almost the exclusive workers of signs and wonders. The fact that Philip and Stephen performed signs does not rule out the fact that these are almost exclusively apostolic. Also, the term *sign* refers almost exclusively to miraculous works. When Paul says "signs" and then immediately uses the term again in reference to miracles, it is much more probable that he uses it the same way than that he changes the meaning. As strong as these arguments are, the grammatical argument is more conclusive. If this were a dative of association, meaning "along with," it would usually occur with a verb of association, which is not the case in this passage.[8] In addition, if this were the associative dative with the meaning set forth by Deere, it must relate to or be in association with the noun "signs." However, according to leading authorities of Greek grammar, the associative dative does not occur in association with nouns in the New Testament.[9]

Thus, on grammatical grounds alone the associative interpretation is improbable. In addition, in the New Testament, *katergazomai*, the verb used in 2 Corinthians 12:11, takes the accusative as direct object and the instrument or means by which the action is performed is in the dative case as here. Thus, the construction used here is exactly the construction we would expect if the verse means that the signs of the apostle were performed by means of signs, miracles, and wonders. Finally, it is almost impossible to take this construction as related to anything other than the verb in this particular sentence. To take it as related to the noun is highly unlikely given the structure of the verse. With so many solid grammatical arguments against the associative view, it is an impossible interpretation. The mere fact that a dative case can be associative in some instances does not mean it is possible in this verse. The nongrammatical arguments against the associative view merely confirm what the grammatical argument has definitely shown. The signs of an apostle were performed by means of signs, wonders, and miracles.

In contradiction to this verse, Deere argues that it is illogical for miracles to be a sign of apostleship since Stephen and Philip also performed miracles. The fact that two other individuals in the church performed miracles on some occasions does not rule out the fact they were highly unusual or that it was necessary for someone who claimed to be an apostle to be able to do miracles. Deere also argues that since Jesus performed miracles and they authenticated him, there would be no need to authenticate the apostles. They could preach on the basis of Christ's miracles as we do today. Of course, this is defective both logically and theologically. We know who Jesus is not merely due to his miracles but primarily due to his death and resurrection. He would have been quickly forgotten if the evidence regarding him was restricted only to the miracles he performed. The apostles were the primary witnesses of his resurrection. The gospel concerns his death, burial, and resurrection. The apostles were confirmed by signs as direct representatives of Christ and witnesses to the basics of the gospel, to events that took place after Christ's miracles and after his death.

The Epistles indicate that the gift of apostle was given only at the beginning of the church. Ephesians 2:20 states, "And are built upon the foundation of the apostles and prophets, Jesus Christ himself being the chief corner stone." Some have interpreted this to mean the foundation that the apostles and prophets laid. The expression "of the apostles and prophets" is in the genitive case and is plural. The genitive case in Greek may function in many ways, indicating such aspects as content, possession, or relationship. The only way to determine the function of the case is from the context, since the form does not change. Here in Ephesians 2:20 the genitive is definitely the appositional use of the genitive; that is, we may translate this passage as "built upon the foundation *which is* the apostles and prophets." Thus the apostles and prophets *are* the foundation. The reasons for regarding this as an appositional genitive are as follows. The figure Paul uses is a building that consists of people. The cornerstone is a person, Jesus Christ. According to verses 21–22, the building itself consists of people, believers. Therefore, it is clear that the foundation also consists of people, the apostles and prophets. Also, this is a normal, well-accepted use of the Greek genitive case. Some who have erroneously interpreted this verse to mean that the apostles and prophets laid the foundation of the church have then gone on to state that this verse applies also to the "planting" (i.e., laying the foundation) of local churches. They conclude that God may still be sending out apostles for pioneering ministries on the mission field. But we have already seen that this verse is not discussing the concept of laying a foundation.

The context of Ephesians refers to the universal church, to the entire body of Christ, not to a single, local assembly. The entire letter, especially Ephesians 2, argues that Jew and Gentile are made one in the body of Christ. The figure in Ephesians 2:19–22 specifically demonstrates that in Christ the Gentiles have been brought into the same household of God as the Jews and that we are all built together on the same foundation and cornerstone. Ephesians 2:20 states that the apostles and prophets are the foundation for the universal church. The Ephesian believers are part of the building built on the foundation. The tone of the passage separates them from the foundation. This supports the concept that the foundation is not only basic but is temporally first, and is not being continuously constructed. The tense of "being built" (*epoikodomethentes*, v. 20) is actually past (aorist) and could be better translated "who have been built," indicating that the foundation is already in place and the building set upon it. Just as the cornerstone, Jesus Christ, has been set, so the foundation has been laid and the church built upon it. There is no need for other cornerstones (other messiahs), since Christ accomplished his work, and the church still benefits from it. In the same way there is no need for other foundations (other, later apostles), since the apostles' work is accomplished and the church is built on that foundation and the cornerstone.

Present-day apostles cannot be foundational for the universal church. A foundation of necessity occurs at the beginning, and the rest of the superstructure is erected upon it. A foundation is not without temporal significance. Except for the cornerstone, the foundation must come first. The foundation for the universal church must exist at the beginning of the universal church. The apostles and prophets are the foundation upon which the church has been built down through the years.

First Corinthians 15:8 says, "And last of all he was seen of me also, as of one born out of due time" (a miscarriage). The context refers to a succession of events. Paul says, "Then *(epeita)*, he appeared to James; then *(eita)* to all the apostles. And last of all *(eschaton panton)* he appeared to me also" (15:7–8). Paul was the last of all to whom Jesus appeared. To be an apostle one must have seen the resurrected Lord. Since his last appearance was to Paul, it is improbable that anyone after Paul became an apostle. In Deere's opinion this is not a probable interpretation, yet he attempts to substantiate this by simply referring to a commentator rather than providing any evidence. He makes the statement that this verse does not necessarily mean that Jesus could not appear to anyone else after he had appeared to Paul.[10] However, are we trying to discover what the Scriptures say or merely trying to support a position? Paul could have continued with "then," or "next," or even "last." However, he uses a much stronger statement, "last of all."

The context refers to resurrection appearances that support the basic gospel message. It is not describing some incidental visions or appearances. These are actual physical resurrection appearances to confirm that Christ rose from the dead, and are, in effect, part of the gospel testimony. There is no need to establish this all over again. Scripture shows that although others had seen the Lord in his early appearances, the basic witnesses to Jesus' resurrection were the Twelve. Paul's statements in this passage stress how unusual it was for him to see the resurrected Lord at this later time and to become an apostle along with the Twelve. This was so unusual that he compared it to a miscarriage. Paul certainly was not expecting any future appearances, and when he said "last of all" it was for a reason. There are no further resurrection appearances in Scripture. The Lord appeared in a vision in Revelation 1, but not in a resurrection appearance. Even Deere himself admits that there are no additional apostles nor have there been any. Although it cannot be proved beyond any doubt, it is much more probable that Paul meant "last of all" until the Lord returns.

Jude 17–18 also supports the idea that the time of the apostles is past. These verses say, "Remember the words which were spoken beforehand *(proeiremenon)* by the apostles of our Lord Jesus Christ; that they said *(elegon).*" The tense of the verbs indicates a past time from the standpoint of the writer. This means that the apostles were a specific group that had already spoken.

Some may believe that there is a gift of apostle for today in some sense different from the "apostles of the Lord." However, such an apostle is merely a nonapostle. Such a position lacks biblical justification. There are no apostles today.

The Epistles indicate that an apostle received very special and unique responsibilities and revelation. An apostle has authority over local assemblies. This authority is very strong and extends to much more than mere advice, according to such passages as 1 Corinthians 4:19–21; 5:3–4; and 2 Corinthians 13:2–3, 10. An apostle is specifically appointed or called by the Lord. Paul refers to this often in the opening verses of his Epistles. This concept of appointment or calling is mentioned in passages such as Romans 1:5; Galatians 1–2; and 1 Timothy 2:7. Paul also states that apostles and prophets receive revelation (Eph. 3:5) and that he himself was the recipient of special revelation (2 Cor. 12:1–7).

Apostles Are Unique

The apostles of the Lord Jesus Christ were unique. Grudem attempts to equate them with the Old Testament prophets. This allows him to argue that since New Testament prophets are lesser than the apostles, they are also lesser than the Old Testament prophets. Thus, the Holy Spirit gives lesser or "fallible" prophets, such as today's charismatic "prophets." Those Old Testament prophets who are described as performing miracles seem to perform miracles often as spectacles or warnings, such as Elijah did on Mt. Carmel. In contrast to the apostles, the miracles of the Old Testament prophets seem to be more occasional, and are often warnings directed to specific individuals. The apostles performed miracles on a more panoramic scale, healing multitudes as evidence of the Good News rather than as a warning. Also, the apostles performed them over an extended period of time.

The apostles were a very restricted group who existed during one period of time. They were promised that they will be on twelve thrones judging the twelve tribes of Israel (Matt. 19:28) and their names will be on the foundation of the heavenly city (Rev. 21:14). The Old Testament prophets are promised none of these things. Everything about the apostles shows their uniqueness. As seen in passages such as 1 Corinthians 12:28 and 14:37, they have authority over prophets.

We have no information about the existence of any large number of "wonder-working apostles" who were present even in the early church. Although New Testament churches faced numerous problems, apparently no genuine apostle besides Paul was available among the Gentile churches to correct them. Paul never addressed apostles when he wrote the churches or indicated that the church should consult an apostle. Paul's associates, Timothy and Titus, were left in churches to correct them rather than waiting for some circuit-riding apostle to come along and resolve the problem. Thus apostles seem to have been very rare. The Twelve are carefully pointed out as apostles in the Gospels and the book of Acts. They are a very select group in Acts 1–2. Paul is also carefully pointed out as an apostle in the New Testament. Why should we expect others to be apostles who are not likewise carefully designated?

Apostles According to the Testimony of Church History

In general the church has not accepted the notion of the existence of apostles since the first century A.D. In fact many supporters of the charismatic movement do not believe that apostles are present in the church today. The great majority of genuine believers throughout the history of the church have never believed that apostleship was a gift given past the first generation of the church. The arguments of those who do believe that apostles are present today have failed to convince the majority of Christians.

New Testament apostles are *not* present today. The gift of apostleship was given to individuals in the early church but has not been given since.

What Is a Prophet?

An edifying gift of high priority that is also miraculous in its outworking is the gift of prophecy. Today some people claim to be prophets. Since this claim runs counter to the accepted opinion of the church throughout most of its history, the gift of prophet demands further study.

Although the average Christian has felt that the meaning of prophet and prophecy is clear, some confusion regarding these terms exists among theologians. For example, Conzelmann states, "The working ascribed to prophecy makes plain that it is not foretelling of the future."[11] On the other hand, some say that the "element of prediction" is "often minimized, but it should not be overlooked."[12] In contrast to what we might expect, even Pentecostal theologians do not agree on the nature of prophecy. Some believe that it is the ability to predict, while others regard it as exhortation.[13] Hollenweger concludes:

> Apart from a few exceptions, which are, however, important, biblical prophecy seems to me to be absent in the Pentecostal movement. For

biblical prophecy contains more than the edificatory exhortation known as prophecy in the Pentecostal movement of the present day.[14]

Thus, one basic issue regarding the New Testament prophet is whether he is primarily a *forthteller* (i.e., preacher, edifier, exhorter) or a *foreteller* (i.e., one who predicts). Many scholars do not feel that a ministry of prediction is possible. The opinion of such scholars on this subject is suspect. Only the true prophet of God could, in fact, predict. Therefore, in order to determine if a predictive element was involved in New Testament prophecy, only the biblical evidence can provide reliable information. Evidence from nonbiblical literature will naturally not include a predictive element that can be verified. The meaning of *prophet* or *prophecy* in pagan literature, therefore, is not sufficient for a definition of a biblical prophet, who by the power of God could, in fact, predict.[15]

Many interpreters have considered the statement "the one prophesying speaks edification, and exhortation, and encouragement to men" (1 Cor. 14:3) as a definition of the New Testament prophet. This verse, however, does not define the gift of prophecy but merely refers to the fact that prophecy is understandable and, therefore, results in edification, exhortation, and encouragement. This is an argument explaining why prophecy, in the assembly, is preferable to tongues which the hearers do not understand. Those who regard this verse as a definition of prophecy do not understand how it is used in this context. Godet states the issue very clearly:

> The conclusion has often been drawn from this verse, that since to prophesy is to edify, exhort, comfort, whoever edifies, exhorts, comforts, merits according to Paul the title prophet. This reasoning is as just as it would be to say: He who runs moves his legs; therefore, whoever moves his legs, runs. . . . One may edify, comfort, encourage without deserving the title of prophet or prophetess.[16]

Other gifts, such as apostle and teacher, also edify, encourage, and exhort. A definition of a prophet must be based on a study of the New Testament usage rather than on a verse listing some of the results of prophecy. Several gifts edify and communicate God's truths, but each has its own particular features that make it different from other gifts. A gift is defined not by those characteristics that it shares with other gifts but by those that differentiate it from the others.

The same terms are used for *prophet* in the New Testament as in the Greek Old Testament. Furthermore, the New Testament refers to Old Testament prophets and prophecies frequently, and uses the same terms that it does for prophets and prophecies given to the church. The examples of prophets in the New Testament bear a similarity to those in the Old Testament. All of these factors suggest that the gift of prophet in the New Testament is similar to that in the Old Testament. This similarity in terms and description presents a definite obstacle to those who argue for distinct differences. Thus the Old and New Testament prophets seem to be virtually equivalent in both terms and actions, and only very clear evidence will demonstrate otherwise.

Prophet and Prophecy: The Biblical Terminology

Old Testament Background

Prophesy (propheteuo). This verbal form means "to be a prophet" or "to expound or preach under the influence of the Holy Spirit."[17] Secular Greek of the New Testament period uses *prophesy* of interpreting oracular utterance and of taking the divine things and prophesying to men.[18] The Septuagint (Greek Old Testament) uses this verb of foretelling, although sometimes the fulfillment aspect is immediate.[19] We may tentatively conclude that the verb *prophesy* signifies the communication of information that is derived in a supernatural manner (by revelation), and in biblical references it concerns events that are future.

Prophet (prophetes). The noun *prophet* in the common use of that day referred to a person who speaks for God and interprets his will to people.[20] The Septuagint uses the term of a representative of God who brings God's Word directly to the people. His information is gained by a direct revelation, such as a vision or dream.[21] For example, the prophet Nathan gave David an incorrect opinion of God's will concerning the temple, but later received direct revelation from God that changed his initial instructions to David (2 Sam. 7). This example shows that a prophet, as we would expect, does not always speak due to a direct revelation from God and may err unless he speaks by revelation.

Prediction is a prominent aspect of the Old Testament prophet. Scholars argue and make endless studies trying to remove the idea of prediction from the word "prophet" and the verb "prophesy." Some of this must be due to a bias against the supernatural aspect involved in prediction, since the predictive aspect is so prominent. Deuteronomy 18:20–22 states:

But the prophet, which shall presume to speak a word in my name, which I have not commanded him to speak, or that shall speak in the name of other gods, even that prophet shall die. And if thou shalt say in thine heart, How shall we know the word which the LORD hath not spoken? When a prophet speaketh in the name of the LORD, if the thing follow not, nor come to pass, that is the thing which the LORD hath not spoken.

The Hebrew word *nabi* is translated here by the Greek word for *prophet*. These verses not only indicate that a prophet speaks by direct command (revelation) of the Lord, but they imply that prediction is normally involved in prophecy. They also clearly state that the test of a prophet of God is whether he can predict (foretell). Therefore, a prophet must be able to predict by means of direct divine revelation. Since this is *the* test, given only to prophets, it must be an essential characteristic of a prophet. Many gifts concern speaking to men on behalf of God, but the ability to foretell is the ability that differentiates the prophet from other gifted individuals. All alleged prophets claim to speak by divine revelation; however, unless a prophet can make accurate predictions, he is not a true prophet of God.

Prophecy (propheteia). This term was used in the culture of that day for the oracular gift, the prophecy itself, or sometimes the office of prophet.[22] The Septuagint refers to the book of Isaiah as a *propheteia* (2 Chron. 32:32). In 2 Chronicles 15:8 and Ezra 5:1 the term is used for a word from God.[23] In the Greek Old Testament this noun form never refers to the *office* (gift) of prophet; rather, it always refers to the *content* of a prophet's message. We may conclude that prophecy *(propheteia)* means either the message of the prophet or in secular Greek it may refer to the office of a prophet. The Old Testament uses it only in reference to the message, that is, the content of the prophet's communication.

New Testament Usage

Prophesy (propheteuo). This verb occurs twenty-eight times in the New Testament. It occurs eleven times in 1 Corinthians, the only occurrences in Paul's Epistles. In the Gospels and book of Acts it occurs thirteen times. The remaining four occurrences are in 1 Peter 1:10, Jude 14, Revelation 10:11, and 11:3. Several occurrences refer only to Old Testament instances. These are Matthew 15:7, Mark 7:6, 1 Peter 1:10, and Jude 14, all of which refer to acts of foretelling; Matthew 11:13 implies prediction. In the following paragraphs we will look at the use of "prophesy" in the New Testament.

Although the nature and content of the prophecies is not stated, we learn that some individuals will prophesy falsely in Jesus' name. Those involved will also claim to cast out demons and perform miracles, implying that the prophesying is thought to be supernatural (Matt. 7:22–23).

On one occasion Jesus was blindfolded, then hit and sarcastically told to prophesy who hit him. This implies that in the people's minds prophesying did not always require prediction, but it did require supernatural revelation. Mere edification and exhortation do not fit this passage (Matt. 26:67–68; Mark 14:65; Luke 22:64).

According to Luke 1:67, Zacharias prophesied after he was filled with the Spirit. This appears to be an oracular type of utterance. It apparently is based upon direct revelation from God, since the content is a prediction, even though some of the information was given by the angel in Luke 1:14–17. Also, the details of the prophecy (1:68–79) are more than what would normally be known by a human, and the prophecy in this instance was a result of the Holy Spirit filling Zacharias.

According to John 11:51, Caiaphas, the high priest, prophesied unwittingly on one occasion. There is no evidence of a vision, dream, or revelation. Apparently in this verse John uses the verb "prophesy" to indicate unintentional foretelling. This predictive element is the only basis upon which Caiaphas' statement can be considered as prophesying. This shows that prediction is the prominent concept in prophesying.

In some passages, the content is not indicated, so it is impossible to determine whether it is predictive. In most instances it can be clearly differentiated from mere edification or exhortation (Acts 2:17–18; 19:6; 21:9; 1 Cor. 11:4–5; 13:9; 14:1–39). As a result of the imparted information, the person prophesying edifies, exhorts, and consoles others (1 Cor. 14:3–5). In short he edifies the church since, as 1 Corinthians 14 indicates, prophesying can be understood by the hearers; no interpretation is necessary. However, the passage does not indicate the content of the prophecies.

At first glance, the statement in 1 Corinthians 14:31, "For you may all prophesy one by one," seems to indicate that everyone can prophesy. But this is not what the passage means. The entire chapter is based on the fact that not all prophesy, only some. The chapter would make no sense if all prophesied.[24] This verse is introduced by "for" (*gar*), showing that it is the reason for the statement of verse 30, which refers only to the prophets, not to everyone. They are to prophesy in an orderly fashion because they will all eventually have opportunity to prophesy. The entire context in verses 29–32 refers to the prophets and not to the congregation as a whole. Paul says explicitly in 1 Corinthians 12:29 that all are not prophets. A study of the passage shows that prophets are the ones who prophesy. Paul also states specifically in 1 Corinthians 14:5, "I would that ye all spake with tongues, but rather that ye prophesied." The statement "but rather that ye prophesied" means "but I wish more that ye all prophesied." They did not all prophesy or Paul would not wish that they did. Finally, 1 Corinthians 14:37 indicates that only certain ones in the Corinthian church would consider themselves to be prophets.

Revelation 10:11 and 11:3 reveal little for the purpose of our study, although the idea of prediction seems to be present. The verb "prophesy" describes certain actions by prophets and is not used of everyone who speaks for God. In the historical books it is not used of Jesus, the apostles, Paul, or anyone in the church except Philip's daughters and to describe the initial reception of the Spirit by the men in Acts 19. Otherwise, except for the statements in 1 Corinthians 11–14, the verb "prophesy" is not used to describe the activities of the church.

Prophecy (propheteia). This word occurs nineteen times in the New Testament. Of these, seven occurrences are in Revelation and five are in 1 Corinthians. Matthew 13:14 uses it to refer to Isaiah 6:9–10, an Old Testament prophecy. Matthew's use of it with the verb *pleroo*, "fulfilled," shows that Matthew regards it as a prediction. Apparently it refers to a prophecy (content) in 1 Corinthians 13:8; 14:6, 22; 1 Thessalonians 5:20; 1 Timothy 1:18; 4:14; 2 Peter 1:20–21; Revelation 1:3; 19:10; 22:7, 10, 18–19; and probably 11:6. Direct revelation seems to be involved in 1 Timothy 1:18 and 4:14. Prediction is implied in 2 Peter 1:20–21 as well as the passages in Revelation. The remaining passages provide no information on the content of the prophecies.

Only Romans 12:6, 1 Corinthians 12:10, and 13:2 refer to the office or gift of a prophet, and this understanding of its use in the latter two verses is questionable. The noun *propheteia* usually refers to a "prophecy," that is, to the message or content delivered by prophesying. It refers to the gift of prophecy in perhaps only three instances. In Revelation 11:6 it seems to refer to some prophetic activity.

Prophet (prophetes). "Prophet" occurs much more frequently than the other terms (thirty-four times in Matthew; five times in Mark; twenty-nine times in Luke; fourteen times in John; thirty times in Acts; and twenty-seven times in the remainder of the New Testament).

In the great majority of occurrences the Gospels use *prophetes* to refer to Old Testament prophets. There is little help for this study in the synoptic Gospels except in Luke 7:39. The word is used of Old Testament prophets in John except in 7:52; however, John 4:19, 6:14, 7:40, and 9:17 appear helpful. The Gospels suggest a similarity between the use of the term in the New Testament and the Old Testament.

Luke 7:39—Here the Pharisees expected a prophet to have supernatural discernment, so the idea of edification or exhortation does not fit this passage.

John 4:19—The woman at the well credited Jesus with being a prophet when told of her past life. Supernatural knowledge indicated to her that he was a prophet. Edification is not in view here.

John 6:14—After performing the sign of feeding the five thousand, Jesus was regarded as "the Prophet" by the crowd. The idea of edification or exhortation is absent in this passage.

John 7:40—Jesus was regarded as "the Prophet" after he spoke at the feast.

John 9:17—The man healed of blindness regarded Jesus, who healed him, as a prophet. The idea of edification or exhortation is absent in this passage.

Since John 6:14 and 7:40 refer to "the Prophet," they may not be applicable to prophets in general. The verses listed above all describe events that occurred historically before the gift of New Testament prophet, but they indicate certain things that Israel regarded as typical of a prophet, including supernatural insight, knowledge, and speaking truths about God. The performance of miracles seemed to indicate that Jesus was more than a prophet. It indicated that he was special; he was "the Prophet" in fulfillment of Deuteronomy 18:18. This implies that miracle working was not associated with the average Old Testament prophet.

The book of Acts describes the time of the early church; therefore, it will directly bear on the nature of the New Testament prophet. Of the numerous occurrences in Acts, the following are deemed significant. The rest refer mainly to Old Testament prophets.

Acts 2:30–31—This passage states regarding David, "Therefore since he was a prophet and knowing . . . he, foreseeing, spoke of the resurrection of Christ . . . ." In this passage Peter stresses that because David was a prophet, he foresaw and predicted the coming of Christ, thereby directly linking the prophet with the ability to predict.

Acts 3:18–25—In this section verse 18 says, "But those things, which God had declared beforehand by all his prophets, that Christ should suffer, he has thus fulfilled." All of the prophets had a predictive ministry regarding Christ.

Acts 7:52; 10:43—Both Stephen and Peter refer to predictions made by the prophets in regard to Christ.

Acts 11:27–28—Agabus is the first example of a New Testament prophet. He acted much like an Old Testament prophet. Receiving information that was given by the Spirit, he predicted a famine that came to pass.

Acts 13:1; 15:32—The church at Antioch included prophets and teachers. We know little of their specific ministry as prophets. Judas and Silas were prophets from the Jerusalem church who encouraged the brethren with many words.

Acts 21:10—Agabus came from Judea and foretold Paul's captivity. Agabus acted precisely like an Old Testament prophet and explicitly stated that his prediction was from the Holy Spirit. According to the book of Acts, his prophecy was precisely fulfilled.[25]

Acts 26:22–23—Paul indicated that the Old Testament prophets foretold the events concerning Christ.

From the book of Acts we see that the prophet in both the Old and New Testament was involved in ministry that included foretelling. The only specific examples we have of a New Testament prophet are Acts 11:27–28 and 21:10, which refer to Agabus; and Acts 15:32, which refers to Judas and Silas. In both cases Agabus predicted a future event. He specifically stated in Acts 21:10 that his information was received by direct revelation. Also, Luke stated in Acts 11:27–28 that Agabus "signified by the Spirit." Although his "home church" was probably Jerusalem, he appears to have had an itinerant ministry. It is impossible to determine the specifics of Judas and Silas's ministry in Antioch, since it is described under the general statement "exhorted the brethren with many words, and confirmed them." It is not specifically stated that they prophesied.

In the book of Romans all of the references refer to Old Testament prophets. The following passages in the remaining Epistles appear to be significant for study of the New Testament prophet.

1 Corinthians 12:28-29—This passage clearly refers to New Testament prophets. They are second in rank in the church. Since the list is not given in chronological order, it is difficult to regard "second" in any sense besides that of prominence, priority, or authority. The aspect of priority is also suggested by the close connection with the apostles in other passages (Eph. 2:20; 3:5). Although this is an important gift, it is stated that not all have it.

1 Corinthians 14:29-32—In the assembly, prophets are to speak one at a time, and no more than a total of two or three are to speak. A prophet who receives a direct, immediate revelation has the priority in speaking over another prophet who is speaking apart from immediate revelation. A revelation is no unusual thing for a prophet; in fact, it is expected. Such revelation is immediate and cannot be merely equated with biblical knowledge. A prophet may receive revelation at some other time and communicate it later to the assembly. However, the one receiving the revelation during the assembly has priority. The other prophets are to discern (Gk. *diakrino*) all utterances by prophets. Since Paul says that the "spirits of the prophets are subject to the prophets," no one may claim to be carried away and therefore avoid these restrictions.

Ephesians 2:20—As shown in the previous discussion of this verse, the apostles and prophets themselves are the foundation for the universal church. This is a strong implication that prophets are not only of very high priority but are a gift for the beginning of the church as a whole. Since Christ, apostles, prophets, and Christians are all a part of the building in this figure, the prophets referred to in this verse are part of the church; therefore, they are New Testament prophets.[26]

Ephesians 3:5—Apostles and prophets are again closely connected, here as recipients of truth (revelation) by the Spirit. This verse, which says "which in other ages was not made known unto the sons of men, as it is now revealed to his holy apostles and prophets by the Spirit," refers specifically to the prophets of that respective time, New Testament prophets. The close connection between apostles and prophets in Ephesians 3:5 implies that Ephesians 2:20 also refers to New Testament prophets.

Ephesians 4:11—The gift of prophet is a gift intended for building up the church to maturity in Christ. Like the gift of apostle, it is a leadership gift, although the two gifts are separate.

Titus 1:12—This verse refers to a prophet of the Cretans, a pagan prophet.

1 Peter 1:10—This passage refers to Old Testament prophets. It clearly indicates that they foretold by means of revelation. Since Peter does not delineate the prophets as Old Testament prophets, and the same term is used for both, it is probable that the New Testament office of prophet differed little from the Old Testament office.

The book of Revelation uses the term *prophet* frequently, but adds little new information to this study. Apparently prophets will be present during the period of the great tribulation. The prophets are linked with foretelling (see Rev. 22:6). In 22:9 the angel states that he is a fellow servant with John and "thy brethren the prophets."

From this study we may conclude that not all believers have the gift of prophet. A prophet is usually involved with a predictive ministry. Prophets are the recipients of direct divine revelation, which may occur immediately before speaking. Prophets may speak apart from immediate revelation; however, it is doubtful that their speaking is described as prophesying if it is not based on direct revelation. Prophets are given to edify the church. When the prophet speaks due to an immediate revelation, his ministry exhorts and causes hearers to learn. A prophet can control his gift. Finally, Ephesians 2:20 shows that prophets were given to the church only at its inception.

Are New Testament Prophets Fallible?

Numerous charismatics testify that their "prophets" are not infallible.[27] Hollenweger, a well-known Pentecostal researcher, sees no prophets in the worldwide Pentecostal movement who are biblical prophets.[28] In attempting to show that such "fallible prophets" are the New Testament gift, some have argued that New Testament prophets are of a lesser order and have less authority than Old Testament prophets had. They are fallible and may even convey incorrect messages. They are no more reliable than any preacher or counselor.[29] This is in contrast to the infallible prophets of the Old Testament and to what most people expect a prophet to be. Since this concept is necessary to maintain that today's fallible charismatic prophets are the gift from the Spirit, and since Wayne Grudem has presented one of the most extensive arguments for this position, we will need to discuss his arguments in some detail.

Grudem has a two-pronged approach to the issue of the New Testament prophets. First, he tries to show that the apostles are equal to the Old Testament prophets. Since the New Testament prophets obviously have less authority than the apostles, the New Testament prophets likewise have less authority than the Old Testament prophets. Thus, we end up with infallible Old Testament prophets and fallible New Testament prophets. Second, Grudem argues that the New Testament prophet is unreliable and nonauthoritative, which is a position with which Carson agrees.[30]

Grudem's argument that the apostle equals the Old Testament prophet has two weaknesses. First, he never seems to consider the possibility that apostles are of *greater* authority than either Old or New Testament prophets. The unique aspect of the apostles, the special place assigned to them in the heavenly city, and the statement that John the Baptist as forerunner of the Messiah is greater than the prophets, opens a definite possibility that these special representatives of the Messiah also have a unique authority. If this is so, then most of Grudem's arguments fall since they all are based on the assumption that the Old Testament prophet is the highest authority figure and the apostles are only equal to them in authority. Second, Grudem uses only a few selected Old Testament prophets to compare the apostles and New Testament prophets with Old Testament prophets.

Grudem's argument states that there is no evidence for a group of prophets in the New Testament who, like the Old Testament prophets, could speak with absolute divine authority and who had authority to write books of Scripture.[31] However, there is direct evidence that the New Testament prophet did speak with divine authority comparable to the Old Testament prophet, as we shall see in this discussion. With regard to the authority to write Scripture, did all of the Old Testament prophets have the authority to write Scripture? Old Testament prophets did not have authority to write Scripture as part of their prophetic office.

In reality only a few specially selected men had this privilege. Likewise, did the apostles have the authority to write Scripture as part of their apostolic office? Could Thomas or Matthias have written Scripture if they were so inclined? Again it seems that neither Old Testament prophets nor the apostles had the authority as part of their office to write Scripture. Only those men specifically chosen by God had such authority. Neither Mark nor Luke were apostles, yet both wrote Scripture. Neither apostles or Old Testament prophets had any more authority to write Scripture than these two who were neither. The fact that both Mark and Luke wrote Scripture, though neither were apostles, severely weakens Grudem's thesis.

Another argument used by Grudem is that both apostles and Old Testament prophets were sent by God and are therefore identical.[32] But Ananias was also sent by God in Acts 9 and Agabus was sent by God in Acts 11 and 21, yet neither was an Old Testament prophet. Grudem also argues that the apostles are "connected with" Old Testament prophets in several passages, but New Testament prophets are not connected in the "same way" with Old Testament prophets.[33] However, apostles are also connected with New Testament prophets. If connection with Old Testament prophets proves that apostles are equal to Old Testament prophets, then connection with New Testament prophets also proves that apostles are equal to New Testament prophets and all three groups are equal. Of course, this is not true since apostles have higher authority than New Testament prophets. If apostles are connected with Old Testament prophets in some passages and with New Testament prophets in other passages, then a more logical conclusion would be that Old and New Testament prophets are equal, and that apostles are superior to both. Actually, "connected with" is such a loose idea that it proves nothing in regard to relationship.

In one of the instances where apostle is "connected with" Old Testament prophets, Grudem refers to the statement in Hebrews 1:1–2, which says, "God . . . spake in time past unto the fathers by the prophets, hath in these last days spoken unto us by his Son." On the basis of this statement, he argues that Jesus is called an apostle in Hebrews 3:1 rather than a prophet, thereby connecting apostle with Old Testament prophets. He then argues that the statement that Jesus is an apostle contrasts in the same passage with Moses, the "archetypal prophet," thus connecting apostle with an Old Testament prophet.[34] But this so-called connection proves just the opposite. In Hebrews 1:1–2 the point is that the revelation by Jesus the Son of God is far superior to that of the Old Testament prophets; and in Hebrews 3:1ff. the point is that Jesus the apostle is the Son of God and far superior to Moses the archetypal prophet. Thus, this connection, if it proves anything, argues for the superiority of apostle over the Old Testament prophets, including Moses the archetypal prophet.

The fact that Paul asserts authority over New Testament prophets means little unless it is proved that he could not exercise authority over Old Testament prophets in the same circumstances.[35] Likewise, the argument that apostles are sometimes called prophets is meaningless as well, since they are also called teachers and preachers. Yet this does not equate them with Old Testament teachers and preachers, and thereby mean that New Testament teachers and preachers are inferior to Old Testament ones.[36] Thus, neither can it mean this with relation to prophets. The gift of apostle included all of these abilities such as prophet, teacher, and preacher, but it was more than any of them.

The fact that the apostles are not called prophets presents a serious obstacle to the concept that they are equal to Old Testament prophets. If they are equal to Old Testament prophets, then why not call them prophets? Why have a different title if they are the same? Grudem realizes that this is an obstacle. He uses two arguments to explain this.

First, Grudem argues that Joel and others predicted that one day all of God's people would be prophets; therefore, a different term was needed to differentiate the apostles from the others.[37] This argument fails on two accounts. All of God's people are not prophets at the present time. Joel's prophecy refers to the future, so why would a different term be needed at the present time? In addition, if this were so, then why would God use the term "prophets" for one of the most important groups in the church since they would also need to be differentiated from the other prophets?

Second, Grudem argues that the term *prophet* had come to have a broader connotation in the world of that day, so that it would not carry the idea of "one sent with absolute divine authority." Thus a different word such as "apostle" was needed.[38] But did the term *prophet* ever carry the idea within the broader culture of "one sent with absolute divine authority?" Certainly, the word *apostle* had a much broader connotation in Greek culture than the word *prophet*. Why choose an even broader term if this were the problem?

Moreover, the term *prophet* had a broad connotation in Old Testament times and could even refer to false prophets. So, why did God use it to refer to Old Testament prophets if this were such a problem? Finally, if there were some such problem with the term *prophets*, then why did God use it at all and, in particular, why did he use it to refer to the second ranking group in the church? The reason why the apostles are called apostles and not prophets is because they are in fact a special group, the apostles.

The Significance of Ephesians 2:20

In an attempt to prove that apostles are equal to Old Testament prophets, Grudem employs an unusual interpretation of Ephesians 2:20. This verse refers to Christians who are "built upon the foundation of the apostles and prophets, Jesus Christ himself being the corner stone." Grudem interprets the "apostles and prophets" to mean the "apostles who are prophets" or the "apostle-prophets."[39] In other words, he regards the nouns as identical. The basis upon which he makes this claim is that there is only one article ("the") with the two nouns ("apostles and prophets") joined by "and" *(kai)*. He refers to eleven verses where he says, "one person or group of persons is meant, but the same construction as in Ephesians 2:20 and 3:5 is used."[40]

Not one of his eleven examples, however, is precisely the same construction as Ephesians 2:20 or 3:5. The precise construction used here always means just the opposite of Grudem's claim; that is, the construction indicates two separate groups rather than one. Also, the fact that these nouns are plural is significant in this construction, yet many of Grudem's examples have singular nouns. There is, however, a more glaring difference between Ephesians 2:20 and 3:5 and the examples supplied by Grudem. As many as seventy-one occurrences of this general construction have been found with plural nouns.[41] However, less than one-third of these have this precise construction that occurs in Ephesians 2:20 and 3:5. The construction in Ephesians 2:20 and 3:5 has two independent nouns, yet none of Grudem's examples fit this pattern. His examples use participles (verbal adjectives), adjectives, or nouns in an adjectival relationship to some other noun in the verse; they refer to some other actual or understood noun referent in the verse. This is the factor that ties them together and, therefore, they are not independent.

In Ephesians 2:20 and 3:5 the two nouns refer to no other

noun, either stated or implied; they are independent. Thus, they cannot be considered the same construction since in the one case there is some factor tying the two nouns together that is not present in Ephesians 2:20 and 3:5. Grudem's first example, Romans 16:7, will illustrate this. This verse says, "Salute Andronicus and Junias, my kinsmen and my fellow prisoners." There is one article before "kinsmen" (an adjective used as a noun) and "fellow prisoners" and they refer to the same people, Andronicus and Junias. However, the one article does not make them the same; it is the fact that both "kinsmen" and "fellow prisoners" refer to the specific nouns, "Andronicus and Junias," stated in the verse, which makes them the same. Otherwise they could not be considered the same. All of Paul's kinsmen are not also fellow prisoners, nor are all of Paul's fellow prisoners his kinsmen. Only Andronicus and Junias, who are specifically referred to in this verse, fit these criteria. The two "nouns" coincide only in the case of these two people. The nouns in question function in an adjectival, or modifying relationship rather than as independent nouns. Thus the single article is not the factor that indicates that they are the same since if there were an article before each noun, they would still refer to the same people.

Four other examples given by Grudem are all singular and all have some specific referent in the verse (see Eph. 6:21; Phil. 2:25; Philem. 1; Heb. 3:1). Thus they do not have the same construction as Ephesians 2:20 or 3:5. In Colossians 1:2 "saints" and "faithful brethren" are both plural, but both modify a specific referent. Even the statements "God and Saviour" in 2 Peter 1:1 and "Lord and Saviour" in 1:11, although they are singular nouns, in each instance has a specific referent, "Jesus Christ." Galatians 1:7 and 1 Thessalonians 5:12, the two remaining passages, have participles (i.e., verbal adjectives) rather than nouns. Not only are they adjectival but commonly two verbal ideas accompany one subject. Each has the same understood subject represented by the article. As Wallace has shown, two participles with one article commonly refer to one group or person; however, two nouns refer to two different groups or persons.[42] This is the case in Ephesians 2:20. Thus the construction used in Ephesians 2:20 and 3:5 does not refer to identical groups.

Even if the two nouns were interpreted as identical, which is contrary to Greek grammar, Grudem's interpretation "apostle-prophets" would still be unacceptable. It requires a specific but highly questionable way of viewing the two nouns. Normally, if two nouns are identical, they refer to the same thing. Thus apostles and prophets would be the same. This is obviously not so, which should be sufficient to settle this question. But Grudem's interpretation requires that the noun "prophets" refer not to the well-known group of prominent individuals in the church, but only to some prophets, namely, apostles. But, apostles are not elsewhere called "prophets." This is particularly obvious since Grudem has actually gone to great lengths attempting to show why the apostles are not called "prophets." Is there any example of such an interpretation elsewhere?

Let us look at a construction similar to Ephesians 2:20 in which the same term *apostle* is used together with the term *elders*. The same construction—one article before two plural nouns joined by "and"—is used in Acts 15:2 where it refers to the "apostles and elders." If we apply the same principle as Grudem does in interpreting Ephesians 2:20, we will have a new group of individuals called "apostle-elders," which will exclude those at Jerusalem who are normally called "elders." However, this interpretation in incorrect. There were elders in Jerusalem. The "apostles and the elders" are mentioned in Acts 15:4 where the grammatical construction clearly indicates that the apostles and elders are two separate groups. Also, the article appears before each group in Acts 15:6, 22–23. Yet in Acts 16:4, referring to the same incident, the two groups are once again preceded by only one article. Thus, in Acts 15:2 and 16:4 the same groups are referred to with one article, as in Ephesians 2:20; and in Acts 15:6, 22–23 they are also referred to with two articles, indicating that the author has in mind two separate groups. The instances that have only one article merely group the two separate groups, "apostles and elders," due to something the author views as common to both. For example, as Wallace points out in Matthew 3:7, only one article precedes the "Sadducees and Pharisees," yet they are two distinct entities.[43] Therefore, the idea that Ephesians 2:20 refers only to one group is both grammatically and logically untenable.

Carson's assertion that the exegesis of this verse is so complex that any deductions from it should be used with caution is incorrect, as is his taking Gaffin to task for using this verse as an argument.[44] Ephesians 2:20 could not be more clear. The verse contains no difficult words, nor any difficult or unusual grammatical constructions. The grammatical construction of one article preceding two nouns joined by "and" is a familiar and well-known construction. Any alleged complexities in interpreting this verse arise not from the verse itself but from the presuppositions of the interpreter. Because a few scholars do not agree on the meaning of the verse has nothing to do with the alleged complexity of this verse. Most scholars have had no difficulty with it. Therefore, cessationists are completely justified in using this perfectly clear verse to support their position. There is no valid reason to avoid stressing it merely because those who disagree with it have had difficulty fitting it into their thinking.

The Allegation That New Testament Prophets Are Deficient

Grudem uses several indirect arguments in attempting to prove that New Testament prophets are deficient when compared to those of the Old Testament. In a somewhat strange argument, he contends that when Paul instructs the prophet who may already be speaking to stop and allow another to speak who is receiving a direct revelation (1 Cor. 14:30), Paul is directing that these words be lost. Thus, he concludes they cannot be God's words.[45] However, the passage does not even intimate such an idea. There is no reason to assume that the original speaker is not allowed to finish his message as soon as the revelatory speaker has finished his revelation.

Another argument that the word "revelation" does not imply divine authority may mislead those unfamiliar with Greek, since they may think that this Greek word itself may be the basis of Grudem's argument.[46] However, this argument has no more force than it would with the English word "revelation." We may say that it was revealed to me that I should study harder. The fact that this does not imply a divine revelation has no bearing at all on the meaning of "revelation" in the statement, "The prophet of God communicated a revelation to us." The context and the identification with a prophet of God, together with the fact that prophets commonly communicate divine revelation, makes the divine revelatory aspect clear. To take it otherwise would be to ignore the context. Neither does the statement, "What? came the word of God out from you? or came it unto you only" (1 Cor. 14:36) imply that the prophets in Corinth did not speak with divine authority as Grudem claims.[47]

Paul is not referring to some fallible prophecies in this verse. He is merely asking the Corinthians in this somewhat caustic statement if they think they received some special information so that they can do things their own way different from the other churches. It has no bearing on the actual accuracy of their prophets. He also argues that since women may prophesy according to 1 Corinthians 11, this implies that New Testament prophecy is nonauthoritative.[48] This argument depends on one possible interpretation of 1 Corinthians 14:34–35, and assumes that 1 Corinthians 11 refers to the assembly. It says nothing about the assembly. Whenever the assembly is specifically in mind in Corinthians it is expressly stated. Regardless, the point in 1 Corinthians 11 is that women should be covered, specifically because prophecy is authoritative.

This seemingly endless series of tenuous and indirect arguments is due to the fact that there are no direct statements of Scripture to support the "fallible prophet" concept. He also argues that the expression "let the others discern" in 1 Corinthians 14:29 refers to the entire congregation and thus makes the New Testament prophets subject to the entire congregation.[49] However, this is contrary to the context, which is only speaking in regard to prophets, which uses the same term specifically of the prophets in the following verses and concludes that all may prophesy definitely, referring only to all the prophets. In any case, how this can indicate that New Testament prophets are inferior to Old Testament prophets is not clear, since the entire congregation of Israel was also told to scrutinize their prophets (Deut. 18:22).

Another argument, that the word "discern" (Gk. *diakrino*) means that the hearers are to sift out the good from the bad in a prophecy, thus indicating that it may contain both good and bad, is based on an untenable meaning for the word.[50] The word *diakrino* does not imply that there is both good and bad to be sifted out. It is often used in a context such as this in reference to rendering judgment between two people, that is, determining which one is right and which one is wrong. In contrast to the assertions that it differs from *krino*, "to judge," is the fact that it is used thirteen times in this way in the Septuagint, and in nine of these passages it is explicitly equated with either *krino* or *krisis*. Thus, Carson's and Grudem's statements about the meaning of *diakrino* here have little basis in fact. In the New Testament it can also mean to judge or evaluate people. In fact, it is used earlier in this epistle (1 Cor. 6:5) in the same way as in the Septuagint (see, e.g., Exod. 18:16; 1 Kings 3:9; Zech. 3:7 and many other passages in the Old Testament). If there is any sifting out, it is only in order to pass judgment regarding the persons being judged. Carson's statement that "discern" refers to judging the prophecy itself,[51] if correct, would mean to judge whether the entire prophecy were true or false. It would not mean to sift out the good from the bad and consider the good parts as from God and the prophet as a genuine prophet. This is contrary to biblical practice.

The normal use of *diakrino* in this kind of context would mean to render a judgment in regard to people. It would fit well with the admonitions to test the spirits and with Paul's statement at the beginning of this section that speakers can communicate from different sources of revelation. This is the precise word to indicate a judging to determine whether the prophet speaking is true or false. It seems clear from the ministry of Agabus as well as 1 John 4:1 and other historical documents that itinerant prophets needed to be verified. In any case, the entire point about sifting and evaluating is meaningless to prove that all New Testament prophets are "fallible" or inferior to Old Testament prophets, since the content of the prophecy would need to be "sifted" or evaluated to pass judgment on the veracity of the prophet or even to determine the meaning of the prophecy. How else could anyone determine whether a prophet was true or false? Therefore, the idea of sifting or evaluating proves nothing to support the argument that true New Testament prophets were "fallible." However, the fact that *diakrino* is commonly used in contexts of judging persons and not for evaluating isolated details is decidedly against Grudem's view. *Diakrino* definitely does not imply that both good and bad may need to be sifted out from the prophecy. It does not imply that there are true and false statements in all New Testament prophecy or that a genuine prophet may give false prophecies.

Agabus: Is He Treated Fairly?

Agabus the prophet has suffered some extremely critical treatment at the hands of a few scholars. Agabus came to Paul and his companions in Caesarea and said, "Thus says the Holy Spirit, So shall the Jews at Jerusalem bind the man who owns this girdle, and shall deliver him into the hands of the Gentiles" (Acts 21:11). Regarding Agabus and his prophecy, Carson says that he "can think of no reported Old Testament prophet whose prophecies are so wrong on the details."[52] Carson asserts that the Jews did not bind Paul; the Romans did, and they did not hand Paul over to the Romans. Instead, the Romans rescued Paul. Although Gaffin attempts to defend Agabus, Carson accuses Gaffin of not paying attention to the details.[53] In a moment we will examine who has paid attention to the details.

Grudem is even stronger in his comments regarding Agabus. Grudem says, "by Old Testament standards, Agabus would have been condemned as a false prophet, because in Acts 21:27–35 neither of his predictions are fulfilled."[54] He says, "Luke tells us twice that it was not the Jews but the Romans who bound Paul." He also states that Agabus's second "mistake" was saying that the Jews would deliver Paul into the hands of the Gentiles. Grudem insists that this word "deliver" in all of its 119 other uses in the New Testament always means "to willingly, consciously hand over."[55] Perhaps he should have been more temperate in making such charges. First, Luke does not tell us even once that it was not the Jews who bound Paul. Luke tells us that the Romans bound Paul but he says nothing that implies that the Jews did not. Carson asserts that the Jews did not bind Paul, but he fails to tell us how he knows this. There certainly is no statement to this effect in the Scripture. There is no logical reason to assume that because the Romans bound Paul this somehow means that the Jews could not have bound him previously. Certainly Paul did not voluntarily go along with the Jewish mob; he must have been bound in some sense. Since the Greek word *deo*, "bind," can have several broader meanings, including the meaning "to take captive," which the Jews obviously did to Paul, it is illogical to state that the Jews did not "bind" Paul as Agabus said. However, there is no reason to assume that the Jews did not actually bind Paul with some physical restraints.

The assertion that Paul was not handed over to the Gentiles as Agabus said is a statement that contradicts Paul himself. Describing the events to the elders in Rome, Paul said about himself, "yet was I delivered prisoner from Jerusalem into the hands of the Romans" (Acts 28:17). Here he uses exactly the same verb as Agabus to describe this event (*paradidomi*, "deliver"). Paul describes this event in the same way as Agabus, and Paul, more than anyone else, should know what happened and be able to state it correctly and accurately. Therefore, Agabus made no errors. Rather the errors are being made by those accusing Agabus of mistakes.

Carson also states that it is rare for a New Testament prophecy to be "in the form of a direct quotation from God, prefaced perhaps by a stern 'thus says the Lord.'"[56] However, every place where the explicit words of a prophecy by a New Testament prophet are quoted it is prefaced by the words, "Thus says the Holy Spirit." Admittedly, this is "rare," because it occurs only once in the New Testament, and that is in the passage we are discussing. It is Agabus who makes the statement, "Thus says the Holy Spirit." This formula parallels the Old Testament prophets' "Thus says the Lord," except for the fact that the Spirit is explicitly specified in the New Testament. In the few remaining places where the prophecy of a New Testament prophet is referred to in general terms but not directly quoted, Luke explicitly states that it is from the Spirit (Acts 11:28; 21:4). The occasion when Jude and Silas were sent by the Jerusalem church to the Gentile churches does not describe any prophecy but gives only an overall summary of their ministry (Acts 15:32). Thus we see that Agabus did not make any mistakes. Furthermore, he presents himself and his prophecy in almost exact correspondence to the Old Testament prophets and prefaces it with "Thus says the Lord," claiming divine authority for the words of his prophecy.

We do not have the exact words of the prophecy in Acts 21:4, which concerns the same subject as that of Agabus's prophecy. Therefore, it is inappropriate to claim with Carson and Grudem that Paul disregarded this prophecy, thereby showing that he did not regard it as authoritative.[57] This is particularly true since there is a direct correspondence to this situation in the same passage. When Agabus gave his prophecy, warning Paul what would happen to him in Jerusalem, the disciples, including Luke, interpreted the warning to mean that Paul should not go to Jerusalem even though Agabus did not specifically say that Paul should stay away from Jerusalem (Acts 21:12–13). The most logical way to interpret Acts 21:4 is that the prophecy was much the same as Agabus's—a warning rather than a prohibition against going to Jerusalem. Like Agabus's prophecy, this passage was interpreted as a warning.

This warning was then understood by most of those present as a prohibition, just as the similar warning was incorrectly taken as a prohibition in Acts 21:12–13. On the other hand, it was correctly understood by Paul to be only a warning. Since the Lord stands by Paul later in Acts and indicates that this is all according to his plan, he would hardly have given a direct prohibition to Paul in a prophecy. Thus, Paul did not disregard this prophecy as some inferior prophecy that could be disregarded. Rather he interpreted it correctly as a warning rather than a prohibition. We also need to remember that Luke says explicitly that the Spirit supplied this information. In any case, the opinion that the prophecy in Acts 21:4 prohibited Paul from going to Jerusalem will not fit any evangelical idea of New Testament prophecy, since the prophet in Acts 21:4 spoke "by the Spirit," and if he prohibited Paul from going to Jerusalem, then he instructed Paul by the Spirit to disobey

God's will. Even the most flexible idea of what it means for a New Testament prophet to speak "by the Spirit" does not seem to permit falsehood, let alone the blatant contradiction of God. Acts 21:4 was a warning interpreted by those present just as the same warning was in Acts 21:10–13. Paul did not disregard this prophecy as if it had no authority; therefore, this passage provides no support for the concept that New Testament prophets are inferior to Old Testament prophets or that they make mistakes or lack authority.

Conclusion Regarding the Gift of Prophet

Although he may also minister otherwise, a New Testament prophet receives direct revelation from the Lord. Normally his ministry may be described as one that involves foretelling or prediction. Similar to the Old Testament prophet, he functions as a spokesman for God. If someone does not receive direct revelation and does not predict on occasion, he is not a prophet. The Old Testament states that a prophet must be able to predict. The only examples of a prophet's ministry in the New Testament reflect this predictive element.

Prophets apparently ministered both in the local church and in itinerant ministry, but are not restricted to one or the other. More than one prophet may be in an assembly. The prophet is a high-priority gift often linked with the apostle. We have no valid evidence for New Testament prophets in the church who are inferior or deficient, or who lack divine authority when speaking by revelation. Even if these prophets were not fully equal to the Old Testament prophets, this would not imply that their prophecies were incorrect or mistaken or that they spoke without divine authority. Instead the New Testament prophets are comparable to the Old Testament prophets, but dissimilar to the "fallible prophets" found in charismatic circles today.

The prophet was a gift given only to the early church. Apostles and prophets are the foundation of the church established by Christ, the cornerstone. No one has shown that individuals demonstrating the biblical qualifications for a prophet are present in the church today. Based on the description of the prophet in the New Testament no one can demonstrate that they are a prophet apart from the ability to predict the future. The predictions are not vague, general statements, but rather quite specific predictions that may be verified within reasonable time. They must also receive direct, immediate revelation. Any individual who claims to be a prophet merely because of an insight into Scripture is making an erroneous claim. Those who claim that anyone who encourages, exhorts, and consoles is a prophet are also making erroneous claims. Exhorting and encouraging are the results of the prophet's ministry, but they also are the results of the ministries of others who are not prophets.

In the early church individuals described as prophets were rare. In fact only Agabus, Philip's daughters, and some at Antioch are called prophets. It is implied that prophets were in the assembly in Corinth and by extension would be in other churches. However, little is said of their activity elsewhere in the New Testament.

Summary

Second Corinthians 12:12 directly states that miracles are a sign of an apostle. New Testament examples bear this out. The teaching that an apostle must have seen the resurrected Lord is given by Peter in Acts 1 and by Paul in 1 Corinthians 9:1-2. The limitation of apostleship to a narrow group is indicated in direct statements of Scripture. The unique authority of an apostle is declared by direct statements of Scripture (see 1 Cor. 4:19-21; 5:3-4; 2 Cor. 13:2-3, 10; 1 Tim. 1:20). The teaching that apostles and prophets receive revelation is made in Ephesians 3:5 (see also 2 Cor. 12:1-11), and that a prophet receives direct, immediate revelation from the Lord is stated in 1 Corinthians 14:29-32. The teaching that apostles and prophets comprise the foundation of the church along with Jesus Christ, the cornerstone, is directly stated in Ephesians 2:20.

All of the important conclusions reached in this chapter regarding apostles and prophets are directly taught in Scripture. The only important point not directly taught is the aspect of foretelling in the prophet's ministry. However, the New Testament writers assume this. For example, Peter explicitly states regarding David that "since he was a prophet he foresaw" (Acts 2:30-31). Elsewhere in Scripture are numerous statements that the Old Testament prophets foresaw (see, e.g., Acts 3:18-25) and the few examples of New Testament prophets include foretelling as a part of their ministries. Since the terminology is the same and the functions are similar, a parallel exists between Old Testament and New Testament prophets. None of the arguments for the New Testament prophet as an inferior or "fallible" prophet, such as those within the charismatic movement, have stood up to inspection. Therefore, after an examination of the evidence, we conclude that biblical apostles and prophets are not present in the church today.

* * *

1. James Hope Moulton and George Milligan, *The Vocabulary of the Greek New Testament* (London: Hodder and Stoughton, 1930), 70; and Henry George Liddell and Robert Scott, *A Greek-Lexicon*, rev. ed. (Oxford: Clarendon Press, 1968), 220.
2. Edwin Hatch and Henry A. Redpath, *A Concordance to the Septuagint and the Other Greek Versions of the Old Testament*, 2 vols. (Graz, Austria: Academische Druck-u Verlagsanstalt, 1954), 1:145.
3. If they are "apostles" of a lesser sort, they do not possess the gift of apostle and therefore are still of no help in determining the nature of the gift of apostle.
4. Except for the miracles performed by Philip in Samaria and Stephen in Jerusalem, all of the numerous miracles in the book of Acts were performed by apostles. The next chapter discusses the miracles.
5. Deere, *Surprised by the Power of the Spirit* (Grand Rapids: Zondervan, 1993), 104–5; Philip E. Hughes, *Paul's Second Epistle to the Corinthians* (Grand Rapids: Eerdmans, 1962), 457.
6. Deere, *Surprised* , 278.
7. Ibid., 104–5.
8. F. Blass and A. DeBrunner, *A Greek Grammar of the New Testament and Other Early Christian Literature*, trans. and rev. Robert W. Funk (Chicago: University of Chicago Press, 1961), 101–2.
9. Blass and DeBrunner, *Greek Grammar*, 100–102; Nigel Turner shows only occurrences with words other than nouns, such as verbs. In these instances he also points out that the associative dative presents "the means by which" but has strong emphasis on accompaniment or nearness, and if it describes accompaniment adds *en* (*Syntax*, Vol.3, *A Grammar of New Testament Greek*, James H. Moulton, 4 vols. [Edinburgh: T. & T. Clark, 1963], 240). A. T. Robertson mentions a few possibilities, such as John 12:12 (*A Grammar of the Greek New Testament in Light of Historical Research* [Nashville: Broadman, 1934], 528); however, it is questionable whether this is really accompaniment.
10. Deere, *Surprised*, 290 n. 37. Deere should give some evidence for his claim that it is not probable that Paul means "last of all," rather than merely referring to someone else who supports his position.
11. Hans Conzelmann, *First Corinthians*, Hermeneia (Philadelphia: Fortress, 1975), 234.
12. Leon Morris, *The First Epistle of Paul to the Corinthians* (Grand Rapids: Eerdmans, 1958), 172.
13. Walter J. Hollenweger, *The Pentecostals* (London: SCM, 1972), 345.
14. Ibid.

15. Of course, others have different views of the gift of prophet, such as Watchman Nee, who believes that the prophet is a gifted individual in the local church who by revelation can determine who has the gift of apostle (*The Normal Christian Church Life*, rev. ed. [Washington, D.C.: International Students, 1969], 30).
16. F. L. Godet, *Commentary on the First Epistle of St. Paul to the Corinthians*, 2 vols. (1898; reprint, Grand Rapids: Zondervan, 1971), 2:267–68.
17. Liddell and Scott, *Lexicon*, 1539–40.
18. Moulton and Milligan, *Vocabulary*, 555.
19. Hatch and Redpath, *Concordance*, 1231–32.
20. Liddell and Scott, *Lexicon*, 1540.
21. Hatch and Redpath, *Concordance*, 1232–33.
22. Liddell and Scott, *Lexicon*, 1539; and Moulton and Milligan, *Vocabulary*, 555.
23. Hatch and Redpath, *Concordance*, 1231.
24. 1 Cor. 14:24, "But if all prophesy," is a hypothetical example introduced by "if." It does not state that all do or can prophesy.
25. The claims of a few scholars who disagree will be discussed in the section on defective or "fallible" prophets.
26. The novel but incorrect idea that the prophets in this verse are the apostles, will be discussed in the section on "fallible prophets."
27. Grudem, *Gift of Prophecy*, 109–12.
28. Hollenweger, *The Pentecostals*, 345.
29. Grudem, *Gift of Prophecy*, 109–12.
30. D. A. Carson, *Showing the Spirit* (Grand Rapids: Baker, 1987), 97–98.
31. Grudem, *Gift of Prophecy*, 18–25.
32. Ibid., 25–26.
33. Ibid., 26–27.
34. Ibid.
35. Ibid., 30–31.
36. Ibid., 27–44.
37. Ibid., 32ff.
38. Ibid., 33–41.
39. Ibid., 50–60.
40. Ibid., 50–51.
41. Daniel A. Wallace, "The Article-Noun-*kai*-Noun Plural Construction," *Grace Theological Journal 4:1* (Spring 1983): 59–84.
42. Ibid.
43. Daniel A. Wallace, *Exegetical Syntax*, A preliminary draft, 203.
44. Carson, *Showing the Spirit*, 96–97.
45. Grudem, 79–81. Grudem's argument that the first speaker would not resume speaking misses the basic point of the passage. The

speaker who has the immediate revelation has the right of way due to that very fact. That is why he is not to retain the revelation until the other has finished, and that is why the first speaker is to be interrupted. This "interruption" in no way precludes the first from finishing his message once the revelatory speaker has finished.
46. Ibid., 81–83.
47. Ibid., 83–85.
48. Ibid., 86–87.
49. Ibid., 70–79.
50. Ibid. Carson (*Showing the Spirit*, 95–96) agrees with Grudem, but a study of *diakrino* in no way bears out the conclusions drawn by Grudem and Carson. In Exod. 18:16, Moses judges between two parties. In 1 Kings 3:9, Solomon judges God's people discerning between the good and bad. Psalms 50:4; 82:1; Eccl. 3:18; Joel 3:2, 12; Zech. 3:7; Ezek. 17:20; and 20:35–36 all refer to God's judging of people. Prov. 31:9 refers to the king as judging people. Ezek. 44:24 refers to the priests as judging people. All of these refer to passing judgment, right or wrong, guilty or not, condemned or not. This is the most common meaning in the Greek Old Testament. As for the contention that this verb differs significantly from *krino*, did they ignore the fact that Moses' actions described by *diakrino* in Exod. 18:16 are described also by *krino* and by *krisis* in the immediate context? Moses describes it as *krino* in v. 13. In addition, both *krino* and *diakrino* refer to the same judgment by the king in 1 Kings 3:9. Psalm 81:1–3 also seems to use *krino* and *diakrino* in the same way. The same can be said of Job 23:10, 13. In Eccl. 3:16–18 the same action is described by both *krino*, *krisis*, and *diakrino*. One of the most telling passages is Ezek. 20:35–36 where not only are both words used, but the Lord says, "I will judge *(diakrithesomai)* you. . . . In the same way which I judged *(diekrithen)* your fathers in the wilderness of the land of Egypt, thus I will judge *(krino)* you." This explicitly equates the two words. Ezek. 34:20, 22, are another instance where *krino* and *diakrino* are the same. Ezek. 44:24 uses *krisis* and *diakrino* to describe the same thing. There is no justification for claiming that there is some difference between these two words that would imply that New Testament prophets are fallible or inferior.
51. Carson, *Showing the Spirit*, 95.
52. Ibid., 98.
53. Ibid., 97–98.
54. Grudem, *Gift of Prophecy*, 96.
55. Ibid., 97.
56. Carson, *Showing the Spirit*, 94.
57. Ibid., 97; Grudem, *Gift of Prophecy*, 94, 110.

CHAPTER 5

The Gift of Miracles and the Gift of Healing

ALTHOUGH MIRACLES AND healing are two separate gifts in the New Testament, incidents of outright miracles exclusive of healing are rare. The principles and conclusions are similar for both gifts; therefore, they will be discussed together.

Biblical Facts Regarding Miracles

We will study passages using the terms *miracle* (Gk. *dunamis*), *sign (semeion)*, or *wonder (teras)*, as well as the other passages referring to miraculous happenings. Since very few claims today deal with miracles other than healing, the passages will be studied particularly with respect to the gift of healing.

The Evidence of the Gospels
Since we are studying gifts given to individuals in the church, the miracles before the day of Pentecost are only an incidental part of this discussion. Mark 16:15–20 is the only passage in the Gospels that deals with gifts exercised by believers after the day of Pentecost.[1] Mark 16:15 connects the statements in the following verses with preaching the gospel, that is, with evangelistic outreach. Casting out demons, speaking in tongues, taking up serpents, drinking poison, and healing are called *signs*. This is the same word *(semeion)* that John uses in his Gospel to describe Christ's miracles, which were performed in order to confirm his person and message (see John 20:30–31).

According to Mark 16:15–20 the miraculous acts, such as healing, casting out demons, and speaking in tongues are to be *signs* that will accompany the preaching of the gospel and confirm the gospel message. Some interpreters believe that Jesus Christ was promising that these signs would always accompany believers; that is, that they would be present throughout the history of the church. If this were so, then these signs would have been evident throughout church history in all sections of the church, regardless of the church's attitude. Jesus said that they would accompany those who had believed (past tense). He gave no conditions; therefore, they accompanied those persons who believed for whatever the duration intended by the Lord. Grammatically, the passage does not require that these signs accompany all believers for all time. Jesus said that these signs would accompany "those who have believed." The expression *those who have believed* is related in time to the main verb, "shall follow," and is antecedent to it. It could refer either to the believers at that time only or believers throughout church history. The past tense opens the possibility that this refers to those who had already believed at the time Jesus made the statement.

This is an unequivocal statement that these signs would follow the believers involved. The presence of these signs does not depend on faith or on seeking the signs or sign gifts involved. It does not await revival or some other contingency, nor does it refer only to the beginning and the latter times of the history of the church. The statement does not require that all believers exercise all of these signs. The conditional statement, "if they drink any deadly thing, it shall not hurt them," applies to any of those believers to whom Jesus referred. Thus none of "those who have believed" will be harmed by drinking any deadly thing. The same also applies to handling snakes. If this refers to believers of the entire church age, then no believer shall ever die from drinking anything deadly and no believer shall die from snakebite. The preceding is true regardless of their faith, knowledge, or belief in spiritual gifts since it is a direct, unconditional prophecy. This is improbable; therefore, it is improbable that it refers to the entire church age.

Mark 16:18 states, "They shall lay hands on the sick, and they shall recover." This is not conditioned on any response of the sick person. His faith has no bearing on the result. There is no allowance for failure. They *shall* get well. But these signs have neither followed all believers nor been present throughout the greater part of church history. The sporadic claims to speaking in tongues during the past nineteen hundred years have not been validated and have occurred only in isolated cases. Tongues have not always followed believers. The same may be said of the other signs mentioned in this passage. Healers have neither always been present nor even claimed to be present in the church.

The belief that these signs have not been present during most of church history due to a lack of faith on the part of Christians is contrary to this passage. Jesus said that these signs would accompany believers. There are no "ifs" or conditions. Believers have died from drinking poison and other deadly things, and we have no evidence that believers are immune to poison today. If Mark 16:15–20 means that miracles and tongues are present today and have always been present in the church, it also means that believers today may drink poison without harm. If these signs are to accompany believers today and since there are no conditions stated (such as seeking such gifts or exercising faith in charismatic workings), why aren't they demonstrated among all groups of genuine believers? Therefore, this passage does not mean that all believers will do these signs or that these signs will always be present in the church.

We must interpret this passage carefully in order to see what it means. Notice the following three points. First, Jesus did not say that these signs would always follow believers. Since in reality they have not, this omission is significant. Second, the fact that this was addressed to the apostles and referred to "those who have believed" (aorist tense) makes it grammatically possible to refer these statements to the early group of believers, that is, those who had already believed. Third, Mark 16:20 states that this preaching and confirmation by signs *was accomplished* (past tense) by those present. It was accomplished by the time Mark wrote his Gospel. The rest of the New Testament confirms this fact. This is all that is necessary to fulfill the promises of Mark 16:15–20.

In many instances the Gospels show Jesus healing people who could not have exercised faith. An obvious example of this is the healing of the ten lepers in Luke 17:11–19. Ten were healed, but only one had faith and was saved. In Matthew 8:5–13 the centurion's servant was healed, but only the centurion had faith. Since the two demoniacs in Matthew 8:28–29 were fierce and hostile, it is unreasonable to imagine that they came to Jesus by faith to be healed. The man possessed by a demon in Mark 1:23–26 could not have exercised faith. The boy in Mark 9:17–29 did not exercise faith. When the disciples wondered why they were unable to cast out the demon, Jesus did not refer to the boy's faith but to the disciples' need for prayer and fasting in order to cast out the demon. Since the man healed at the pool of Bethesda did not even know who Jesus was, he was not healed due to his faith (John 5:1–16). Jesus also healed an epileptic boy who was in a seizure. How could he have exercised faith at this time? These examples, as well as the healing of multitudes, show that the healing of afflicted individuals was not contingent upon their faith. On the contrary, Jesus explicitly states that the failure to heal is due to the lack of faith and prayer of the healers (Matt. 17:19–20; Mark 9:17–20).

Some object that verses such as Matthew 9:22 and 29 show that faith is necessary to be healed. However, these verses do not say that it is necessary; they state only that Jesus responded to their faith. They do not demonstrate that he could not have healed them unless they exercised faith. The same is true of Mark 5:34; 10:52; Luke 7:50; 8:48; 18:42. In many of these instances it is difficult to determine if the expression, "thy faith hath saved thee" (e.g., Luke 7:50; 18:42), refers to healing or to salvation since the verb *sozo*, "save," is used. According to Mark 2:5 and Luke 5:20 those who brought the sick man possessed the faith, not the sick man himself. The final objection that some raise is the statement that Jesus was not able to do any miracle in his own country due to their unbelief (Mark 6:5). However, the verse does not directly state that healing depended on their faith. Neither does it imply or state that Jesus tried to heal them but failed because of their lack of faith. On the contrary, some were healed. Those who came to Jesus for healing were healed. Perhaps due to hostility, only a few came to be healed. Certainly the open disbelief shown by these people cannot be compared with the attitude of those who come to be healed but do not receive healing in present-day healing meetings. Jesus never attempted to heal and then failed. When the disciples failed, Jesus blamed the failure on their faith.

The Evidence of the Book of Acts

The book of Acts deals with the beginning of the church when the miraculous spiritual gifts were operative. This is the only account that we have that describes the exercise of the spiritual gifts where we have no doubt that the genuine gifts are in view.

Acts 2:1–14—This is the first of the miraculous happenings during the time of the early church. This miracle includes the sound from heaven, tongues like fire on the participants, and speaking in languages (vv. 2–4). The miracle was performed publicly, before multitudes of unbelievers (vv. 5–13, 37–41). It served the purpose of gathering a crowd for the evangelistic sermon by Peter. In spite of the claims of some that there have been numerous "Pentecosts," the church has not experienced anything like that which took place on the original day of Pentecost.

Acts 2:22—This verse may be translated as follows: "Men, Israelites, hear these words. Jesus the Nazarene, a man proved [confirmed] to you by God, by means of miracles and wonders and signs which God did through him in your midst...." The verse states that God verified Jesus to Israel by the miracles he performed. The terms *dunamis, semeion,* and *teras* are used. The miracles performed by Christ were to confirm or verify his ministry and deity and were not primarily for the benefit of the recipients.

Acts 2:43—"Many wonders and signs were done by the apostles." The miracles were performed by the apostles. Notice also that these miracles apparently were performed before *unbelievers* rather than in some type of special meeting.

Acts 3:3–16—The lame man was healed by the apostle Peter outside the gate of the temple. This miracle was performed by an apostle and was in public rather than in a meeting. There is no intimation that the lame man was a believer nor that he exercised any faith on this occasion. The context and the fact that he asked for alms from Peter and John demonstrate that he not only did not seek to be healed but that he had no idea that this was about to take place. The lame man gave attention to Peter and John, "expecting to receive something from them" (Acts 3:5). That he was expecting money rather than healing is clear from Peter's statement, "Silver and gold have I none" (3:6). The reference to faith in 3:16 refers to Peter's faith, rather than to the faith of the lame man. This healing was apparent to all in the vicinity and resulted in gathering a large crowd, which primarily consisted of unbelievers. The miracle was so evident and undeniable that the rulers examined Peter and John concerning the matter and were unable to refute it in spite of their desire to do so (see 4:9–10, 14, 16). They said, "for that indeed a notable miracle hath been done by them is manifest to all them that dwell in Jerusalem; and we cannot deny it" (4:16). Notice the contrast between this miracle of healing and present-day healings. The former healing was performed immediately and directly by the apostles. It was done publicly on someone not seeking to be healed, and the authorities were unable to deny its veracity. Today healings are seldom if ever immediate, are in meetings rather than in public, are connected with prayer and other religious acts rather than directly by the healer, are performed on the faithful or seekers (failures being blamed on a lack of faith on the part of the sick), and are seldom if ever recognized by all so as to be past denial.

Acts 4:29-30—In reaction to the interrogation and subsequent release of Peter and John, the church prayed, "Grant unto thy servants, that with all boldness they may speak thy word, by stretching forth thine hand to heal; and that signs and wonders may be done by the name of thy holy child Jesus." The stretching forth of God's hand to perform miracles was to occur while the word was spoken. "By stretching forth" should be translated "while stretching forth," since the Greek denotes contemporaneous time. Nor does the Greek text separate "healing" from "signs and wonders," as the KJV does. The preposition *eis* should go with the infinitive *ginesthai*. Thus the translation should read, "Give to your servants to speak your Word with all boldness while you stretch forth your hand to perform healing and signs and wonders through the name of your holy servant Jesus." In this translation the word "while" *(en to . . . ekteinen)* denotes contemporaneous time. The miraculous workings were to confirm the message.

Acts 5:5, 10—Ananias and Sapphira died at Peter's word after they lied regarding their offering. This apparently took place in the assembly and was an immediate result of Peter's word. We do not see incidents such as this today, nor have we seen such throughout church history. This indicates that all things did *not* remain the same.

Acts 5:12-16—This passage teaches several important aspects in regard to miracles. For example, many miracles were performed by the apostles in public to unbelievers. Verses 14-16 state that multitudes came, and that *everyone* was healed. The people came from the entire region; many were placed in the streets, and some were healed merely by Peter's shadow falling upon them. Besides the miracles of healing, demons were also cast out. We have no record of failures, no requirements for the sick to exercise faith, and no "meetings." Certainly nothing resembles this magnitude or type of ministry today. If the same operations were present today, then we should be able to see the same types of miracles. Although we see no failures in the book of Acts, we witness a multitude of failures by healers today. Thus far in our study of the New Testament, we have observed that only the apostles have performed miracles or healing.

Acts 5:19; 12:7–9—Peter was miraculously released from prison. Paul's release was also made possible by a miracle (Acts 16:26). If all things are to continue throughout the church age as they were in the beginning, then why don't we have any evidence of miracles such as these?

Acts 6:8—Described as being "full of power," Stephen performed great wonders and miracles among the people in public. This is the first instance in which miracles were performed by someone other than an apostle. There was no meeting and no indication that the sick had to exercise faith. The same terminology that is used to describe Stephen's ministry of performing "great wonders and miracles" is used to describe the apostles' ministry (see 2:22, 43). Thus his ministry was on the same level as that of the apostles rather than on some lower, fallible level.

Acts 8:6, 13—Philip performed miracles of healing and casting out demons among the Samaritans, which served to confirm his evangelistic preaching. Like Stephen, Philip's miracles are called signs and miracles and are of the same order and quality as those of the apostles. The entire city was aware of this. Note that this confirms the initial thrust of the gospel into a new area. Besides the apostles, Stephen and Philip are the only other persons to whom miracles are attributed. Thus far in our study of the book of Acts, we have no evidence that the ability to perform miracles was common in the early church.

Acts 9:1–18—Paul's salvation and call to ministry were miraculous. Struck down by an outburst of glory and blinded for three days, Paul was spoken to directly by Jesus Christ. Simultaneously, Ananias was spoken to directly by the Lord and later ministered to Paul, whose sight was restored when Ananias came. The unique manner of Paul's salvation is one of the many differences between the apostolic age and the following periods of church history.

Acts 9:32–34—The apostle Peter healed Aeneas, who had been paralyzed for eight years. All who lived in the area saw it and turned to the Lord. The healing was immediate, complete, and performed by an apostle. It confirmed the gospel to those who knew of it.

Acts 9:36–42—Peter raised Dorcas privately, but all in Joppa heard of it and many believed on the Lord. This is the first instance where we know that a miracle was performed by a gifted Christian upon a believer. Previously, miracles and healings were performed for and upon unbelievers in order to authenticate the message of the gospel to them. The result was the same when Dorcas was raised, since many believed in the Lord (v. 42). This miracle was performed at the specific request of the believers in Joppa. This is also the first recorded instance in the church of a miracle performed privately rather than in public. The question with which we are left is, Why don't we see miracles like this performed today? Has anyone today raised a specific dead person upon request?

Acts 13:11–12—Paul blinded Elymas the sorcerer simply by saying, "Thou shalt be blind." Not only did the miracle confirm Paul's message, but the deputy witnessed it and consequently believed. Do we see opponents of the gospel silenced in this manner today?

Acts 14:3—Describing Paul's ministry in Iconium, Luke says, "Long time therefore abode they speaking boldly in the Lord, which gave testimony unto the word of his grace, and granted signs and wonders to be done by their hands." The conjunction "and" is absent in the Greek text. "Granted" *(didonti)* translates a word that is an adverbial participle of means. Thus the sentence should be translated, "they spoke boldly in the Lord, who testified to the word of his grace by giving signs and wonders to be done through their hands." Acts 14:3 is a straightforward and clear statement that the Lord gave miracles to confirm the message to unbelievers in Iconium, an idea that is consistent with the passages studied thus far.

Acts 14:8–10—Paul healed the crippled man at Lystra. This healing was in connection with preaching the gospel, and it made an impact on the entire town. This is the only place where the faith of the person who is being healed is mentioned. However, this case is somewhat different from the preceding. Paul was already in the process of preaching the gospel, and the crippled man was responding by faith. He did not come seeking physical healing, and there is no reason to assume that he expected to be healed. Seeing that the man had faith to be saved (i.e., that he was responding to the gospel), Paul took the initiative and healed the man. The man's faith was in the gospel that Paul was proclaiming, not in healing.[2]

Acts 19:11–12—Paul performed special miracles in Ephesus. Many were healed, some by handkerchiefs carried from Paul's body. Evil spirits were cast out. This miraculous ministry continued for some time, so that Luke says, "all in Asia heard the word of the Lord Jesus, both Jews and Greeks" (v. 10). The miracles resulted in the public testimony of God's miraculous power.

Acts 20:9–12—Paul raised Eutychus, who had fallen out of an upper window during Paul's sermon. This is the second recorded instance of healing performed specifically for a believer. This was done not in a meeting but at the scene of the accident. Why don't we see miracles like this performed today?

Acts 20:17–38—This passage does not describe a miracle; however, it describes Paul's ministry in Ephesus, especially to believers. Paul mentions many things regarding his ministry but does not mention the miraculous works, such as healing and casting out demons. Despite the amazing magnitude of such works by Paul at Ephesus (Acts 19:11–12), Paul apparently considered all of this miraculous work insignificant as far as his ministry to believers was concerned. Notice that his emphasis is on ministry that edifies, such as teaching. In Acts 20:32–38 he commends the Ephesians to the Word of God, tells them to labor to help the weak, and prays for them, but he does not tell them to perform miracles or any of the sign gifts, nor does he tell them to seek or emphasize such. He makes no mention of the miraculous gifts.[3]

Acts 27—Paul prophesies of shipwreck and the details concerning it, which happened as he said.

Acts 28—Paul was not affected by snakebite (vv. 1–6), and he healed some people on the island of Malta (vv. 8–9).

The miracles described in the book of Acts are of a magnitude never seen since that time in church history. Because these miracles were performed by miracle workers, they cannot be placed in the same category as miracles performed by God in response to the prayers of the church. The huge crowds who were healed and the quality and immediate nature of the healing have not been repeated. Apostles performed all of the miracles, with the exception of Stephen and Philip, whose miracles were qualitatively the same as those of the apostles. The miracles were performed publicly on unbelievers by men who relied upon God's power rather than at special healing or prayer meetings. Miracles were performed primarily to confirm the gospel, though the recipients obviously benefited from the miracles. The faith of the recipient did not alter the miracle. Also, every attempt to heal was successful. There were no failures. Today we do not see erring church members die at the word of an apostle (5:5–10), nor do we see opponents blinded by the word of a miracle worker (13:11–12). Where is the evidence today that anyone has raised a specific dead person in answer to the request of others?

The Evidence of the Epistles
We will now look at the evidence for miracles in the Epistles. Although 1 Corinthians 12:10, 28–29; 2 Thessalonians 2:9; Hebrews 6:5; and the references in the book of the Revelation refer to miracles, they are not significant for this study.

Romans 15:19—The context of this verse is definitely speaking of evangelistic outreach to the Gentiles, for Paul speaks of "ministering the gospel of God, that the offering up of the Gentiles might be acceptable" (Rom. 15:16). In 15:18–19 Paul speaks of the obedience of the Gentiles and states that God worked by him, "to make the Gentiles obedient, by word and deed, through mighty signs *(dunamei semeion)* and wonders *(teraton)*, by the power of the Spirit of God; so that from Jerusalem, and round about unto Illyricum, I have fully preached the gospel of Christ." Paul clearly says that miracles, signs, and wonders were God's confirmation of Paul's evangelistic ministry. God worked miracles through Paul so that the Gentiles would believe.

1 Corinthians 2:4—Paul states that his gospel came to the Corinthians in demonstration of the Spirit and power. This power *(dunamis)* is related to the initial evangelistic ministry to Corinth. It is not definite, however, that Paul refers to miracles in this passage.

2 Corinthians 6:7—It is impossible to determine if this passage refers to miracles.

2 Corinthians 12:12—Paul states that miracles, signs, and wonders are the signs of an apostle. If they are evidence of apostleship, then they could not be common in the church. He apparently refers to his initial visit to Corinth. Since the book of Acts does not mention any of Paul's miracles performed at Corinth, Luke must have not regarded them to be as significant as other aspects of Paul's ministry, such as teaching. As mentioned earlier, this conforms to Paul's attitude toward the miraculous aspect of his ministry in Ephesus (Acts 20:17–28).

Galatians 3:5—This verse refers to God as the one who supplies the Spirit and performs miracles. It says nothing about any person performing miracles. Since they are contrasted with works of the Law, connected with faith and joined with "supplying the Spirit," then they must be connected with the initial reception of the gospel. Perhaps regeneration is the main miracle in the mind of Paul.

Hebrews 2:3–4—This passage connects miracles, signs, and wonders with eyewitnesses of the Lord. It implies that this was the initial presentation of the gospel to the recipients. The verb "confirmed" *(ebebaiothe)* is in the past tense, indicating that this confirmation was done in the past and was not going on when Hebrews was written. The miraculous works were to confirm the gospel testimony of eyewitnesses of the Lord and were not going on at the time.

James 5:14–15—These verses are often quoted to support modern claims to healing. James says, "Is any sick among you? Let him call for the elders of the church; and let them pray over him, anointing him with oil in the name of the Lord: And the prayer of faith shall save the sick, and the Lord shall raise him up; and if he have committed sins, they shall be forgiven him." Notice that the sick person calls for the "elders" of the church and not for a "healer." The use of the article with "church" probably specifies the specific church or assembly to which the sick man belongs. The elders pray for the man and anoint him with oil; there is no indication that they lay hands on the sick man. The agency that makes the healing effective through God's power is the prayer of the elders, not an individual with a gift of healing. We need to observe several aspects of healing here. First, James speaks of elders from the sick man's church who pray for healing. This differs from the gift of healing which is the performance of healing miracles by a specific individual. Instead, this is the response of God to the prayer of believers. God performs the healing without a human agent. However, the healings performed in the book of Acts used people as direct agents of the miracle. Second, apparently no healers or miracle workers were available for believers when James wrote, otherwise it would seem only reasonable that James would have instructed the sick man to find someone with the gift of healing. This verse clearly implies that no healers were present or even available. Third, we find no evidence here of a public meeting of any type, nor do we see any suggestion that the sick person is supposed to seek out a traveling preacher or healer. Fourth, the prayer and faith of the elders restores the sick man. We see no indication that the faith of the sick man is a factor.

James 5:16—This verse says, "Confess your faults one to another, and pray one for another, that ye may be healed." In this section of James we have instructions regarding the sick that fit the normal church practice. Believers, specifically elders, are to pray for the sick person. God can heal the person in answer to prayer. This is a miracle in that God performs the healing. Apparently no individuals were available who had the gift of healing. It is impossible to reconcile James 5:14–16 with the opinion that individuals with the gift of healing were common in the early church or are present today. We can explain this passage in two possible ways: (1) the gift of healing was no longer given to the church when James was written; or (2) the gift of healing was not exercised toward church members but was reserved for ministry to unbelievers to confirm the gospel among them. In either case the present emphasis on healers is not in agreement with James 5:14–16.

The Charismatic Concept of Inferior Gifts

The modern charismatic gifts and miracles fall far short of those described in the New Testament. Hollenweger, a Pentecostal, says, "Apart from a few exceptions, which are, however, important, biblical prophecy seems to me to be absent in the Pentecostal movement."[4] Grudem, also a charismatic, describes the situation as follows: "There is almost uniform testimony from all sections of the charismatic movement that prophecy is imperfect and impure, and will contain elements which are not to be obeyed or trusted."[5] Deere says, "I don't see anyone who has the quality and quantity of miracles that took place in the apostles' ministry."[6] For many years charismatics attempted to prove that their gifts are the same as the biblical ones; however, this is impossible to maintain. The fact that their gifts do not conform to those in the Bible is a severe problem for the charismatics. Since they are unable to maintain that they are the same, Grudem has argued for inferior, fallible prophecy as the New Testament gift, and Deere argues for inferior or lesser gifts of miracles and healing. The arguments for a gift of fallible prophecy in the New Testament, as we have already seen, do not stand up to examination. Now we must examine Deere's arguments for lesser gifts of miracles and healing. Since he has gathered most of the possible arguments, his statements should be examined to determine the validity of this concept.

A prominent feature in his argument is that he does not give one direct scriptural statement that miracles, healings, or any other gift were given on a level less than those described in the book of Acts. Neither does he show one specific biblical example of a gift given to the church which operates on a lesser or inferior level. This seems particularly inappropriate for someone who has stated several times and who represents a group which states vociferously when arguing against cessationism that there is not one verse which specifically states gifts will cease. Since there are numerous instances recorded of miracles and healing and there are several references to gifts, it is specially significant that there are no direct statements or examples to support the concept of lesser gifts.

The Nature of Inferior Gifts

In a twofold argument, Deere first argues that gifts are not "automatic." By this he means that the healer or miracle worker cannot heal "at will," that is, "anywhere, anytime, under any conditions."[7] The key idea is that they cannot heal "at will." Although he only makes this argument in regard to the gift of healing, logically it must also apply to all gifts. In Deere's opinion even Jesus and the apostles could not heal at will. He asserts that Jesus could not heal "at his own discretion," since God "dispenses his power to heal and at other times withholds it."[8] The significant point is that Deere is not saying that Jesus did not heal or do miracles at his own will but that he could not. As evidence for this, Deere refers to incidents in Jesus' life that allegedly show that "he was not free to heal at will." In other words, Jesus could only heal at times when God dispensed power for him to heal; at other times, when God withheld power, Jesus could not heal. The same concept is also applied to the apostles and other gifted Christians. This is then presented as the reason why today's healers often cannot heal.

The first incident is Luke 5:17, which refers to an incident where the Pharisees and others were observing Jesus. The "evidence" is in the statement by Luke, "And the power of the

Lord was present for him to heal the sick" (Luke 5:17). Deere asks, "Why would Luke say that 'the power of the Lord was present for him to heal' if Jesus could heal at any time, under any condition, and solely at his own discretion?"[9] Before we study the verse let us look at the logic of this argument. Does the concept that something is present imply that it is only present some of the time? The English translation of 2 Corinthians 5:8, a verse using a different verb but the same concept as Luke 5:17, states that Paul desires to be present with the Lord. Does this imply that Paul desired to be only temporarily with the Lord? Of course not. The statement that something is present does not imply that it is at sometimes also absent. The past tense of the verb "was" in Luke 5:17 has no bearing on the issue, since Luke is describing a past event and the power was present at the time of Luke 5:17.

An even more glaring error is the fact that, although Deere's entire point depends on the word "present," the verse does not say that the power was present. The word *present* is supplied by some translators in order to render the verse in smooth English. The verse uses the verb "was" with a construction that usually denotes result or purpose. The verse does not contrast the presence of power at one time with its absence at other times. Rather the verse stresses the direction of the power toward healing. The Lord's power "was" directed toward, or resulted in healing. Using the same verb and tense, "was," but without the purpose construction, Luke 2:36 states, "Anna was a prophetess." Does this suggest that sometimes she was not a prophetess? Luke 5:3 says, "the boat was Simon's." Does this mean that it was his boat only at that moment but not at other times? Thus we conclude that Luke 5:17 provides no support for Deere's contention that Jesus received power to heal only on certain occasions.

The second argument focuses on the healing of only one man at the pool of Bethesda (John 5). The argument then narrows its focus to the statement in John 5:19, that "the Son can do nothing by himself, but what he sees the Father do: for whatever the Father does, the Son also does likewise." Deere argues that Jesus healed only the one man at the pool of Bethesda because this was all that God enabled him to do. He argues that Jesus "could not heal" unless the Father was doing the healing.[10] However, this passage does not teach that Jesus cannot do things at will, but that everything Jesus does is in agreement with the Father. Jesus does not say that he lacks the ability or power to do anything on his own but that he does nothing contrary to God. If this passage means that Jesus does not have the ability to do, as Deere interprets it, it says he does not have the ability to do anything. Logically this would mean that he cannot eat, sleep, stand up, or sit down at will, apart from a special dispensation of power from God, a power that might be withheld so that he would be unable to do these things. Obviously, this is not the meaning of John 5:19. Actually, it means just the opposite. It does not mean that Jesus lacks the ability to do anything without a special surge of power from God. Rather it means that Jesus has the ability to perform "at will" in accordance with God. Everything he does at will is in accordance with the Father's will. Notice particularly in John 5:21 what Jesus says: "For as the Father raiseth up the dead, and quickeneth them; even so the Son quickeneth whom he will." The Father raises whom he wills. The Son raises whom he wills just like the Father does. The stress is that the Son does as the Son wills, just like the Father does as the Father wills. This is due to the fact that the Father has given all judgment to the Son, so that people will honor the Son just as they do the Father (5:22–23). Jesus introduced these verses with the statement, referring to the Father, "for whatever that one does, the Son does in the same way" (5:19). They both act at will, yet they do the same things. This passage does not teach the Son's inability but rather the Son's equality with the Father.

Someone may be puzzled by the statement, "The Son can do nothing" (John 5:19). The phrase *can do nothing* does not necessarily mean "not to have the ability." It is used in various ways that must be determined from the context. The specific statements of this passage do not fit with the meaning "inability." Let us look at some other uses of *dunatai*, the word used here. For example, the Son is able (i.e., permitted) to ask the Father for help, but of his own will restricts himself so that Scripture will be fulfilled (Matt. 26:53–54). The householder was not able (i.e., it was inconvenient) to get up and give bread to his neighbor (Luke 11:7). A potential disciple said, "I have married a wife, and therefore I cannot (i.e., it is inconvenient) come" (Luke 14:20). The steward is no longer able (i.e., permitted) to be steward (Luke 16:2), Christians are not able (i.e., it is inconsistent) to drink from the table of demons and from the Lord's table. All are able to prophesy (i.e., permitted) one at a time (1 Cor. 14:31) and the church at Ephesus was not able (i.e., did not tolerate) to bear sin (Rev. 2:2). Thus, when Jesus said he was not able, this does not mean he lacked the ability or power. In this context it means that of his own will, he did not do it because it was inconsistent with his will, his person, and his mission.

As a third argument Deere uses Mark 6:5–6 as additional evidence of Jesus' alleged inability.[11] The passage says, "And he could do no miracle there due to their unbelief except he laid his hands on a few sick, and healed them. And he was amazed at their unbelief." This does not mean that Jesus lacked the ability to perform miracles, nor does it mean that he attempted to perform miracles and failed. Matthew 13:58 says, "And he did not do many miracles there because of their unbelief." While Jesus did some miracles there, the fact that "he did not many . . . there" may mean that few came to be healed due to their unbelief, or it may mean that healing them would be inconsistent with their rejection or inconsistent with restrictions Jesus placed on his actions. In any event it does not mean that he desired to heal them but was unable to do so since he healed many who could not have responded by faith. In any case, this verse does not support the idea that Jesus could heal only on occasions when God sovereignly dispensed his power since it was the unbelief of the people that restricted the healing, not God's withholding of power. Moreover, this is not in a context where the issue was merely a lack of faith but of outright definite unbelief and rejection. Therefore, it provides no support for healers who fail to heal afflicted persons who come to them for healing.

Deere also presents the apostles as unable to perform miracles at will. To demonstrate this he refers to several verses. For example, in Acts 3:12 Peter stated that he and John did not heal the afflicted man "by our own power or godliness." Deere, however, modifies the meaning of this statement by adding the word *apostolic*, so that it says, "by our own *apostolic* power or godliness."[12] But Peter did not say, "by our own *apostolic* power." He said "by our own power." One's own power is power apart from the Holy Spirit. In this case, apart from the apostolic gift. Thus, this verse does not refer to Peter's ability when exercising his apostolic gift. Apostolic power and the gift are from God through the Holy Spirit; they are not one's own power. Neither does this passage imply anything about God's sovereign will or power operating momentarily to perform this healing. Peter is merely stating that he healed this man by God's power rather than his own; therefore, he is a messenger of God to be heard.

Another passage that Deere employs to buttress his claim that the apostles were unable to heal is Acts 14:9–10. This text includes the statement that the man listening to Paul "had faith to be healed." Deere asserts that Paul simply "saw that the man had faith to be healed and then proclaimed him healed."[13] But nothing in this verse indicates that Paul did not initiate this healing. Since the phrase can be translated "had faith to be saved," it is more probable that Paul did initiate the healing, and the man was responding to the message of the gospel that Paul was proclaiming. Seeing that the man was responding to the gospel, Paul healed him. Whatever the case, this verse provides no evidence that Paul could not heal at will. There is nothing in this verse to indicate that the healing was not under Paul's control. It seems to imply just the opposite.

Contrary to what Deere has stated, Epaphroditus, Trophimus, and Timothy are not examples of individuals who Paul could not heal.[14] First of all, we have no evidence that Paul even tried to heal them. The gift of healing was a sign to unbelievers, not a guarantee for the physical well-being of believers.

In response to this, Deere mentions the incident of Eutychus, a believer healed by Paul.[15] Although the healing of Eutychus took place among a group of Christians, it probably became widely known (Acts 20:7–12). Also, the one exception of a believer being healed does not disprove the general principle that healing was typically performed on unbelievers. In the light of this incident, several important questions need to be answered by Deere. If Paul made a practice of healing believers, then why is Eutychus the only recorded instance of Paul healing a Christian? Why are the three men who Paul "could not heal" all Christians? And why are the miracles and healings described in the New Testament almost always in public and among crowds rather than in meetings of believers?

As we saw in the earlier discussion on miracles, numerous direct scriptural statements indicate that miracles and healings are signs to authenticate the gospel to unbelievers. They are not for ministry to believers. If healers were available for believers, then why did James tell believers to call for the elders to pray rather than to seek a healer?

As an argument opposing this, Deere claims that 1 Corinthians 12:7 says the gift of healing is for the edification of those in the church.[16] As we have already seen, this is not what 1 Corinthians 12:7 actually says. The word *edification* is not used in this verse, much less the unwarranted addition *of those in the church*. Instead, the word used in 1 Corinthians 12:7 is *profit*, not *edification*, and the verse refers to all of the gifts, but only some of the gifts are for the edification of believers. This alone makes Deere's statement improbable. In this same passage Paul explicitly states that tongues are a sign to unbelievers, in contrast to prophecy, which is for believers (1 Cor. 14:22). As a sign to unbelievers, healing and miracles are profitable for those who respond to the signs. Likewise, the gift of evangelism profits those who respond to the gospel message. Both profit the body of Christ as well, in that more are added to the body.

As we have already stated, a great deal of evidence, both direct and indirect, indicates that the gift of healing was not given to heal believers but was intended as a public sign for evangelistic ministry to unbelievers. James 5:14 clearly shows that Christians did not expect that fellow believers would be healed by anyone with the gift of healing. Rather they were to ask for prayer by the church leaders. The fact that three Christians, Epaphroditus, Trophimus, and Timothy, were not healed by Paul merely reinforces this idea, since we know that Paul could heal. In no way does the experience of these three men support the claim that Paul tried and failed to heal them.

The disciples' failure to heal the epileptic boy in Matthew 10:1 is not an example of a gift given to the church. The church did not start until Pentecost, the disciples had not received the indwelling Holy Spirit, and the gifts were not yet given. This event furnishes no evidence for the healer's inability to heal apart from a sovereign dispensing of God's power since Jesus said the problem was insufficient faith rather than the will of the healer. The timing, person, place, and situation were not the factor. With faith the disciples could have exercised their healing "at will."

When one receives a gift it can be exercised at will. Otherwise, it could not be exercised by faith if the person had no way to know it would work until he tried it, and would then in many instances discover that the power had been sovereignly withheld. In addition, Paul not only expects the gifts of tongues and prophecy to be under control of the person possessing the gift but states that they are (1 Cor. 14:26–36). Are the gifts of teaching, ruling, showing mercy, and helps exercised apart from the individual's control and not at will? Do they function only on occasions when a special dose of power is given to exercise that gift, a power which may be withheld? If these gifts are exercised under the control and will of the gifted person, then why not the miraculous gifts? Why would miraculous gifts not be allowed to function at the will of the possessor but the nonmiraculous gifts which are every bit as important would? If someone can exercise the gift of healing or miracles only on occasion when God sovereignly gives a special spurt of power, then what is the point of gifts? God could give out these special spurts of power first to one person, then to someone else. First Corinthians 13:1–3 shows that a person may exercise a gift, including the miraculous gifts, with the wrong motive. First Corinthians 14 also shows that a gift, including the miraculous gifts, may be exercised at the wrong time, several at the same time, and contrary to proper restrictions. Does God sovereignly empower persons to exercise these gifts erroneously or for improper motives, and yet withhold the power on legitimate occasions? Rather, these concepts show that a gift is controlled by the possessor and exercised "at will." The argument that the genuine gift of healing could not be exercised "at will" totally collapses.

In this system advocated by Deere, believers do not really have a gift of healing or performing miracles. They merely receive occasional power, apart from their own will, and are able to perform only at the time that the power is given. This conveniently places the responsibility for failures on God. However, Deere and other charismatics maintain that failure is due to a lack of faith by the healer or a lack of faith by the person who needs healing. But which is it? Does a healing only work when God dispenses the power to heal, provided the healer exercises the proper amount of faith and the afflicted person has faith to be healed? Does the healing fail if any of these three is missing? Is it God's sovereign will to heal and dispense power, only to be thwarted by the healer or the sick person? If God can sovereignly dispense temporary power to accomplish healing, can't he also give power that will last for an extended period of time? Are the gifts of teaching or ruling only temporary? God allows believers to minister in other aspects of ministry at their own will. Cannot He allow the gift of healing to also be exercised at will? These and other questions need serious answers. The solution provided by Deere, however, seems to be merely an attempt to explain the failures and deficiencies of the gifts in the modern charismatic movement. Deere's concept is contrary to the biblical information.

The Distribution of the Gift of Miracles and the Gift of Healing

In order to show that the apostolic gifts of miracles and healing were of a higher quality than those given to the church at large, it must be shown that the church at large exercised these gifts. The expression *as every man hath received a gift* in 1 Peter 4:10 does not prove the widespread distribution of the gift of miracles and healing.[17] It merely implies that each believer has a gift; it does not indicate what gifts they have. First Corinthians 1:7 says, "you lack in no gift." It is improbable that the gift of apostle was exercised by any individual permanently resident at Corinth. This verse could mean that the Corinthians did not lack any gift normally received by average church members. Gifts such as that of apostle and other gifts generally reserved for apostles, such as healing and miracles, would then be excluded. Thus there is some limitation to the idea that this verse means that all gifts were operative at Corinth.[18] Or it could mean that the Corinthians had received ministry from all the gifts, including the apostles. If so, then it does not mean that all of the gifts were necessarily present and operative at Corinth. It seems quite unlikely that the church at Corinth, which was overly excited over "showy" gifts such as tongues, would have been performing miracles and healings without making any mention of it. These gifts would be even more "spectacular" than tongues. Thus it seems unlikely that the gifts of healing and performing miracles were functioning at Corinth or in other local churches. If they were, then why would James make a suggestion to call for the elders to pray for the sick rather than to seek a healer?

First Corinthians 1:7 does not say, "You have every gift," nor does it say, "You do not lack any gift." Literally, it says, "You do not lack *in* any gift." When the verb "lack" (Gk. *hustereo*) is used in the New Testament, the item lacking may be in the accusative case, but more often it is in the genitive case. In 1 Corinthians 1:7 neither of these is used. The context is as follows: "You were enriched by him in all things, in all utterance and in all knowledge; just as the testimony of Christ was confirmed in you: so that you do not lack in any gift" (vv. 5–7). In verse 5 the word *all* is specifically oriented toward speech and knowledge. They had been enriched by the Lord in (or by) all speech and knowledge. The result is that they did not lack *in* any gift. Thus, this does not require that every gift was being performed by the church members at Corinth. They had received ministry so that they were enriched by all the gifts, particularly in speech and knowledge and, therefore, did not lack in any gift. Miracles and healings had been performed by the apostle Paul. Thus, they were not lacking in these gifts.

If this verse refers to the possession and operation of gifts, it would only refer to gifts understood to be distributed to church members and would not include those distributed only to the apostles. Since several other interpretations are viable, this verse alone cannot demonstrate that every gift was being performed by church members at Corinth. It must be interpreted by a comparison with the rest of the New Testament.

First Corinthians 14 does indicate that prophets functioned in the local assembly (see also Acts 13:1; 15:32). The statement in 1 Thessalonians 5:18 does not require that local church members actually prophesied since it refers to prophecies and does not say prophesying was in progress. The incidents of speaking in tongues in Acts 2, 10, and 19 and prophesying in Acts 19:6 indicate a single occurrence in each instance rather than recurring incidents of speaking in tongues.[19] Both prophesying and speaking in tongues apparently occurred at Corinth. Apart from the references in 1 Corinthians and a few instances in the book of Acts, speaking in tongues is not mentioned in the New Testament.

As evidence for miracles and healing in the local churches, Deere provides only one verse, Galatians 3:5. Yet this verse does not say that anyone in the Galatian churches performed miracles, nor does it say that anyone had the gift of miracles or healing. Rather it refers to "the One who supplies the Spirit, and performs miracles among you." This verse says that God performs miracles among the Galatians. Therefore, this verse does not serve as evidence of people having the gift of healing or miracles. The verse concludes with the question, "does He do it by works of the Law, or by the hearing of faith?" This latter expression is used in Galatians 3:2 of the reception of the Spirit upon salvation. The same terminology is used in Romans 10:14ff. in reference to salvation. The details and the argument of Galatians 3:1–5 also deal with salvation. Hence, the miracles referred to in Galatians 3:5 are performed by God and are primarily oriented toward salvation. In any case, nothing in the verse says that the Galatians performed miracles. Thus, apart from the examples of the apostles, Stephen, and Philip, we find no direct statement in Scripture that the gift of healing or the gift of miracles occurred in the churches. Even if it could be proved that the gifts of miracles and healing were widely distributed in the churches, this still would not be evidence that they have continued or that they were inferior or lesser gifts.

The Question Regarding the Quality of Certain Spiritual Gifts

In case the previous arguments designed to explain the inferior nature of charismatic gifts are insufficient, Deere also argues that the gifts given to the church were of a lesser quality than that given to the apostles. In other words, the spiritual gifts given to the church today cannot be expected to compare with those we read about in the book of Acts. If the power to perform a healing or miracle only comes by the sovereign will of God so that the gift can operate at only that moment, why would God provide power that would be ineffective and incapable of doing the job? The concept that the Holy Spirit, the third member of the Trinity, would give gifts that are of a lesser or fallible quality seems illogical.

Several arguments are advanced to support the concept of lesser gifts. In Romans 12:6 the apostle Paul writes, "we have different gifts according to the grace that is given to us. If someone's gift is prophesying, let him use it in proportion to his faith." On the basis of this verse, Deere believes that Paul admits that "spiritual gifts occur with varying degrees of intensity or strength," and "there are different measures of grace and faith given with which to exercise the various gifts."[20] The passage, however, says none of these things. First, it does not say that the gifts vary, but that there are various gifts. This is explicit from the overall statement, "Having different gifts according to the grace that is given to us," whether it is prophecy, or ministry, or teaching. The difference is the difference of the gift of prophecy or teaching from other gifts. The part of the verse that refers to prophesying does not even imply that the gift of prophecy varies in its quality.[21] If this common translation is accurate, it would still only mean that the amount of faith is the problem, not the gift itself. The faith might vary, but not the quality of the gift. In explaining this, Deere adds words that are not in the verse. Rather than "proportion to his faith," he interprets it in the sense of "the measure of faith given him to exercise his gift."[22] This changes the meaning from "according to the individual's faith" to "the faith God has given" to exercise his gift. This suggests the idea that some believers have been given a greater amount of faith—thus, in effect, greater performance of gifts. The meaning of the verse is changed from what it actually says. But how could someone use their gift of prophecy other than according to what God has given them? Why then would Paul exhort to do this?

Romans 12:6 is commonly understood as saying "prophesy in proportion to the amount of faith you have." However, the meaning of the word translated "proportion" (Gk. *analogia*) is not completely clear in this context. Often it means "in proportion to," but it can also mean "corresponding to, in correct relation to." In addition, the meaning of "faith" is uncertain, particularly since it occurs with the article "the." Does it mean faith as an attitude, or does it mean "the faith," that is, the truth we believe? Therefore, this verse could be saying "prophesy in accordance with the doctrine we believe." Such an instruction would fit well with other admonitions regarding prophecy. In addition, regarding the next several gifts listed in Romans 12, Paul instructs that they are to be exercised in the sphere of ministry corresponding to the respective gift. It is likely then that this is instruction to exercise prophecy in the sphere appropriate to prophecy: "the faith."

If this refers to the person's own faith, why is this mentioned only in regard to prophecy since it would be true of all or most of the gifts? Also, does it seem realistic that Paul would be instructing the person to prophesy *in proportion* to their own faith or even the faith given to them? If his faith were at 5% or 50%, his prophecy would not only function at that level, but Paul would be instructing him to prophesy at that reduced level. Would Paul say, "If your faith is 5%, then prophesy at 5%," rather than urging them to increase their faith? What would it mean to prophecy at 5%? Such ideas are unlikely. Also unlikely is the idea that Paul would tell someone to prophesy at a low level if their faith were low. If this verse refers to the person's own faith it must mean they either have enough to prophesy or they do not. Even this would have the improbable meaning "prophesy only if you have enough faith." In this list Paul gives appropriate guidelines or instructions as to how or with what attitude or in what sphere to exercise the gift. He gives a guideline related to a primary feature of the gift. The main feature in prophecy is information; it would be appropriate that his instruction relates to the truth. Regardless of which view is taken, Romans 12:6 provides no support to the idea of lesser gifts.

Based upon Paul's statement in 1 Corinthians 14:18, Deere concludes that Paul had a greater gift of tongues. However, this notion is groundless. The verse only says that he used this gift more often; it says nothing about the quality of the gift.[23] Likewise, when Timothy is told to rekindle his gift in 2 Timothy 1:6, the variable is Timothy's attitude, not the quality of his gift.[24] These verses say nothing about varying qualities of gifts.

Deere's remaining arguments are actually a series of speculations. He asserts that the nonmiraculous gifts, such as teaching and evangelism, vary in strength; therefore, so do the miraculous ones.[25] However, there is no evidence that the nonmiraculous gifts vary in strength. This is an assumption based solely upon the varying results that gifted persons, such as teachers and evangelists, may accomplish. But the comparison is logically incorrect.

The gifts of miracles and healing are accomplished entirely by the power of the Holy Spirit apart from any human effort. For instance, raising the dead is not a human ability nor does it depend on the cooperation of the dead person. The nonmiraculous gifts are in areas that often have a corresponding human ability. For example, teaching is an ability common to many people, and many exceptional teachers do not belong to the body of Christ. Individuals may teach without the gift, but they do not perform miracles in their own power. Thus, another factor, human ability, is involved in teaching, which is not involved in performing miracles. Both teaching and evangelism also depend on the recipient in areas such as attitude and receptivity. Thus, the results of nonmiraculous gifts are affected by human factors in a way not possible in the miracle-working gifts. Varying results in the nonmiraculous gifts do not demonstrate varying quality of gifts. Although Apollos was "mighty in the scriptures" (Acts 18:24), he did not necessarily have a greater teaching gift.[26] It simply means that he could use the Scriptures effectively, due to knowledge, interest, and speaking ability.

The fact that Peter and Paul are the main characters in the book of Acts does not mean that their gift of apostleship was superior to that of the other apostles.[27] The particular ministry and the ways that God uses believers does not depend on the strength or quality of their gifts. Interestingly, Deere implies that Peter and Paul's gifts are superior since they are the only ones who raised the dead. This, however, is an argument from silence, a concept which Deere argued against earlier in his book. It is pure speculation. Not only does Deere argue that the other apostles did not raise the dead, but he uses this fact to argue that Peter and Paul had stronger gifts. Thus, he suggests that the other apostles *could* not do so.

Deere also argues that since no one is equal to Paul as a teacher or evangelist, then gifts must vary in quality.[28] But by his own logic, Deere cannot use such an argument. His argument that no one else has taught or evangelized like Paul is an argument, to use his own words, based on a lack of experience. It only means that Deere has not seen anyone who teaches or evangelizes like Paul. According to Deere's own logic, his "limited experience cannot be used" as evidence.[29] Therefore, the church may be full of teachers and evangelists like Paul. In any case, the argument is invalid.

Paul's "success" does not mean that he had higher quality gifts. In fact, in many instances his evangelistic and teaching efforts were thwarted, such as the witness to Agrippa, Festus, Felix, and the Jews in general. He had no magical evangelistic ability. His success was due to a combination of factors. The Lord led him to specific places in the world prepared to receive the gospel. He had been prepared by background and culture for the world he encountered. In most cases he was the first to bring the Good News. He was also able to use miraculous signs to enhance his testimony. In spite of all of this he was often rejected. The same is true of his teaching. He received information by revelation and had the knowledge that made his teaching superior. However, many did not respond to his teaching. Many of the Pauline Epistles were written to correct some error in churches where Paul had been and taught. His opponents at Corinth said that he did not look imposing and was not a good speaker. People did not automatically respond to Paul's teaching anymore than they do to teaching today. If we were present during Paul's teaching and evangelistic efforts, it is doubtful that we would see any obvious qualitative difference in his gift of teaching or evangelism. The success of his ministry was not due to qualitatively superior gifts, but to a combination of factors.

As for the statements regarding discipline of the sinful Christian in 1 Corinthians 5:1–5, they do not even imply that Paul had a greater authority than anyone else in the body of Christ, so that he alone could hand someone over to Satan.[30] Even a cursory reading of the passage will show that it has nothing to do with gifts and that the entire Corinthian church is involved in this decision and has this authority.

The fact that the apostles' miracles are described on some occasions by the terms "signs and wonders," and not by the term *charismata* does not lead to Deere's deduction from these facts. He argues that "signs and wonders" refers to an "unusual outpouring of the Holy Spirit for miracles" where an abundance of miracles occurs, and refers to the revival and evangelistic ministry of the apostles and differs from the gift of healing.[31]

Regarding the term *signs and wonders*, this is used to describe false miracles in the book of Revelation; therefore, it is not just used for revival or evangelistic ministry. The reason that the apostles' ministry is not described by *charismata* is not because the apostles' ministry was superior to others but, as should be evident, because *charismata* does not have this meaning. The word *charismata* means "gifts." Signs and wonders are not gifts; rather they are what one or two of the gifts produce. The terms are not interchangeable. For example, 1 Corinthians 12:4, which uses the word *charismata*, should not be translated "now there are diversities of signs and wonders," nor should Acts 5:12, which refers to signs and wonders, be translated "by the hands of the apostles were many gifts wrought among the people." Teaching, helps, giving, and showing mercy are *charismata*, but they are not signs and wonders.

The reason the term *signs and wonders* is used for an abundance of miracles should also be apparent. This expression, which refers to a large number of occurrences, would hardly be appropriate for one or two miracles, such as the healing of Dorcas. On the other hand, we could hardly expect a citywide performance of many miracles to be described one by one. Hence, the general term *signs and wonders* is used. In addition, the fact that *charismata* is not used to describe the apostles' ministry is meaningless to demonstrate a difference between the apostles' ministries and that of others. In actuality, *charismata* is not used to describe anyone else's ministry. The same is true regarding the term *signs and wonders*. Although Deere leaves the impression that some other term is used to describe the ministry of those other than the apostles, this is not so. Every description of a healing or miracle-working ministry in the New Testament uses the same terms used to describe the apostles' ministry. The only ones described are that of the apostles, Stephen, Philip, and perhaps Ananias in Acts 8. Thus Deere's argument based on the use of the term *signs and wonders* is meaningless.

Summary

The New Testament offers no evidence anywhere of a qualitative difference in gifts given by the Spirit of God. This is as we might expect since God gives perfect gifts (James 1:16–17). All are described in the same way. We have no example of any qualitatively inferior or fallible gift or of any failure by any Christian who attempted to exercise a gift. Neither do we have any evidence that the gifts of miracles and healing were widely distributed in the church. More than once it is specifically stressed that they were performed by the apostles. Paul says that they are the sign of the apostle. Accordingly, they cannot be widespread. If they were exercised throughout the church, why is there such stress on them as apostolic? Apart from the apostles, only Philip and Stephen exercised such gifts, and they exercised them on the same level qualitatively and quantitatively as the apostles.

The overtly miraculous gifts were certainly not for edification but were performed publicly, primarily for unbelievers to confirm the gospel. Only on a few occasions are believers healed. The fact that James 5:14 instructs the sick to call for the elders rather than a healer shows that these gifts were not expected or used in the local churches for the benefit of Christians. When Paul lists in 1 Corinthians 12 the gifts given to the entire body of Christ, he includes apostles, miracles, and healings. However, when he lists in Romans 12:6ff. the gifts to be expected in the local church, he does not list apostle, miracles, or healing.

The excuse is invalid that gifts do not function at the will of the possessor but only when God sovereignly gives or withholds specific instances of enablement. First Corinthians 13:1–4 and 1 Corinthians 14 show that a gift is under the control of the person who has the gift. The biblical evidence that miraculous gifts can be exercised in the wrong situations and for the wrong reasons is against the concept that they are exercised only in God's sovereign will on specific occasions. Why give a sovereign enablement to speak in tongues or prophesy on a specific occasion if it is for misuse? If they are exercised on specific occasions at God's sovereign will rather than the individual's will, how can they be misused? Why would God sovereignly in his will give enablement to perform a specific healing or miracle and yet give some inferior gift to carry out his sovereign will?

Every example of healing or miracles is described in the same way. Every example of a Christian prophet is true. The Old Testament gives only one test for a genuine prophet (Deut. 18:22), thus implying they were all on the same qualitative level. Even if it could be proved that gifts differed qualitatively, there is still no indication that any were defective, fallible, or might fail.

Mark 16:9–20 says that the miracles were to confirm the preaching of the gospel. Both Acts 4:29–30 and 14:3 directly state that the miracles were to confirm the evangelistic ministry. All the other miraculous episodes in Acts support this concept. The Epistles clearly state that miracles, including healing, were for the confirmation of the gospel message. Romans 15:19 is especially clear. This concept is also asserted in Hebrews 2:3–4, which apparently restricts the miracles to eyewitnesses of the Lord and implies that the miracles were past. Such a conclusion coincides with the evidence of the book of Acts. Very few cases of miracles or healing were private. The case of Eutychus, which was unusual, is the only case of a miracle occurring during a meeting of believers.

The miracles in Acts were performed publicly, flawlessly, and independent of the recipient's faith. This fits perfectly with the scriptural evidence that the miracles were to confirm the gospel to unbelievers. They were not primarily for the benefit of the faithful. Modern-day claims of healing bear little resemblance to the practice, purpose, or results of miracles that occurred in the early church as recorded in the book of Acts.

There are other indications that such gifts were not exercised for the benefit of the local church. James 5:14–15 implies either that these gifts had ceased or that they were not for the church, since it assumes that no healer was available. Paul writes to Timothy regarding Timothy's physical condition (1 Tim. 5:23) and yet does not tell Timothy to search for a healer. In contrast to a lack of exhortation to perform or expect miracles, the Epistles abound with commands to be holy, to teach, to minister, and to pray. For example, Timothy was not instructed to perform miracles but to read, preach, and exhort in sound doctrine. Miraculous sign gifts are not even mentioned in many passages where gifts are discussed and where local church members are exhorted to use their gifts (see Rom. 12:6–8; Eph. 4:11; 1 Pet. 4:10–11).

Today claims of miracles usually narrow down to healing. We need to be perfectly focused in our thinking. The gift of working miracles means that a specific individual can directly perform miracles. The gift of healing means that a specific individual can heal other people directly. The same applies to casting out demons if it is considered a gift. The individual has the ability to perform the miracle or healing. Instances where people are healed in answer to prayer are not instances of the exercising of spiritual gifts but are the direct work of God in response to prayer. If believers gather and pray for a sick person and that person is healed miraculously, this is not evidence that the gift of healing exists today. This demonstrates that God answers prayer.

None of today's claims of miracles or healings are of the magnitude or quality of those in the New Testament. Little correspondence exists between the biblical descriptions and today's so-called miracles and healings to allow any credence to the allegation that they are the spiritual gifts of the New Testament. Very few people claim to perform miracles directly, and those who claim to do so fail frequently. But the Holy Spirit never fails. The incidents in the early church involved multitudes of healings without any failures.

The alleged evidence for "lesser" gifts amounts to no evidence at all. We find nothing in Scripture that describes an instance of lesser gifts, nor does it suggest that such gifts ever existed. Without doubt the scriptural gifts were miraculous, but the modern-day charismatic gifts do not compare to those in Scripture. We must not miss the important fact that the very admission of "lesser" gifts and the need for charismatic defenders to find them in the Bible is a direct admission that even the charismatics know their gifts do not conform to Scripture.

Not only do today's claims fail to live up to the New Testament, but this has been true throughout church history. No one in the history of the church since apostolic times has performed miracles and healing as those described in the book of Acts. The purported instances of postapostolic miracles are few and are not validated. The rarity of claims is in itself evidence that God is not giving this gift to the church at large.

Many Christians have said that they desire to have the power of the early church. They are disenchanted with the lack of power in the present-day church and are convinced that we should expect the same power of the early church to be with us today. First of all we might ask, Which New Testament church do you desire to imitate? Certainly no one would desire to imitate the Corinthian church since they were in worse shape than many churches today. Although the Thessalonian and Philippian churches were commended, we have no indication that they had any more power (in the sense of miraculous working) than churches do today. Also, we have no reason to believe that any church other than the church of Jerusalem had any more power than we have today. As far as the church at Jerusalem is concerned, the power was in the apostles, not in the church as a whole. When people speak of the power of the early church, they usually refer to the ministry of the apostles and mistakenly attempt to apply this to the entire church. Apart from the apostles, only Stephen and Philip were involved in miraculous workings.

If we are to follow the example of the first-century church, as so many propose today, then we should refer to the church rather than to the apostles and eyewitnesses of the Lord. The early churches seem to have been much like the average Bible-believing church today. They had problems much as we do today, including adultery, theft, lack of love, and factions. Some were weak doctrinally. The Corinthian church was saturated with problems. James 5:14–16 makes it plain that no healers or other miracle workers were in the local churches in the New Testament. Despite what some people may naively assume, we have no evidence that the New Testament churches were "turning the world upside down." This is said in regard to the apostle Paul. Only a few churches were commended for outreach, and this mainly by report rather than by conscious "evangelistic outreach." This is not to criticize those churches, but it is to keep us from following a church that exists only in someone's imagination. Revelation 2–3 gives us a realistic evaluation of the first-century church. Of the seven churches mentioned in this passage, only two could be construed as "spiritual" while the five remaining churches experienced serious spiritual problems. None of the seven, however, were characterized by either possessing or exhibiting miraculous powers.

Conclusion

We have no evidence from any source to demonstrate that sign gifts from the Holy Spirit, such as the gift of miracles or the gift of healing, are present today. The biblical evidence is conclusive that the sign gifts were given to confirm the truth of the gospel message to the world. James 5:14–15 shows that the early church was instructed to react to sickness in much the same way as the noncharismatic Bible-believing churches do today. Apparently, healers and miracle workers were not available. God's miraculous answers to the prayers of his people do not prove that individuals have the gift of miracles or healing. Since not all miraculous experiences are from God (Matt. 7:22–23), all experiences must be verified by Scripture. Thus, until modern-day charismatics can provide adequate biblical support for their claims in regard to the gifts of miracles and healings, we have no warrant to give any credence to their claims.

※ ※ ※

1. John Broadus, "Style of Mark xvi. 9–20, as bearing upon the question of genuineness." *The Baptist Quarterly* (July 1869); John William Burgon, *The Last Twelve Verses of Mark*, (Grand Rapids: Associated Publishers and Authors, n.d.); and more recently, W. R. Framer, *The Last Twelve Verses of Mark* (Cambridge: The University Press, 1974) have adequately demonstrated that these verses are genuine.
2. If the statement in verse 9 is taken to mean that this man had faith that he could be physically healed, the verse only states that Paul *responded* to this and healed him. It does not say that his faith was *necessary* for Paul to heal him.
3. The word for wonders *(teras)* does not occur after 5:12. The word for

signs *(semeion)* does not occur after 15:12. The word for miracles *(dunamis)* does not occur after 19:11. The six occurrences of *teras* (wonders) in Acts describing actual ministry and the seven occurrences of *semeion* (signs) describing actual ministry all occur in the first half of the book of Acts. Four of the five examples of *dunamis* (miracles) describing actual ministry occur in the first eight chapters of Acts. These three words occur a total of thirty-two times in Acts, but only six are after Acts 8. Apparently the main part of the miraculous ministry occurred during the early days of the church; that is, in the first third of Acts. A study of the miracles themselves supports this implication. The frequency of miracle working seems to have been on the decline during the lifetime of the apostles.
4. Walter J. Hollenweger, *The Pentecostals* (London: SCM, 1972), 345.
5. Wayne A. Grudem, *The Gift of Prophecy in the New Testament and Today* (Westchester, Ill.: Crossway, 1988), 110.
6. Jack Deere, *Surprised by the Power of the Spirit* (Grand Rapids: Zondervan, 1993), 68.
7. Ibid., 59.
8. Ibid., 59–61.
9. Ibid., 59.
10. Ibid., 60.
11. Ibid., 61–62.
12. Ibid., 62.
13. Ibid., 63.
14. Ibid.
15. Ibid.
16. Ibid.
17. Ibid., 65.
18. Ibid.
19. Ibid., 64.
20. Ibid., 65.
21. Ibid.
22. Ibid.
23. Ibid.
24. Ibid.
25. Ibid.
26. Ibid.
27. Ibid., 65–66.
28. Ibid., 67.
29. Ibid., 58.
30. Ibid., 67.
31. Ibid., 66–67.

CHAPTER 6

Tongues: The Nature of the Gift

NICHOL STATES THAT every Pentecostal believer believes in healing and in a postconversion baptism by the Holy Spirit which is demonstrated by speaking in tongues.[1] In addition to the main Pentecostal groups, there are other groups and individuals who stress speaking in tongues. However, there is disagreement over most aspects of speaking in tongues.

What was the genuine gift of tongues? Do today's alleged tongues seem to be the same? What was the purpose for the gift of tongues and the proper use of tongues? These issues must be studied in order to determine whether today's tongues fit the biblical description. The primary issue is to determine if the tongues of today are genuine. This chapter will answer the first question, What was the gift of tongues described in the New Testament? Charismatics hold a veritable tangle of different opinions on the nature and practice of tongues speaking. They agree only that this gift is available today. However, large segments of orthodox Christians do not believe that this gift has been present since the apostolic age. This has been the position of orthodox Christians since the first century. The opinion that tongues are given today by the Holy Spirit is a modern view contrary to the accepted opinion of Christians for eighteen hundred years. This orthodox opinion cannot be dismissed lightly. The "new" opinion of the charismatics needs to be biblically verified.

The apostle Paul instructed the Corinthians regarding the necessity and the way to verify those claiming to speak by the

Holy Spirit. He wrote, "No one speaking by the Spirit of God says Jesus is anathema" (1 Cor. 12:3). This passage was a warning to the Corinthians that everyone who claimed to do so did not necessarily speak by the Holy Spirit. Paul felt the necessity to verify those speaking. Certainly we should attempt to verify such claims today.

A Word Study of "Tongue"

The Greek word *glossa*, "tongue," is a crucial term for understanding the nature of the gift of tongues. The following presents a detailed study of this term.

In Classical Greek

One recognized authority on the use of Greek words in classical times and up to A.D. 500 is the *Greek-English Lexicon* by Liddell and Scott. Herein the word *glossa*, or "tongue," is defined as the organ of speech or a language, including obsolete or foreign words which need explanation or anything shaped like a physical tongue.[2] Notice that an "obsolete or foreign" word is still part of a known human language and is intelligible. There is no claim that *glossa* means ecstatic unintelligible speech. It is either the physical tongue or some aspect of normal human language.

Liddell and Scott in their *Lexicon* and Behm in the article on *glossa* in the *Theological Dictionary of the New Testament*[3] refer to certain passages from classical Greek in order to demonstrate that *glossa* may refer to obscure or difficult speech. These references are then assumed as proof that the word *glossa* may refer to ecstatic unintelligible speech such as is present today in the tongues movement. However, these passages do not refer to ecstatic or unintelligible speech.

Under references supporting the use of *glossa* as "an expression which in speech or manner is strange and obscure and needs explanation,"[4] in his study Behm refers to various writings, including Aristotle *Poetics* 21, 1457b, 1ff., wherein the word *glotta* is translated "rare."[5] However, *glotta* (the Attic dialect for *glossa*) does not describe strange, obscure utterance in this reference. It refers to normal language, which in this case is not used by everyone. The difference in usage depends on geographical or local differences. This is also true of Behm's second reference, Aristotle *Poetics* 22, 1458a, 22ff., where *glotta* is used of rare words in the same sense as above. In both cases *glotta* refers to normal Greek words. Another writing used as evidence by Behm is a discussion of the words which produce "smart and popular sayings."[6] The word *glottai* is translated as "strange words." This could be translated "obsolete" or "rare" just as well as "strange." The entire discussion concerns normal language. *Glottai* does not refer to ecstatic or unintelligible speech. It is possible that the expression here means words from foreign languages. It refers to words with which the hearer is unfamiliar in contrast to those he already knows.

The next reference is to a statement of Sextus Empiricus where he writes concerning the grammarians.[7] Here again the reference is to words which make up normal language, in this case obsolete words. Another reference given as evidence is from Plutarch, *Isis and Osiris*. But *glotta* is not used here to describe ecstatic, unintelligible speech. It refers to Greek words which the poets attempt to revive and are not familiar to the hearer.[8]

As strange or obscure speech, Behm also refers to uses of *glossa* as archaic expression.[9] But all of his references refer to actual human language, although "out of date." Archaic expressions from human language, however, are not evidence for ecstatic speech. His final group under the general category of strange or obscure speech is uses of *glossa* as select poetic expression."[10] The examples in this group refer to less common words,[11] poetry,[12] and the vague and obscure statements of a pagan prophetess. The statements of the prophetess are not unintelligible, however. They are merely unusual applications of normal words. Some examples are calling men "mountain roamers," rivers "mountain engorgers," and Spartans "snake devourers."[13] In a separate section titled "glossolalia," Behm refers to incidents in pagan religion of "muttering of words or sounds without interconnection or meaning."[14] However, these examples of ecstatic utterance in pagan religion further support the concept of *glossa* which is emerging from our study thus far, namely, that *glossa* was not used to refer to unintelligible ecstatic utterance. Behm lists several examples of such pagan ecstatic utterance. In the first, the word *glossa (glotta)* does not refer to unintelligible ecstatic speech but rather to the words of Cratinus the poet.[15] This statement apparently refers to some statement Cratinus made in a poem or in a speech. There is no evidence that it was ecstatic or unintelligible. Any implication of unintelligible ecstatic speaking is not in the word *glottes*, which in this example merely means speech or word, but is in the term *bakchei*, which refers to Bacchic rites or frenzy. Therefore, this passage cannot be used to prove that *glossa* or *glotta* is used to mean ecstatic unintelligible speech. The remaining examples refer to pagan seers such as the Delphic oracles, the Sybils, and others including Gnostics.[16] However, these examples do not use the word *glossa*. They use other words such as the verb *phtheggomai* ("to utter").[17]

It is apparent that the ancient Greeks did not use *glossa* to mean unintelligible ecstatic speech. This is not due to a lack of references to ecstatic utterance since there are numerous references in Greek literature. Instead they used other terms to refer to the ecstatic utterance of their time.

The uses of *glossa* referred to by Behm all refer to words in actual, known human language. Liddell and Scott include under the broader category of language a section termed "obsolete or foreign words."[18] Their references do not include any which have not already been discussed. Neither of these authorities gives any evidence for the use of the word *glossa* as describing or referring to unintelligible ecstatic speech. All of the references supposedly supporting strange or obscure speech actually refer to human language, although the words may be obsolete or used poetically.

In Pre-Christian Judaism

Some have contended that the word *glossa* as a technical term for unintelligible ecstatic utterance originated in Jewish circles or sects prior to New Testament times.[19] One of the examples commonly cited as evidence is the *Testament of Job*. Behm calls this an example of reference to the "tongues of angels."[20] Harrisville refers to the poetic use of *glossa* and the technical use of *glossa lalein*, "to speak in tongues." He then states that such poetic use is most strikingly illustrated in the *Testament of Job* 48:2–3a; 49:2; 50:1a–2; 51:4; and 52:7.[21] However, despite all of these authoritative statements, the word *glossa* does not appear in the examples cited! Although *glossa* is not used, the verb *apophtheggomai* is used. This is a compound form of the verb *phtheggomai*, which, as we have noted earlier, was used in Greek pagan religion for ecstatic utterance.[22] *The Testament of Job*, rather than providing evidence for the use of *glossa* as a term to describe ecstatic unintelligible speech, does not use *glossa* for such speech. It provides evidence, however, that another term, the verb *phtheggomai*, was normally used to describe such utterance. Other examples cited as evidence of glossolalia in pre-Christian Judaism actually give no evidence whatever for such utterance.[23]

Some scholars attempt to derive the meaning of "ecstatic

utterance" from the word *glossa* by reference to Philo. As examples of parallel phenomena in religious history, Behm cites several references from Philo.[24] Harrisville adds several references.[25] However, there are two basic flaws in these parallels. None of them uses the word *glossa* in the sense of speech of any kind, and none of them seems to refer to incidents of unintelligible utterance. They provide no evidence whatsoever for *glossa* used of unintelligible ecstatic speech.[26]

The references to Philo may be dismissed as evidence for glossolalia or for the use of *glossa* as unintelligible speech. Their use as evidence can only be explained as a move of desperation to support the preconceived opinion that *glossa* refers to unintelligible ecstatic utterance in 1 Corinthians 14.

In Secular Literature in New Testament Times

Moulton and Milligan's *Vocabulary of the Greek Testament* is a recognized authority listing examples of the use of secular Greek around the time of the New Testament. The papyri and other evidence of everyday transactions support the fact that at that time *glossa* meant normal human language, local peculiarities of speech, or the physical tongue.[27] There is no intimation that *glossa* meant unintelligible ecstatic speech. Since "local peculiarities" refer to normal language, the evidence supports the two basic meanings for *glossa* in agreement with the findings based on classical Greek. There seems to be no basis in secular Greek, up to and including the New Testament period, to conclude that *glossa* was used of unintelligible ecstatic speech.

In the Septuagint

The Greek Old Testament, the Septuagint, was translated from Hebrew by Alexandrian Jews. This reveals how they used the Greek language when referring to religious or biblical topics and provides the background for the "religious Greek" familiar to the New Testament writers. A study of *glossa* in the canonical books of the Old Testament reveals that this word is used of the physical tongue, of a tongue-shaped object, of speech, of human languages, and sometimes of a nation in the sense of a language unit.[28] *Glossa* occurs 114 times in the canonical books of the Septuagint and 41 times in the apocryphal books, providing a total of 155 examples of its usage. In spite of this large number of occurrences, *glossa* never means unintelligible speech. It always refers to the tongue itself (including one reference to an object shaped like a tongue or wedge), or to normal coherent speech or language.²⁹ *Glossa* is not used in the Septuagint to mean ecstatic, trancelike, or oracular utterance. The evidence supports the same conclusion that was reached in the study of the papyri and the classical literature. *Glossa* means the physical tongue or some aspect of normal human language. There is no support for the use of *glossa* in a special sense to describe ecstatic unintelligible speech.³⁰

In the Old Testament

Many have stated that ecstatic speech occurs in the Old Testament, concluding that it is therefore biblical. They then try to link this with the New Testament gift of tongues. Although the examples do not use the word *glossa*, it seems appropriate to discuss this claim. Behm attempts to demonstrate that such speech occurs in the Old Testament by citing 1 Samuel 10:5ff., 19:20ff., and 1 Kings 18:29ff. as examples of "ecstatic fervor"; 2 Kings 9:11 as an example of "broken cries and unintelligible speech"; Isaiah 28:10ff. as a reference to Isaiah's "ecstatic babbling of obscure words"; and Numbers 11:25ff. as an example of "ecstatic frenzy; that is, in raving gestures and outcries."³¹ Behm's examples are the ones commonly used; therefore, we will examine them.

First Samuel 10:5ff. refers to the fact that Saul prophesied when the Spirit of God came upon him. There is no suggestion that the prophesying was unintelligible or was accomplished in ecstatic fervor. First Samuel 19:20ff. refers to Saul's prophesying when the Spirit of God came upon him. In 1 Samuel 19:24 he stripped off his clothes and prophesied. The action of stripping off his clothes and lying down all night may imply ecstatic fervor, but such is not stated. This case is unusual since Saul was not one of the prophets and at the time was opposing God's will. The case in 1 Kings 18:29ff. concerns the false prophets of Baal and their pagan practices. It is an example of pagan practice, not of a true working of God.

The prophet's speech in 2 Kings 9:11 is definitely intelligible rather than "broken cries and unintelligible speech." The content is recorded in 2 Kings 9:6–10. It is clear and lucid. Jehu expresses this when he says, "You know the man and his communication." There is no suggestion of any ecstatic state of fervor. The men called the prophet "mad" because of the content of his speech which they clearly understood. Isaiah 28:10ff. says nothing to imply any kind of ecstatic speech; rather, it refers to the foreign language of future conquerors of Israel. Numbers 11:25ff. merely states, "When the spirit rested upon them, they prophesied and did not cease." There is no mention of "raving gestures and outcries"; in fact, there is no indication of glossolalia or unintelligible speech. None of these references proves that unintelligible ecstatic speech (glossolalia) was practiced in the Old Testament by believers.

There is no evidence in secular Greek of classical or koine times, nor in pre-Christian Judaism, nor in the biblical Greek of the Septuagint that *glossa* was used to mean ecstatic unintelligible speech. Such speech, although common to pagan religion, was not described by *glossa* but by other terms such as *phtheggomai* which were available in the Greek language. Numerous scholars have attempted to explain the origin of such a meaning for *glossa*, revealing that they realize there is no firm evidence that *glossa* was ever used to mean unintelligible ecstatic utterance. In addition, it cannot be demonstrated that the Spirit of God in the Old Testament ever moved individuals to unintelligible speech. Thus, there is no linguistic or Old Testament background that furnishes evidence for interpreting *glossa* in this manner.

In the New Testament

The New Testament uses the word *glossa* in the normally accepted sense of the physical tongue or human language. *Glossa* occurs 50 times.[32] All of the passages using *glossa* are clear and undisputed except those describing the gift of tongues. Of these passages, the one most seriously disputed is 1 Corinthians 14. No proof from the Greek language has been presented to demonstrate that *glossa* was used to mean unintelligible ecstatic speech. A word must be interpreted according to its normal usage unless the context demands otherwise. Those passages describing the gift of tongues cannot be interpreted as referring to other than known human languages, unless it is impossible for this meaning to fit the passage and its context. Since many feel that language, in the sense of normal human languages, makes the best sense in these passages, certainly such an unsupported meaning for the word *tongues* as unintelligible ecstatic speech is not demanded by the passages. The disputed passages are Mark 16:17, Acts 2:4ff., 10:46, 19:6, and 1 Corinthians 12–14.

Acts 2:4–11. The tongues spoken on the day of Pentecost refer to languages normally spoken and do not refer to unintelligible ecstatic utterance. This is directly stated in verse 6 and verses 8–11.

> And they were all filled with the Holy Ghost, and began to speak with other tongues, as the Spirit gave them utterance. And there were

dwelling at Jerusalem Jews, devout men, out of every nation under heaven. Now when this was noised abroad, the multitude came together, and were confounded, because that every man heard them speak in his own language. And they were all amazed and marvelled, saying one to another, Behold, are not all these which speak Galilaeans? And how hear we every man in our own tongue, wherein we were born? Parthians, and Medes, and Elamites, and the dwellers in Mesopotamia, and in Judaea, and Cappadocia, in Pontus, and Asia, Phrygia, and Pamphylia, in Egypt, and in the parts of Libya about Cyrene, and strangers of Rome, Jews and proselytes, Cretes and Arabians, we do hear them speak in our tongues the wonderful works of God. (Acts 2:4–11)

The same speaking is described twice by the word *glossa* and twice by the term *dialektos*, which means the language of a nation or region.[33] The hearers stated explicitly, "We hear every man in our own tongue, wherein we were born" and "We do hear them speak in our tongues." The use of *dialektos*, "language," together with such statements as "our own" and "wherein we were born" rules out unintelligible utterance. Writing under the inspiration of the Spirit, Luke states, "Every man heard them speaking in his own language *(dialektos)*." Both Luke and the hearers stated that this speech was in the language of the many pilgrims gathered in Jerusalem. Luke emphasizes that the hearers came from "every nation" (v. 5; see vv. 9–11) and that they were amazed that Galileans could speak thus. There is a stress on the geographical differences which clearly fits if the speech is language. Why the amazement that Galileans, in contrast to other people, could speak as they did? The hearers would not be amazed to hear Galileans speak unintelligibly, but they were surprised to hear Galileans speaking a variety of foreign languages. No one would have been amazed to hear ecstatic unintelligible speech, which was common in paganism. Gundry states it well:

> It could not be clearer that Luke here uses *glossa* and *dialektos* synonymously for the languages spoken in the countries from which the listeners had come and the audience was amazed that uneducated Galilean Jews could speak languages foreign to themselves but understandable to non-Palestinians.[34]

Acts 2:4–11 is the only passage in the entire Bible which directly describes the gift of tongues. Therefore, this passage should be determinative for the nature of "speaking in tongues" by the Holy Spirit.

Some interpreters have claimed that the miracle was in the hearing. This is to reject Luke's inspired statement that "they began to speak with other tongues as the Spirit gave them utterance" (Acts 2:4). This is an explicit statement that they actually spoke with other tongues. The hearers did not regard this as a miracle of hearing. A miracle of hearing also requires a (less likely) miraculous working of the Holy Spirit on an entire multitude of unbelieving onlookers, in contrast to a miracle of speaking produced in a few believers.

A few have rejected the clear statements and stated that foreign language is not involved in this passage.[35] Despite the clarity of the passage, some have still argued that Acts 2:4–11 involves ecstatic unintelligible utterance. The most common arguments for this position are: (1) the accusation of drunkenness would not fit someone speaking foreign languages; (2) the verb *laleo*, which means "to utter," is used for tongues speaking in Acts 2:4ff. and throughout the New Testament, rather than *lego*, which means rational or logical speech; (3) Acts 2:4 describes the tongues as "other," using the Greek word *heteros*, which means "others" in the sense of a different kind; (4) the word *apophtheggomai*, which is commonly used to describe ecstatic speech, is used in Acts 2:4 and suggests ecstatic, often unintelligible speech; and (5) it was unnecessary to speak foreign languages since the hearers could all understand Peter's speech in Aramaic.[36] An additional argument states that the speaking began before any outsiders arrived. Therefore, why speak foreign languages when no foreigners were present?[37]

None of these arguments will stand up to inspection. The accusation of drunkenness does not demonstrate that the speaking was ecstatic and unintelligible. The passage states that Jews from various parts of the world heard them speaking in "our own language wherein we were born" (2:8). It is inconceivable that large numbers of pilgrims from many different countries could all simultaneously and mistakenly think they heard the languages of their homelands and then decide this was merely drunken babble. Thus, there are only two possibilities: either the hearers recognizing the languages accused the speakers of being drunk because they heard their own languages (an illogical supposition), or many of the hearers recognized the languages spoken (as the passage states) but others present did not recognize them as languages because they were not familiar with the specific languages spoken. This latter group made the accusation of drunkenness.

The second possibility is not only logically superior but is implied in the passage. The group described as "out of every nation" (2:5) is the same group which stated that the speaking was in "our own language" (2:8). It is described in verses 9–11 by the respective countries from which they came. It is this same group which is described as "amazed" (2:12) and that asked the question "What does this mean?" (2:12). Verse 13 states that "others" (*heteroi*), another group from that already described, made the accusation of drunkenness. It is stated very clearly that there were two basic groups of individuals present, that is, those who recognized the languages and others who thought the speakers were drunk. That this latter group was mistaken is clear. How could the first group mistake drunken babble for their own language? In addition, Luke states explicitly that they spoke in languages (*dialektos*, v. 6).[38]

The statements of those who recognized the languages support the concept that they were different from those who thought the speakers were drunk. They were surprised that Galileans were speaking thus (2:7). Why should they be surprised to think Galileans could be drunk? Certainly they did not think drunkenness was involved. Why would they ask, "What does this mean"? If they regarded the speakers as drunken, certainly they would ask no such question. Who would be concerned about the significance of what they considered to be drunken babbling? It is not difficult to understand why those who did not recognize the languages might consider a group of people uttering unfamiliar languages as drunken, particularly if none of the typical aspects of pagan religious ecstasy was present. If the speech was clearly "religious ecstasy," a familiar event in the world of that day, why wasn't it recognized as such by all rather than mistaken for drunkenness by some? The solution as we have seen is clear from the passage itself. Gundry states it as follows:

> The accusers were "others" (*heteroi*) than those who had come from foreign countries. "All" the non-Palestinians were "amazed and perplexed" (v. 12). That is, the "others" who charged the disciples with drunkenness were Palestinian Jews who did not understand the foreign languages being spoken. Consequently they mistook those languages for drunken babbling. By way of contrast the non-Palestinian Jews recognized the languages with astonishment.[39]

The argument that tongues are ecstatic unintelligible speech due to the fact that the Greek verb *laleo* is used rather than *lego* is equally futile. This same contention is often used in an attempt to prove that the tongues in 1 Corinthians 14 are ecstatic. It is not valid in either passage. Gundry states the argument and shows its erroneous nature in a discussion of its use with reference to 1 Corinthians:

> Yet further, it has been maintained that the exclusive use of the root *lal-* in references to speaking in tongues favors "ecstatic utterance." The argument is that since no other root for "speaking" is used in connexion with tongues and since *lal-* can indicate incoherent speech like animal sounds and the sounds of musical instruments, it does indicate inarticulate speech here. But *lal-* did not ordinarily mean incoherent speech in Hellenistic times. See the lexica and concordances. Furthermore, a number of facts make it quite evident that *lal-* carries no thought of incoherence in this section of 1 Corinthians. Paul does use another word, *lego*, for glossolalia in xiv. 16 ("when he does not know what you are saying *[legeis]*"). And *lego* does not have the desired connotation of incoherence claimed for *lal-*." Moreover, Paul uses *laleo* in xiv. 19 of speaking "with the mind *(toi noi),*" that is understandably, in contrast to speaking in an uninterpreted tongue. Again, *laleo* occurs in xiv. 29 in the connexion with prophesying, that is, speaking a revelation in the commonly understood language: "Let two or three prophets speak *(laleitosan).*" *Laleo* also occurs in Paul's prohibition of women's speaking in church, which includes the asking of questions—hardly incoherent speech: "they are not permitted to speak *(lalein),* . . . it is a shameful thing for a woman to speak *(lalein)* in church" (xiv.34f.). Not ecstasy, therefore, but probably the use of *laleo* in Isa. xxviii.IIf. LXX, an Old Testament proof-text for speaking in tongues, caused the predominance of *lal-* in this connexion.[40]

A simple concordance and lexical study verifies his statements. The standard Greek lexicons do not indicate that *laleo* is used solely or even primarily for unintelligible sound or chatter.[41] The use of *laleo* in the New Testament is easy to check and does not support the idea that *laleo* implies ecstatic speech. In this very passage (Acts 2:6) *laleo* is used to mean speaking a *dialektos* (language). *Laleo* is used approximately 295 times in the New Testament; 60 of these are in the book of Acts. Excluding the 30 instances where *laleo* is used of "speaking in tongues," 265 instances remain. None of these seem to refer to ecstatic unintelligible speech. Many instances occur such as Peter's clear, lucid, rational gospel message to Cornelius (Acts 10:34–43). Verse 44 states, "while Peter yet spake *(laleo)* these words." Other instances seem just as clear (e.g., Acts 2:31; 17:19; Rom. 3:19; 1 Cor. 2:6; Heb. 2:5). The verb *laleo* is used of prophesying in 1 Corinthians 14:3, 29. The point of that entire chapter is that prophesying is understood by the hearers. *Laleo* is used in 1 Corinthians 14:6 to refer to various modes of understandable speech Also, as Gundry points out, it is used of speaking "understandably in contrast to speaking in an uninterpreted tongue" (1 Cor. 14:19) and in 1 Corinthians 14:34 in a prohibition of women speaking and asking questions in church.[42] In this long chapter on the subject of tongues, there are at least 5 instances where *laleo* is used of speech that can be understood in contrast to tongues (languages) which the hearer does not understand.

The final blow to the argument based on *laleo* is the use of *lego* in 1 Corinthians 14:16 to refer to the tongues speaking, which the congregation is not able to understand or respond to: "How shall he say Amen when you give thanks, since he does not understand what you say *(lego)*?" The statement is not true that *laleo* implies ecstatic speech.

The argument that the use of "other" *(heteros)* tongues in Acts 2:4 means others of a different kind is just as weak as the other arguments. If *heteros* always and clearly meant "a different kind" this still would not imply unintelligible ecstatic speech. The issue would depend upon what the difference in kind is related to. It could easily mean different in the sense that this speaking in languages was miraculous, immediate endowment from the Spirit in contrast to the normal learned language.

Neither will the argument that *heteros* always means "different in kind" hold up under scrutiny. The two Greek words translated "other" are generally synonymous.[43] If a difference is stressed in a given passage, *heteros* may imply difference in kind in contrast to "another of the same kind" *(allos)*. However, in many cases where the words appear to be contrasted it is very difficult to determine whether this distinction is implied. The difference is so nebulous that Ramsay actually argued for the reverse meaning, that:

> When the two words are pointedly contrasted with one another, *heteros* means "a second," "another of the same kind," "anew" (e.g., a new king succeeds in regular course to the throne"), while *allos* implies difference of kind.[44]

Moulton and Milligan refer to this opinion of Ramsay's and add that he

... agrees with the opinion expressed by Professor A. W. Mair who has supplied a long list of passages from Demosthenes and others, showing that any distinction in usage between the two words results naturally from the fact that one is a positive, or absolute word *(allos)*, while the other is a comparative, or relative *(heteros)*, and further that, where this is not essential, they are used indifferently.[45]

Any distinction between *allos* and *heteros* cannot be maintained unless the two words are directly contrasted in a given passage, and even in such a case the distinction should not be overly pressed. In Acts 2:4 the word *heteros*, "other," is not contrasted with *allos*; therefore, no argument for the nature of the tongues can be built on the use of *heteros*; certainly no argument may be built that can offset the plain statement of the passage that the speaking was in normal human languages. It is clear that the *heteros* tongues (2:4) are the same as *hemeterais* (our) tongues (2:11), and that both are the same as the *idia* (our own) *dialektos* (language) (2:6, 8). Even if *heteros* means different in kind, the passage states that the tongues are our languages, our tongues." Therefore the difference in kind cannot mean "ecstatic unintelligible speech."

The word *apophtheggomai* is sometimes used to describe ecstatic speech by pagan oracles; however, this does not prove that the tongues in Acts 2:4ff. are ecstatic and unintelligible. This is merely a compound form of the verb *phtheggomai*. Both verbs *(phtheggomai* and *apophtheggamai)* are used to describe pagan oracular speech, both intelligible and unintelligible.[46] The verb itself *(phtheggomai* or *apophtheggomai)* means "to speak out" or "declare" and has nothing to do with the content or coherence of the speaking.[47] Liddell and Scott's *Lexicon* define it "to speak one's opinion plainly."[48] Arndt and Gingrich state that it "also refers to ecstatic speech."[49] The three occurrences of *phtheggomai* in the New Testament are all intelligible speech.[50] In this same passage in Acts (i.e., 2:14), Peter's sermon, given in intelligible words, is described by the verb *apophtheggomai*. This use in the same passage is enough to discount the argument that *apophtheggomai* in this passage implies ecstatic unintelligible speech. Acts 26:25, the only other occurrence of this verb in the New Testament, describes intelligible speech. The two occurrences of *apophtheggomai* in the New Testament other than Acts 2:4 definitely refer to nonecstatic intelligible speech. The argument that *phtheggomai* implies ecstatic unintelligible speech, just as the other arguments, does not stand up as fact.

It is quite probable that the hearers all knew Greek and Hebrew;

therefore, it was not necessary to speak foreign languages in order to communicate with the hearers. But this does not imply that the tongues were ecstatic. If communication were the primary goal, it not only would also be unnecessary to speak ecstatic utterance, but it would be impossible to communicate. Smith argues that there was no need to speak the various languages, thus if the tongues were languages, this would be an unnecessary miracle. Who is to say that miracles are necessary? What is the necessity of ecstatic speech or of Jesus telling the blind man to wash his eyes or of Jesus' walking on the water? All miracles are primarily necessary as signs. The miraculous ability to speak languages is definitely a sign. Incoherent utterance or babbling similar to pagan oracles would be no sign. Languages as a sign are far more necessary than unintelligible speech. As Gundry states,

> *Neither at Corinth nor on the Day of Pentecost is speaking in tongues presented as the overcoming of a communications barrier.* Everyone spoke at least Greek in Corinth. At Pentecost the disciples and the Diaspora Jews and proselytes could have communicated in Greek, Aramaic, or Hebrew, all three of which we now know were regularly used in first century Palestine. *The New Testament presents* glossolalia *primarily as a convincing miracle, only secondarily as the communication of a message; for communication alone could be accomplished more easily without "other tongues."*[51]

The speaking in many foreign languages served as a sign that attracted the crowd. Once the crowd was gathered, Peter preached to them in Hebrew or Greek. The statement that no "foreigners were present" while the tongues speaking occurred is contrary to Luke's statement as well as the statement of the crowd who said they heard the speaking.[52]

All of these arguments attempting to prove that the tongues on the day of Pentecost were unintelligible and ecstatic are contrary to Luke's clear statements that they were languages. Thus, they could not outweigh the clear statement of the passage. However, we have seen that none of these arguments are valid as evidence since the facts are not as their proponents state.

Acts 10:46 states, "For they heard them speak with tongues, and magnify God." Although some argue that these tongues were ecstatic (unintelligible), there is no description of any kind in this verse. Since they are not described, we may assume that Luke expects the reader to have prior knowledge of what he means.

This must be the tongues speaking already mentioned in Acts 2:4. There is definite proof that this is the case since Peter states in Acts 11:15-17, describing the incident in 10:46, that "the Holy Ghost fell on them, as on us at the beginning. . . . Forasmuch then as God gave them the like gift as he did unto us." There is only one "beginning" similar to this tongues speaking in Cornelius's house—Pentecost. Cornelius and his house received the same *(isen)* gift as Peter and the others did on the day of Pentecost. Peter says specifically that the tongues in Acts 10:46 are the same as those on the day of Pentecost (2:6-11). Therefore, they are languages in both passages, and are both called a gift (11:17).

Acts 19:6 does not give a description of the tongues to which it refers. Normal interpretive procedure would regard these tongues as the same as those in the previous passages in Acts, that is, as language.

Mark 16:17-18 states, "And these signs shall follow them that believe; In my name shall they cast out devils; they shall speak with new tongues." Again, there is no description of the tongues referred to in this passage. The entire list of items refers to miraculous abilities such as those performed by the apostles; therefore, it may be safely assumed that the tongues referred to are the miraculous gift of tongues mentioned in the New Testament. They are stated to be part of a group of miraculous items classified as "signs" *(semeion)*. The only item of description is the adjective *kainos*, "new." Some argue that the use of *kainos* rather than *neos*, another Greek term also meaning "new," implies ecstatic unintelligible speech, since *kainos* implies new in the sense of a difference in quality.[53] Two simple facts are sufficient to answer this argument. First, a word study shows that *kainos* does not necessarily imply "new in quality" or "strange."[54] Second, the idea of "new in quality" or "strange" could easily mean "miraculously inspired by the Spirit." Such a gift was not only different in quality but previously unheard of (strange). A miraculous ability (i.e., from the Spirit of God) to speak previously unfamiliar foreign language could easily be described as "not there before," "just appeared," "unfamiliar," "strange," "unusual," or "new in kind." The use of *kainos* does not in any way require or even imply ecstatic speech in contrast to languages.

First Corinthians 12-14. This passage is the longest section in the Bible on the subject of tongues speaking. Despite its length, the passage does not state explicitly what the tongues are. Many, however, have attempted to derive the definition of the gift of tongues from this passage alone. Some have concluded that the tongues in 1 Corinthians are ecstatic speech and then read this definition into Acts 2:4–11.[55] A more common view is to regard the tongues in 1 Corinthians 12–14 as ecstatic utterance and Acts 2:4–11 as a different kind of tongues, that is, foreign languages.[56] Although the opinion that different tongues are referred to in Acts 2:4–11 and in 1 Corinthians is also held by some noncharismatics, it is standard among Pentecostals, as Nichol states:

> It is necessary to understand the fact that they make a sharp distinction between the ecstatic utterances that are recorded in Acts and the tongues phenomena related by Paul in 1 Corinthians 12–14. In referring to the former, they employ the term "evidence" or "sign"; in referring to the latter, the word "gift" is used.[57]

Numerous charismatic authors state that this is the common Pentecostal view.[58]

The New Testament apparently presents only one kind of tongues. However, it will be necessary to study 1 Corinthians 12–14 in order to determine what kind of tongues are denoted in that passage before further studying this alleged difference between the tongues at Pentecost and those in Corinthians. In 1 Corinthians 12:3 the apostle Paul says, "No one speaking by the Spirit of God says Jesus is anathema: and no one is able to say Jesus is the Lord, but by the Holy Spirit."

One test of validity, according to this verse, is what the speaker says. Paul implies that the speaking is understandable; no allowance is made for unintelligible speech. It is clear in the context and from other statements in this passage that this verse does not refer to mere statements made by any Christian at any time but refers to those speaking under the direct influence of the Holy Spirit (prophesying and speaking in tongues).[59] It is so stated in the verse ("by the Spirit"). The immediate context refers to gifts of the Spirit (see v. 4). The same expression, *en pneumati* or *pneumati*, "by the Spirit," is used in 14:2 and 14:16 to refer to "speaking in tongues." Rather than a statement of the individual's beliefs that he might state at any time, 1 Corinthians 12:3 refers to the intelligible utterance of the individual while he is speaking "by the Spirit" as a test of the spirit prompting the speech. As Beare says, "The test lies in the intelligible content of the utterance."[60] This verse implies and fits well with the view that tongues are intelligible. First Corinthians 13:1–3 says,

> If I speak with tongues of men and of angels, but I do not have love, I am as sounding brass or a tinkling cymbal. And if I have a prophecy, and know all mysteries, and all knowledge; and I have all faith, so that I move mountains, but I do not have love, I am nothing. And if I give away all my possessions, and if I hand over my body to be burned, and I do not have love, I receive no profit.

Many agree that the gift of tongues refers to a supernatural ability to speak languages, but on the basis of the phrase "tongues of men and of angels" (13:1), they assert that the gift is the ability to speak "angel" or "heavenly" languages; therefore, it is ecstatic and in effect unintelligible. This removes the utterance from any possibility of verification as a language. There are no other passages in the Bible that refer to the "tongues of angels" or to men speaking a heavenly language. First Corinthians 13:1 must be examined to determine the validity of the opinion that "tongues" are angel languages.

Paul does not state that he or anyone else speaks or has ever spoken the languages of angels. He says, "If I speak with the tongues of men and angels." This is the first in a series of three parallel statements (vv. 1–3), each of which begin with "if" (*Ean*, "if," v. 1; *kai ean*, "and if," v. 2; *kan*, "and if," v. 3). The "if" presents

> ... mere objective possibility connected with the future; "If I should speak with the tongues of men and of angels," not "Though I speak" (AV). . . . "Supposing that I had all the powers of earthly and heavenly utterance.[61]

Each of the parallel statements begins with "if" and ends with the expression "but have not love. . . . " Each is a hyperbole or exaggeration referring to a spiritual gift or quality and then to an extreme or theoretical example of its application. The statement, therefore, points out that not only the normal exercise of the gift apart from love is profitless to the exerciser, but even if it could be used to such an exaggerated or extreme (theoretical) use, it would still be profitless.

This argument is most clear in the second example (13:2). The first part of the statement, "If I have prophecy," refers to something that Paul and others actually had. However, the second part, "and know all mysteries, and all knowledge," refers to that which no one exercises or will exercise. In this very passage (13:9)

Paul states that in this life we have only partial prophecy and partial knowledge. No one knows all mysteries and all knowledge. This second part of the hyperbole continues with the statement, "if I have all faith, so that I move mountains." This also is a theoretical extreme that no one possesses or exercises. Prophecy is the basic gift; "knowing all mysteries and all knowledge" and "having all faith" are the hypothetical, unobtainable extremes or hyperboles that Paul uses to convey his point that even such exaggerated cases would profit nothing apart from love. The basic gift is first; the extremes are then connected by "and." In effect Paul says, "If I have prophecy and even if I could go all the way to the extreme of knowing all mysteries and knowledge, and having all faith so that I could move mountains, and did not have love, I am nothing."

The third example (13:3) functions in the same way, thereby supporting this interpretation. Paul states, "If I donate all of my goods to feed the poor [Paul may have done this; see Phil. 3:8],[62] and I give my body to be burned [Paul had not actually done so], and have not love. . . ." While it is not impossible to do so, Paul had not performed the more extreme of these examples (i.e., handing over his body to be burned). The first action is probable; the second is connected to the first by "and"; it is an extreme action even if a possibility.[63]

This same structure functions in Paul's first example: "If I speak with the tongues of men and of angels" (13:1). "Tongues of men" refers to the basic gift or quality. Connected to this by "and," the expression "tongues of angels" refers to the exaggeration or hypothetical extreme that is impossible to do, or at the very least that Paul had not done. Paul says, "If I exercise the gift of tongues and, in fact, could even go to such an extreme as to speak angel language, it means nothing (it is mere noise) apart from love."

Each of these three examples is parallel in structure and in thought. The second is very clear. The fact that the three fit the same pattern is definite evidence that they are all, in fact, examples of hyperbole. Hodges states,

> If the expression "tongues of men and angels" (1 Cor. 13:1) be appealed to, it is sufficient to note that the first three verses of the chapter have a pronounced hyperbolic character. While angels no doubt have languages of their own, the apostle no more implies that he expects the readers to use them than that he expects them to give their bodies to be burned (v. 3).[64]

Gundry also says,

> As matters of fact, Paul does not claim to possess all prophetic insight and knowledge or to have all faith or to have given up all his possessions or to have delivered his body to be burned (obviously not, since he is writing a letter!). These are "suppose-so" statements only partially true of Paul's experience. By the same token, although Paul claims to speak in tongues, it is not necessary to infer that he claims to speak in the tongues of angels.[65]

Rather than proof that Paul spoke in "angel" or "heavenly" languages, this passage is evidence that the tongues he spoke were the "tongues (languages) of men."

A normal multilingual ability or speaking one's own language would provide no basis for the parallels with the spiritual qualities involved in prophecy, faith, and giving. Neither would an everyday, normal use of the tongue provide a basis for the conclusion "without love I am merely clanging brass." The "tongues of men" must refer to the spiritual gift. If someone insists on "angel language" as part of the gift of tongues, the gift must also include the "tongues of men" (foreign languages) as the basic gift.

There is further implication in this same chapter that the gift of tongues is not the ability to speak angel or "heavenly" language. First Corinthians 13:8 states that at some time tongues will cease. Several opinions regarding the time of cessation have been advanced, including the completion of the canon, the rapture, the second advent, and the eternal state. However, there is no reason why angel or heavenly language should cease. Such language would continue in eternity.

There is no apparent need for more than one language in heaven; at the most there would be few. It is beyond reason to assume that the angels have different nationalities or geographical provinces so that they speak many different languages. All who claim to speak angel language should be speaking the same language, or at the most a few angel languages. Linguistic studies of glossolalia do not support this.

There is no apparent purpose for a gift of tongues that consists of "angel" languages. The numerous examples in the Bible show that angels can communicate with men in human language. God understands us in our own language. Angel language is not necessary to speak to God. There is no example in the Bible of angelic tongues used in prayer or self-edification. Such a gift would not help men communicate to God or to angels. It would be useless to communicate to men. It is unlikely that God would give a gift of speaking "angelic language" which, when interpreted, at best can communicate and profit no more than direct communication in the hearer's own language.

In summary, it is doubtful that the gift of tongues is "angel language," since the only statement referring to such language (1 Cor. 13:1) is mere hyperbole and there is no other indication of someone speaking angel language in the Bible. Tongues cease, according to 1 Corinthians 13:8, but there is no reason why angel language will cease. No purpose is discernible for a spiritual gift of speaking "angelic languages." There is no reason for more than one "angel language," if even one is necessary. The plural, "angels" (1 Cor. 13:1), does not require plural angel languages. It is certain from this passage that the gift of tongues includes the ability to speak the various "tongues of men."

First Corinthians 14. Many noncharismatics as well as charismatics feel that 1 Corinthians 14:1–40 definitely refers to ecstatic unintelligible speech when it refers to speaking in tongues.[66] Notice that the gift of tongues is not defined or directly described in 1 Corinthians 12–14. Thus, the arguments for ecstatic speech are based solely upon implications derived from chapter 14. But implications are not enough to set aside the facts we have noticed.

Sound exegetical procedure will interpret *glossa*, "tongue," where it refers to the spiritual gift in 1 Corinthians as normal human language. This is a valid use of the word, it agrees with the only passage describing the gift, and there is no evidence that "tongue" is ever used of unintelligible ecstatic utterance. To set aside the fact that languages are referred to in this passage, it must be definitely demonstrated that language cannot fit in the passage. However, this is impossible. It can be demonstrated that language fits the passage very well. There are no conclusive arguments against interpreting the tongues in 1 Corinthians 14 as languages. In fact, many have felt that this is the best interpretation of the passage. Hoekema cites two well-known Pentecostal writers who also feel that 1 Corinthians 14 refers to genuine foreign language.[67] This has been one of the common interpretations of this passage throughout church history.

In order to understand this passage (1 Cor. 14) it is necessary to understand the situation addressed. One of the most important points to keep in perspective is that Paul discusses the use of prophecy and tongues in the assembly. This is not a discussion regarding private use or miscellaneous public use of these gifts.

The entire context refers to a church situation where others are present, where an interpreter may or may not be in the group, where others may sing or speak (or pray or say "amen"), where more than one may speak (so that rules must be laid down for speaking), and where the unbeliever and "unlearned" may visit. Paul also uses specific expressions to designate that this concerns the assembly, such as "edifies the church (assembly)" (v. 4), "the church (assembly) may be edified" (v. 5), "the edifying of the church (assembly)" (v. 12), "in the assembly" (v. 19), "if the whole assembly be gathered together" (v. 23), "keep silent in the assembly" (v. 28), "as in all the assemblies" (v. 33), "let your women keep silence in the assemblies" (v. 34), and "let them ask at home, for it is a shame for women to speak in the assembly" (v. 35). There also are other expressions which make it clear that Paul refers to tongues speaking in the church assembly.

The basic concept in chapter 14 is that the assembly needs to be edified; therefore, in the assembly, prophecy, which the hearers can understand, is superior to tongues, which the hearers do not understand. The stress is not on the unintelligible nature of the utterance, but on the lack of understanding by the hearers (unless the language is translated). This lack of understanding, of course, will be true either with ecstatic speech or with a foreign language unknown to the hearer. Not only does Paul speak with reference to the assembly, Gundry points out two other presuppositions to remember.

> Paul's discussion moves along on two presuppositions. The first is that the tongue is unintelligible not because it is an ecstatic language, but because (and when) neither the speaker nor anyone else in the congregation happens to have the gift of interpretation. It is this presupposition that leads Paul to exhort the glossolalist to pray for the power to interpret so that he may edifyingly exercise the gift of tongues in public meetings (verse 13). It is again this presupposition which causes Paul to prohibit speaking in tongues when no one with the gift of interpretation is present in the assembly (verse 28). It is the absence of an interpreter, not the ecstatic nature of the tongue, which makes the tongue unintelligible.
>
> The other presupposition underlying Paul's words about the unintelligibility of tongues is that in the ordinary church meeting at Corinth there would not be numbers of people with varied linguistic backgrounds such as Luke says were present in Jerusalem on the Day of Pentecost.[68]

To sum up, Paul discusses the use of tongues in the church assembly. The languages are not understood because no translator is present, and the congregation as a whole does not know the languages spoken. A failure to understand another person's speech does not mean the speech is unintelligible ecstasy. No one can understand a foreign language unknown to him.

In every verse which refers to the inability of the hearers to understand, either an unknown foreign language or ecstatic speech may fit. However, due to the evidence of the word study of *glossa*, if either one may fit, then the preference must go to the meaning "language." There are other factors supporting this view. Verse 22 definitely refers to foreign languages rather than ecstatic speech. First Corinthians 14:21–23 says,

> In the law it is written, With men of other tongues and other lips will I speak unto this people; and yet for all that will they not hear me, saith the Lord. Wherefore tongues are for a sign, not to them that believe, but to them that believe not: but prophesying serveth not for them that believe not, but for them which believe. If therefore the whole church be come together into one place, and all speak with tongues. . . .

The quotation in verse 21 is from Isaiah 28:11. This passage prophesies destruction upon Israel. The Hebrew refers to men "stammering in speech, and through a strange tongue."[69] The word translated "stammering" (Heb. *la'ag*) means "mocking," "derision," or "stammering (of barbarous language)."[70] The context speaks of God's judgment upon Israel by a nation which speaks a language foreign to their ears. This prophecy apparently referred to the Assyrians, who spoke a language foreign to the Israelites and later invaded Israel.[71]

The Greek word *hoste*, "so then," begins 1 Corinthians 14:22 and connects it with the statement in verse 21. When *hoste* is in an independent clause, as here, it introduces a conclusion based on the preceding statement. Since verse 21 is a quotation (Isa. 28:11) regarding foreign language, the conclusion in verse 22 must also refer to language. Paul would not base a direct conclusion regarding ecstatic utterance on a passage referring to normal languages. The tongues in verse 22 must be of the same nature as those in Isaiah 28:11, or else the conclusion would not follow. Verse 23 is also connected to the preceding verses by "if therefore" *(ean oun)*, showing that the tongues referred to in verse 23 are of the same nature as those in verses 21 and 22, foreign language. Verse 23, however, clearly refers to speaking in tongues and the Corinthian assembly, that is, to the same tongues discussed in the entire chapter. Therefore, all three verses refer to the tongues spoken in Corinth and to foreign languages as one and the same.

Verse 22 also concludes that tongues are intended to be a sign *(semeion)* to unbelievers. The tongues spoken on the day of Pentecost (Acts 2:4ff.) also clearly served as a sign to unbelievers. Yet these tongues (Acts 2:4–11) are explicitly stated to be foreign languages. A miraculous ability to speak previously unknown languages could be a sign to unbelievers. The ability would be obvious to those who heard and recognized their language, and at the same time it could not be faked. Such a miraculous ability was previously unknown. Ecstatic utterance, however, was common and, therefore, would not function as a sign. Although those at Pentecost who did not recognize the languages thought the speakers were drunk (Acts 2:13), those who recognized their own languages realized that an unusual event was taking place (a sign) and asked the question, "What does this mean?" The tongues in the Corinthian church were misused. They were addressed to a local assembly of *believers* who did not understand the languages; therefore, they were useless unless interpreted. This is why Paul prohibited their use without an interpreter. Used properly, tongues would be addressed to those who spoke and understood the language and so function as a miraculous sign.[72]

First Corinthians 14:11 is additional evidence that the tongues referred to are foreign languages. The verse states, "Therefore if I know not the meaning of the voice, I shall be unto him that speaketh a barbarian, and he that speaketh shall be a barbarian unto me." The term *barbaros*, "barbarian," while originally having the basic meaning of "stammering," came to mean "the one who speaks a strange language," and then, to the Greek mind, "a non-Greek."[73] It is difficult to see why one would classify as a "barbarian" a speaker who was in an obvious state of religious ecstasy. Note that the speaker classifies the hearer as a barbarian, since the hearer does not comprehend the speech. Someone may well expect another to understand his language and classify those who do not as foreigners or barbarians. (This was, in fact, the attitude of the Greeks at the time.) Such thinking is appropriate to language. However, this statement (v. 11) is not appropriate to ecstatic speech. Why would the speaker consider the hearer to be a barbarian if he did not understand unintelligible ecstatic speech? No one could be

Tongues: The Nature of the Gift 143

expected to understand such speech. Although unintelligible ecstatic speech does not suit this verse, "language" makes good sense. We have already seen that spiritual gifts are under the control of the gifted person. This passage explicitly states that both prophecy and tongues are controlled by the speaker and are, therefore, not ecstatic. First Corinthians 14:32–33 says, "And the spirits of the prophets are subject to the prophets. For God is not the author of confusion, but of peace." This explains that the prophets are in control of their prophesying. It serves as an answer to the objection that someone may make to the rules of order which Paul just stated in verses 29–31. Some may say they need to speak even though another is speaking or even though three have spoken. They may refuse to yield the floor, as Paul commands in verse 30. These objections apparently would be based on the idea that the Spirit propelled the speaker contrary to his will. Paul states that this is not so; the prophet is in control (v. 32) and, therefore, can follow the rules Paul has commanded. The proof for Paul's statement that the prophets are in control is stated in the following verse (v. 33). The reason is that God is not a God of confusion, but of peace. The apostle Paul apparently considered uncontrolled speaking as not from God and something that results in confusion.

The same argument applies to those speaking in tongues since Paul has also given a similar set of rules to tongues speakers. How can Paul command tongues speakers to keep quiet unless an interpreter is present, to speak only one at a time and no more than three altogether, unless he expects them to be in control of their speech? They must be able to control the gift and for the same reason—uncontrolled tongues are confusion. There is no evidence that this speaking was in an ecstatic, trancelike state.[74] This expected control of the gift does not rule out unintelligible speech, but it does rule out so-called religious ecstasy. It is difficult to picture ecstatic unintelligible utterance from a calm individual in control of his actions.

The fact that the tongues are not understood is one of the basic reasons that many regard the tongues in 1 Corinthians 14 as ecstatic speech. However, foreign languages unknown to the hearer are not understood by the hearer.

It is often claimed that the expression, "he that speaketh in a tongue speaketh not unto men, but unto God" (1 Cor. 14:2) must refer to ecstatic unintelligible speech.[75] However, neither unintelligible nor ecstatic utterance is required in this verse. The verse says nothing regarding the nature of the speech but speaks only regarding the direction of the communication. One can speak unto God in his own language or in a foreign language, either under supernatural influence of the Spirit or apart from it. Normal prayer is speaking to God but is neither ecstatic nor unintelligible. Thus, the expression "speaks unto God" does not at all imply ecstatic speech. Neither does the use of the word "mysteries" in 1 Corinthians 14:2 imply unintelligible speech. It merely means "secret" or, in this context, "not understood." It is a common term for spiritual truths (Matt. 13:11; Eph. 1:9; 5:32; Col. 2:2; 1 Tim. 3:9) and has no implication of ecstatic or unintelligible speech.[76]

First Corinthians 14:7–9 may seem to lend itself to unintelligible speech; however, this is incorrect. The verses say,

> And even things without life when they give sound, whether pipe or harp, unless they give a distinction in the sounds, how shall what is piped or harped be known? For if the trumpet gives an indistinct sound, who shall prepare for battle? So likewise you, unless you by the tongue give a clear sound, how shall it be known what is spoken?

These verses serve as an illustration of Paul's major thesis in the first half of chapter 14 that speech which is not understood is of no value. The terms translated "distinct" and "indistinct" do not imply unintelligible speech. The emphasis is not on the *indistinct* nature of the sounds, but on the failure of the sounds to communicate as desired. Unless the bugle, for example, gives a recognizable call, no one will know enough to prepare for combat. This illustration from the bugle clarifies the meaning. Distinct sounds in themselves do not communicate a message. A series of random yet distinct notes on the bugle means nothing. The specific bugle call for preparation must not only be distinct but must be familiar to the hearer and mean something to him. The same is true of the harp and pipe. The sounds not only must be distinct but must be familiar to the hearer. A series of distinct but unheard of sounds cannot result in "knowing that which is piped" nor in preparation for combat.

Verse 9 clarifies that the emphasis is on understanding the meaning of the sound when it says, "How shall it be known what is spoken?" The conclusion to this section refers not to distinctness of speech but that the tongue needs to be translated (v. 13) so that it may be understood. If the emphasis were on the indistinct quality of the speech rather than on the communication through understanding, then Paul would be ruling out indistinct speech due to its inherent nature, and so also be arguing against ecstatic utterance. However, the stress is on understanding, rather than on the inherent quality of the speaking; therefore, Paul concludes that, if understood, the tongues may be spoken. First Corinthians 14:7–9 does not demonstrate that the tongues are ecstatic speech, but it does specify that a sound must communicate meaning to be used in the assembly.

The implication that the mind or understanding of the speaker is not involved while speaking in tongues (vv. 14, 19) is not because the speaking is in an ecstatic, trancelike state but due to the fact that the speaker does not understand what he says. It is clear from the entire context and particularly from verse 13 that the solution to the lack of understanding is to have the speech translated (interpreted), thereby showing that when it is interpreted understanding does result. The reason the mind or understanding is deficient is not due to the state of the speaker but is due to the inability of the speaker to understand what is said.

First Corinthians 14:23, which states that outsiders who come into the Corinthian assembly will think the tongues speakers are mad, does not imply ecstatic frenzy or speech. The accusation of madness does not stem from the state of the speaker (ecstatic frenzy), or else Paul's obvious desire to avoid this accusation would require cessation of *all* speaking in tongues, since it would *always* appear that the speaker were mad. But Paul does not stop tongues completely; they are acceptable when understood. Therefore, the issue of madness is not linked to their nature but to the aspect of understanding.[77] The accusation of madness cannot be based upon an alleged ecstatic fervor in speech since a prophet speaking "in the Spirit" is not accused of madness. Verse 24 says that those prophesying are not accused of madness but rather convict the hearers. The only difference between the prophesying and glossolalia is the understanding involved. Therefore, since the prophets who are also speaking in the Spirit are not in danger of this accusation, the accusation must not be linked to "speaking in the Spirit" but to the failure to understand. However, failure to understand is not the only issue involved. Pagan oracles commonly spoke without the hearers' cognizance of what was said. The stress here is on the fact that the entire church is assembled in one place and "all" speak in languages (one at a time or many) which the hearers do not understand.

This did not occur in pagan practices; the speaking was restricted to the oracles. To see an entire assembly speaking in languages which they obviously did not comprehend and, therefore, would appear to be gibberish, would give the impression of madness. Language not understood by the hearers fits this passage as well as ecstatic speech.

First Corinthians 14:28 is often used to argue for ecstatic utterance. It says, "But if there be no interpreter, let him keep silence in the church; and let him speak to himself, and to God." As stated in the discussion on verse 2, the expression "speak to God" does not require ecstatic speech but merely refers to the direction of the speech. Men speak to God frequently in their own language, apart from any ecstasy. This verse provides no evidence that ecstatic speech is in view.

Certain additional objections are hardly worth refuting. The use of the word "unknown" does not imply ecstasy, but is merely an addition to the English text in the hope of clarifying the tongues as unknown to the speakers. The use of the expression, he speaks "in the Spirit," does not imply ecstasy since there are many activities in the Spirit such as prophesying, teaching, and praying which are not ecstatic. Why assume that only ecstatic speech is in the Spirit, and that the miraculous ability to speak foreign languages could not be in the Spirit?

The necessity for rules of orderly procedure which govern the speakers and the statement that "all things should be done decently and in order" (1 Cor. 14:40) does not imply that the problem was indecency and disorderliness due to ecstatic speech; rather, they are aimed at such practices as speaking although not understood, several speaking at a time, refusing to let another speak, and speaking by women. Notice that the rules for orderly procedure apply to prophets and women as well as tongues speakers, even though they did not speak unintelligibly. Likewise, the use of the word "interpret" does not imply ecstatic speech, since it is a common word for translate.[78] The use of a translator does not imply ecstatic speech any more than it implies language.[79] Both would need to be interpreted or translated in order to benefit hearers who did not understand. When understood by the hearers as on the day of Pentecost no interpreter was needed, since the hearers understood the language. However, if the speech was ecstatic no one would have understood and an interpreter would have been necessary even on that occasion. According to 1 Corinthians 14 the interpreter was only necessary when the hearers did not understand.[80]

There are verses in 1 Corinthians 14 where foreign language makes sense but where unintelligible ecstatic utterance does not (e.g., v. 22). However, the reverse cannot be said. A foreign language not understood by the hearer is no different from unintelligible speech in his sight. Therefore, in any passage where such ecstatic speech may be considered possible, it is also possible to substitute a language not familiar to the hearers. In this passage there are no reasons, much less the very strong reasons necessary, to depart from the normal meaning of *glossa* and to flee to a completely unsupported usage.

Second Corinthians 5:13. Although 2 Corinthians 5:13 is not one of the passages discussing spiritual gifts, some have interpreted the phrase "beside ourselves," which is the Greek word *existemi*, as a reference to speaking in tongues or seeing visions.[81] The passage says, "For whether we be beside ourselves, it is to God: or whether we be sober, it is for your cause." The word *existemi* means "to be confused," "lose one's mind," or "be amazed."[82] Excluding 2 Corinthians 5:13, this verb occurs sixteen times in the New Testament. It means "to be amazed or astonished" in fifteen of these instances and has the connotation of being "out of one's mind," or "crazy," in Mark 3:21. It is improbable that Paul is referring in 2 Corinthians 5:13 to an actual experience. This verse must be considered in its context.

Paul's antagonists at Corinth had accused him of many things. For instance, they accused him of being "base" or "cowardly" (2 Cor. 10:1; see also 10:10). Paul is not actually stating that he was out of his mind or was ecstatic any more than he admits that he was "cowardly and contemptible" (2 Cor. 10:1, 10). He used his opponents' accusation that he was mad as part of his argument against them. Even if 2 Corinthians 5:13 were referring to an actual experience in Paul's life, there would be no certainty that it refers to speaking in tongues or ecstasy. Hughes mentions the opinions that this refers to Paul's conversion on the Damascus road, or to 2 Corinthians 12:1ff., where Paul was caught up to the "third heaven." He prefers to regard it as an accusation of religious mania; that is, Paul went to extremes in hardship and hazards as a religious fanatic.[83] His quotation of Plummer seems applicable:

> All that is certain is that *exestemen* refers to exceptional, and *sophronoumen* to ordinary condition, and that these two cover the whole of his behavior, which therefore is never self seeking.[84]

There is no reason to assume that 2 Corinthians 5:13 refers to actual ecstatic experiences of Paul.[85] The context of the passage argues against such a conclusion. Paul is referring to accusations made by his enemies, who stated, "He is mad." In any case, there is no basis upon which to equate this expression with the gift of tongues. If it refers to an actual experience in Paul's life, it may have been any one of a number of possibilities. The totality of evidence that tongues are not ecstatic also argues against seeing this as a reference to tongues.

The Alleged Difference Between the Sign and the Gift

Many scholarly works, often considered as authoritative, distinguish between the tongues in Acts and those in Corinthians.[86] Among noncharismatic scholars who distinguish between the tongues in Acts and Corinthians, the most common view is that Acts 2:4–11 refers to speaking in languages while 1 Corinthians refers to ecstatic speech. This allows acceptance of the clear statements of Acts 2:4–11 and at the same time allows for the ecstatic view of tongues. The main support for such a difference between the tongues at Pentecost and those described in the letter to the Corinthians is the assertion that the tongues in Corinthians are obviously ecstatic. However, it was shown that "foreign languages not understood by the hearer" is acceptable in every instance as the meaning for *glossa*, and that there are several verses where *only* this meaning is appropriate. The evidence from 1 Corinthians shows that the tongues referred to are languages. Any distinction between the tongues in Acts 2 and 1 Corinthians 14 based on the opinion that the tongues in 1 Corinthians are ecstatic is groundless.

Additional arguments for distinguishing between the tongues in Acts and 1 Corinthians are usually due to a failure to understand the situation described in 1 Corinthians 14. One argument is that Paul deprecates the tongues in 1 Corinthians in contrast to the description in Acts 2:4ff.[87] However, Paul does not say anything detrimental to the *proper* use of tongues. Rather, he restricts and otherwise deprecates the *misuse* of tongues in the assembly, a use for which tongues were not intended. At Pentecost the tongues were used as they were intended to be used, as a sign to unbelievers. The same answer applies to the objection that Paul in 1 Corinthians only allows two or three speakers while at Pentecost many spoke; therefore, they must be different. A difference in the number of speakers or in the physical surroundings really has no bearing on the nature of the gift. Tongues were not restricted to two or three speakers at Pentecost because they were used as the gift was intended, as a sign to unbelievers. They were restricted to a few speakers at Corinth where they were spoken in the assembly.

Some have argued that an interpreter was necessary at Corinth, but no interpreter was needed at Pentecost; thus, the tongues must be different. But no interpreter was needed at Pentecost because, as the passage explicitly says, men from many nations were present and could understand their own languages apart from translation. In the Corinthian assembly the opposite was true. The church, with a few possible exceptions, would have been made up of the local populace and therefore would not have spoken foreign languages. They would require that the foreign languages, spoken in tongues, be translated. The need for an interpreter on one occasion but not on another has nothing to do with the nature of the speaking. Someone from the United States needs no interpreter when speaking to a group of people in a street meeting in the United States. However, if he speaks English to a Hungarian church in Budapest, he needs an interpreter. His speaking has not changed; it is still English. The hearers and their ability to understand the language are the element which differs. The same applies to the situation in the Corinthian church and at Pentecost. The nature of the tongues did not change, but the hearers' ability to understand was different. Therefore, an interpreter was needed on one occasion but not on the other. The tongues, however, were the same.

Another objection is based on the use of the word "interpret," (*diermeneuo* and its cognates) in connection with tongues in 1 Corinthians but not in Acts. As mentioned previously, this word, in the great majority of biblical occurrences, means to translate a normal human language. Its occurrence in Corinthians does not even intimate that the tongues are unintelligible utterance.[88] The occurrence of *dialektos*, "language," in Acts 2 but not in 1 Corinthians 14 does not imply as some argue that the tongues of Corinthians differ from those in Acts.[89] This word does not occur in Acts 10 or 19, yet these tongues are definitely the same as those in Acts 2.[90] Luke wrote Acts; however, Paul wrote 1 Corinthians. One of the occurrences of *dialektos* in Acts 2 is in a statement by the crowd. Luke, having this in mind, probably used it in the context where he quotes their statement. Whatever the case, Paul is not required to use all of the synonyms that Luke used. Since *dialektos* is a synonym for *glossa*, there is no reason why Paul should feel any necessity to use *dialektos*. *Glossa* adequately describes *language* and is sufficient for Paul's purpose in 1 Corinthians 14.

The similar terminology and description refute any alleged difference. The same term, *glossa*, is used in all of the passages. Usually the verb *laleo*, "speak," accompanies *glossa*, so that *glossais lalein*, "to speak in tongues," occurs in all the passages on tongues almost in the sense of a technical term for the phenomenon (Mark 16:17; Acts 2:4, 11; 10:46; 19:6; 1 Cor. 12:30; 13:1; 14:2, 4–6, 13, 18, 23, 27, 39). There is never any explanation or statement that different tongues are in mind; rather, it is assumed that the Corinthians, for example, knew what was meant. In each passage the tongues are described as a gift provided miraculously by the Holy Spirit; the speakers were believers in every case. The references to tongues establish that those in Acts 2:4–11 have the same purpose as those in 1 Corinthians. This purpose agrees with Mark 16:17. They are a sign to unbelievers. This is clear from the correspondence between the stated purpose for tongues (a sign to unbelievers) in 1 Corinthians 14:22 and their actual use as a sign to unbelievers in Acts 2:4–11. This correspondence is further emphasized by Paul's stress in 1 Corinthians that tongues are not designed for use in the assembly (1 Cor. 14:19) but outside the assembly, that is, to unbelievers.

There is perfect consistency between the terminology and description of tongues wherever they are mentioned in the New Testament. They are always foreign languages; they are one and the same in nature. Items of the same name and description which have no statements of explanation but are assumed to be recognized by the readers are normally considered to be the same. In this case, those who see two different kinds of tongues in the New Testament have arrived at this position on the basis of their theological presuppositions rather than from biblical evidence. There is only one kind of tongues in the New Testament, the miraculous ability to speak foreign languages.[91]

The General Tenor of the New Testament Gift of Tongues

The description in the New Testament of genuine tongues speaking provides no evidence for regarding this gift as similar to speech which is normally classified as ecstatic utterance, nor is it similar to pagan religious ecstatic speech. The tongues speaking in Acts 2:4–11, 10:46, and 19:6 began apart from any working up or "driving" preliminaries. The phenomena came suddenly on the day of Pentecost (Acts 2:2) and apart from any seeking. Those involved were not familiar with this gift. In Acts 10:46 the tongues speaking came unexpectedly upon those who heard Peter's sermon. Neither Peter nor the hearers expected it. The gathering was calm and orderly; the rest were merely listening to Peter speak. The same lack of working up to the event is clear in Acts 19:6. In each one of these events the tongues came unexpectedly and apart from "warming up." Another aspect is consistent in all three passages: there is not the slightest intimation that the speakers were in a high or trancelike state. Nothing is said concerning a feeling of well-being or any blessing as far as the speakers are concerned. In each case the amazement and emotion were on the part of the hearers.

All three passages are consistent in that the speakers apparently experienced no letdown or sense of depression after the speaking, nor did they appear to lose mental awareness at any time during the speaking. Rather, on the day of Pentecost, Peter and the eleven seemed to be perfectly aware of the events taking place and were never "out of it" in the sense of temporary amnesia. Peter stood up immediately with the explanation (Acts 2:16ff.) for his speaking. This is consistent with the passage in 1 Corinthians. It is clear from 1 Corinthians 14:13 and 14:27–36 that the tongues speaker was in control of the speaking and was not out of it or in a trance. He was to speak only one at a time and then only if an interpreter was present. In order to obey this command, he must be able to control the gift.

There is no intimation in the New Testament that exercise of the gift of tongues is connected with any physical phenomena such as jerking, quaking, convulsions, foaming at the mouth, falling, weaving around, closed eyes, rolling of the eyes and head, or changed pitch or tone of voice. The statements "God is not a God of disorder, but of peace" (1 Cor. 14:33), and "Let all things be done decently and in order" (14:40) seem to preclude such actions. There is no evidence in the Bible to suggest that the gift of tongues or any other genuine gift of the Holy Spirit was exercised in a trancelike, ecstatic state.

Although the Old Testament prophets received their information through visions and other means, it cannot be shown that they communicated such things while in a trance. Actual human languages could, of course, be spoken in a genuine ecstatic, trancelike state as easily as unintelligible utterance. However, it is less probable that unintelligible utterance would be spoken in a mentally alert state.

The nonecstatic tenor to the exercise of the gift of tongues is an additional implication that tongues were intelligible foreign languages. Apparently, for the first seventeen hundred years Christians did not consider the gift of tongues to be either ecstatic or unintelligible. It was considered to be the gift of foreign languages. Therefore, it must have appeared to be a reasonable deduction from the passages.

Summary of the Evidence

The strongest evidence concerning the nature of the gift of tongues for those who accept the authority of the New Testament is the clear and explicit testimony of Acts 2:4–11. The tongues are stated by Luke to be human languages. The hearers heard and also described them as languages. This testimony is as explicit as it could be stated. This is sufficient to settle the issue unless exceedingly strong and clear evidence to the contrary is produced. No such evidence has been produced. If the word *glossa* were used only rarely in the sense of language and often as ecstatic utterance, the clear passage in Acts would still demand the meaning of language in Mark, Acts, and Corinthians (apart from irrefutable evidence to the contrary). However, the study of *glossa* reveals that there is no evidence that this word was used to describe ecstatic speech. It was very commonly used to describe language.

But some might think that there must be evidence for interpreting *glossa* as ecstatic utterance since such recognized and modern authorities as Arndt and Gingrich's *Greek-English Lexicon of the New Testament*[92] and Kittel's *Theological Dictionary of the New Testament*[93] interpret *glossa* as ecstatic speech. Both of these lexical works agree that the normal meanings of *glossa* are language, the physical tongue, or some tongue-shaped object. But they make an unwarranted exception in those passages in the New Testament which refer to the gift of tongues. Arndt and Gingrich admit that they have no evidence for regarding *glossa* as a reference to ecstatic speech by describing its use in the disputed passages as a "special problem" and as a "technical term." Interpreting *glossa* as ecstatic speech is abnormal lexicography. There is no support for such a view; it is indeed "special." They do not include Acts 2:4–11 under this description, since the tongues there are not "special" but are plainly the well-recognized use of the word to refer to languages. Their view is based on the unwarranted assumption apart from any evidence that 1 Corinthians 14 refers to "broken speech of persons in religious ecstasy."[94]

Behm likewise admits that there is no proof for such a meaning of *glossa* when he attempts to explain how the New Testament writers could use the term *glossa* for such an alleged meaning. He also refers to it as a "technical term" and mentions several views advanced by scholars who attempt to explain the origin of such a meaning.[95] Harrisville's entire article (referred to earlier in this chapter) is an attempt to explain the origin of the meaning "ecstatic utterance" for *glossa*. He refers to certain scholarly views attempting to explain where such a meaning for *glossa* originated. But this need to explain such an origin is clear proof that no basis exists for this meaning in the Greek language.[96] They support our study; there is no evidence that *glossa* is used of ecstatic utterance, either in classical, koine, biblical, or parabiblical Greek. The classical Greek examples used to prove "obscure" speech refer in actuality to language, although outdated or figurative. The attempts to demonstrate that Old Testament believers practiced ecstatic speech also fall short of certainty. The New Testament use does not support the idea that *glossa* ever refers to ecstatic speech. The only specific example or description of tongues in the entire Bible is Acts 2:4–11 where they are definitely described as normal human language. Peter specifically states that the tongues in Acts 10:46 were the same as in Acts 2:4–11. The other passages (Mark 16:17 and Acts 19:6), excluding 1 Corinthians, do not describe the tongues in any way; therefore, there is no reason to view these as different from Acts 2:4–11.

The major passage allegedly requiring the meaning of "ecstatic utterance" is 1 Corinthians 12–14. But rather than supporting this meaning, the passage refutes it. First Corinthians 12:3 shows that tongues are intelligible. First Corinthians 13:1 clearly includes the "tongues of men." First Corinthians 14:22 is a deduction regarding tongues based upon an Old Testament passage (Isa. 28:11) that refers to foreign languages, implying that the tongues of the passage refer to languages. The necessity that tongues be a sign and the fact that they are self controlled all favor the meaning of language rather than ecstatic speech. The alleged problems with the view that tongues were languages have all been answered, showing that "languages" is appropriate to the passage. There is no reason to depart from the normal meaning for *glossa* and to flee to a special or technical use. Abundant evidence demonstrates that the gift of tongues is the miraculous ability to speak languages previously unknown to the speaker.

A Possible Reason for the Prevalence of the "Ecstatic" View of Tongues

Glossolalia that consists of ecstatic unintelligible speaking is a common occurrence in the world and requires no belief in the supernatural. In his study of present-day glossolalia, particularly in Pentecostalism, Samarin states, "And it has already been established that no special power needs to take over a person's vocal organs; all of us are equipped with everything we need to produce glossolalia."[97] He also says, "Glossolalia is not a supernatural phenomenon. . . . It is similar to many other kinds of speech humans produce in more or less normal circumstances, in more or less normal psychological states. In fact, anybody can produce glossolalia if he is uninhibited and if he discovers what the 'trick' is."[98]

If the gift of tongues is merely glossolalia (ecstatic and/or incoherent speech), then there is no necessity to regard it as supernatural. To some this is more acceptable and so may explain the preponderance of the view that the gift of tongues was ecstatic speech, despite the evidence to the contrary. The many studies attempting to explain the psychology of glossolalia reveal that many of those who explain tongues do not regard them as a miracle from the Holy Spirit. Another scholar who has studied glossolalia, specifically in a Pentecostal setting, is Felicitas D. Goodman. She apparently does not relate glossolalia to the supernatural. Based on her research, it is common in many cultures and religions and can be self-induced. For many, glossolalia (ecstatic speech) is not evidence of the miraculous. From their perspective, Paul's glossolalia may be compared with that of shamans and pagan oracles.[99]

A miraculous, immediate ability to speak previously unknown foreign languages is unknown in paganism. This is more apparent when the speaking is apart from any frenzied or ecstatic state. It can be verified. It cannot be self-induced or come from mere emotional excitement. Such an ability is clearly from some supernatural power; in the case of the New Testament gift it is clearly a miracle from God. It cannot be explained otherwise. However, mere glossolalia is common and can be self-induced. They are not a manifestation of a miracle from God. As long as the New Testament gift of tongues is equated with mere ecstatic unintelligible utterance (glossolalia), it can be explained apart from the miraculous. This position is more acceptable to many scholars. Dillow also refers to this theological bias.

It is important to note that the ecstatic utterance view came with the advent of the denial of the supernatural and the higher criticism against the Bible in the eighteenth and nineteenth centuries. The critics attempted to identify the tongues speaking of 1 Corinthians 14 *totally* with the psychological pagan tongue speaking of the mystery religions. Their motivations were to remove the supernatural out of the Bible.[100]

The objective data of the Greek language and of the New Testament in particular present the gift of tongues as a genuine miracle, previously unknown and not duplicated elsewhere. It was a convincing miracle, a sign, and not merely glossolalia or ecstatic speech.

To determine if someone has the genuine gift of tongues, they should be asked to speak a given language that they do not know in the presence of native speakers of that language. The tongues are under the control of the speaker. If the speaker cannot control the language, then the tongue could hardly function as a sign to any particular group of unbelievers.

* * *

1. John Thomas Nichol, *Pentecostalism* (New York: Harper and Row, 1966), 8–17. See also William W. Menzies, *Anointed to Serve* (Springfield, Mo.: Gospel Publishing House, 1971), 9, who states that the belief in tongues speaking as a sign of baptism of the Spirit is the factor that makes a group Pentecostal.
2. Henry George Liddell and Robert Scott, *A Greek-English Lexicon* (Oxford: Clarendon Press, 1968), 353.
3. Johannes Behm, "Glossa," in *Theological Dictionary of the New Testament*, ed. Gerhard Kittel, Gerhard Friedrich, and Geoffrey W. Bromiley, trans. Geoffrey W. Bromiley, 10 vols. (Grand Rapids: Eerdmans, 1964–1976), 1:719–26. (Hereafter *Theological Dictionary of the New Testament* is abbreviated as *TDNT*.)
4. Ibid., 720.
5. Aristotle, *Poetics*. 21, 1457b, Loeb Classical Library.
6. Aristotle, *Rhetoric*, Loeb Classical Library, 395, 397.
7. Sextus Empiricus, *Against Grammarians*, Loeb Classical Library, 313.
8. Plutarch, *Isis and Osiris* 61 (375), Loeb Classical Library.
9. Behm, "Glossa," *TDNT*, 1:720. Behm refers to three references, Diodorus Siculus IV, 66, 6, Galen [Kuhn's edition, vol. xix, 62ff.], and Marcus Antoninus, iv, 33.
10. Ibid.

11. Quintilian, *Institutio Oratoria*, I, 1, 35.
12. *Anecdotae Graecae*, I, 87, 12.
13. Plutarch, *De Pythiae Oraculus* 24 (II, 406).
14. Behm, "Glossa," *TDNT*, 1:772.
15. Aristophanes, *Ranae*, 357.
16. Behm, "Glossa," *TDNT*, 1:722–23.
17. The reference to the *Testament of Job* that Behm uses as a witness to the "tongues of angels" does not use the word "tongue." The verb *aphtheggomai* occurs along with a reference to angelic songs and similar terms. This apocryphal work contains no reference to the "tongues of angels."
18. Liddell and Scott, *Lexicon*, 353.
19. Roy A. Harrisville lists examples of Jewish literature and Qumran material that are often cited by scholars to prove that glossolalia (ecstatic tongues speaking) occurred in pre-Christian Jewish sects, and that the terminology was therefore available for the apostle Paul's use to describe ecstatic tongues in the New Testament ("Speaking in Tongues," *Catholic Biblical Quarterly* 38 [January 1976]: 42–47).
20. Behm, "Glossa," *TDNT*, 1:723.
21. Harrisville, "Speaking in Tongues," 46–47.
22. Behm, "Glossa," *TDNT*, 1:722.
23. See the following examples given by Harrisville ("Speaking in Tongues," 47). The *Book of Jubilees* 25:14 uses *glossa* for "mouth" rather than "utterance," and the result is a blessing in intelligible speech. The *Testament of Judah* 25:3 states, "And you shall be the people of the Lord and have one tongue" (R. H. Charles, *The Apocrypha and Pseudepigrapha of the Old Testament* [Oxford: Clarendon Press, 1968], 2:324). This clearly refers to language without the slightest implication of ecstatic unintelligible speech. *First Enoch*, *Similitudes* 40 and 71:11 give no indication whatsoever that unintelligible speech is involved. From Charles's translation apparently the word "tongue" is not used. *Similitude* 40 refers to heavenly beings who bless God and pray for humans; *Similitude* 71:11 states, "I cried with a loud voice, with the spirit of power, and blessed and glorified and extolled" (Charles, *The Apocrypha and Pseudepigrapha*, 2:211, 237). Neither of these statements seem to be ecstatic unintelligible speech. *Fourth Maccabees* 10:21 is an answer to Antiochus, who commanded that the speaker's tongue be cut out. The speaker says, "You cut out the tongue that sang songs of praise unto him" (Charles, *The Apocrypha and Pseudepigrapha*, 2:677). This refers to the physical tongue. There is not even an implication of ecstatic unintelligible speech in this reference. *The Martyrdom of Isaiah* 5:14 states that when Isaiah was

being sawed asunder "he neither cried nor wept, but his lips spake with the Holy Spirit" (Charles, *The Apocrypha and Pseudepigrapha*, 2:162). Once again there is no indication that unintelligible speech is involved, nor is *glossa* used.

24. Behm, "Glossa," *TDNT*, 1:723. Specific references are Philo, *De Specialibus Legibus* I, 65 and IV, 49, and *Quis Rerum Divinarum Heres*, 265.
25. Harrisville, "Speaking in Tongues," 47. The additional references are Philo, *Quis Rerum Divinarum Heres* LI, 249; LII 259; LIII 264–266; *De Vita Mosis* I,274, and *De Decalogo* IX 32–33, 46.
26. As far as evidence for the use of *glossa*, several references do not use the word at all. The few that do use the word *glotta* in the sense of the physical organ, the tongue. It is not used to describe or refer to the actual speaking in the passage. For example, Philo, *De Vita Mosis* states, "I shall use your tongue for each prophetic utterance," and *Quis Rerum Divinarum Heres*, LIII, 266, states, "His organs of speech, mouth and tongue are wholly in the employ of another." One of the references mentions "the divine possession or frenzy" of the prophets and uses Abraham's deep sleep in Genesis 15:12 as an example.

    The fact that the prophets put themselves under the control of another when prophesying is mentioned several times; however, nothing is said indicating that the speech was unintelligible. As a matter of fact, the incidents of prophecy described in the Bible to which Philo apparently refers involve intelligible speech. The example from *De Specialibus Legibus* IV, 49, for example, may be translated, "clearly express its prophetic message" (Philo, *De Spec. Leg.* IV, 49, *Loeb Classical Library*. Vol. VIII, 38). Harrisville seems to think *De Decalogo* IX, 32, 33, 46 is evidence for ecstatic speech. But the only use of *glotta* is in reference to the physical tongue, "for God is not as a man needing mouth and tongue and windpipe" (Philo, *De Decalogo*, *Loeb Classical Library*, VII, 20–22). The speaking which is discussed refers to God and to the sounds from heaven when the Mosaic law was given on Mount Sinai. Human utterance is not discussed. How such constitutes evidence for human glossolalia is difficult to see.
27. James Hope Moulton and George Milligan, *The Vocabulary of the Greek New Testament* (London: Hodder and Stoughton, 1930), 128.
28. Edwin Hatch and Henry A. Redpath, *A Concordance to the Septuagint and the Other Greek Versions of the Old Testament*, 2 vols. (1897, reprint; Graz, Austria: Akademische Druck-u Verlagsanstalt, 1954), 1:271–72.
29. In his excellent article, "Ecstatic Utterance (N.E.B.)?" *Journal of Theological Studies* 17 (October 1966): 299–307, Gundry gives a series

of strong arguments demonstrating that the gift of tongues refers to foreign languages; but he states that Isaiah 29:24 and 32:4 are instances where the Septuagint uses *glossa* to mean unintelligible speech (stammering). However, *glossa* does not mean unintelligible speech (stammering) even in these two passages. In each case the passage states, "The tongues which stammer shall learn to speak peace" *(hai glossai hai psellizousai)*. The verb *psellizo* carries the meaning to stammer; however, *glossa* refers to the tongue itself, not to the stammering or speech. That *glossa* refers to the physical tongue is particularly clear in Isaiah 32:4, where the immediately preceding parallel statement refers to the "heart of those who are weak." *Glossa* in Isaiah 29:24 and 92:4 (LXX) does not mean stammering or unintelligible speech. It has its normal meaning, "tongue." The idea of stammering is conveyed solely by the verb *psellizo*.

30. Harrisville erroneously assumes that *glossa* is used in Mark, Acts, and 1 Corinthians as a technical term (in a special sense) describing ecstatic utterance. This assumption invalidates his basic arguments, his examples of parallel phenomena, and his overall thesis. However, he apparently has made a thorough study of the use of *glossa* and states, "The Septuagint translator appears to have known nothing of a technical term for speaking in tongues" and "profane or nonecclesiastical Greek knew of no technical term for speaking in tongues" ("Speaking in Tongues," 39, 41). By "technical term" Harrisville means the use in a hitherto unknown way to describe what he assumes is ecstatic unintelligible speech. His statement does conclude that neither secular Greek nor the LXX uses *glossa* in such a way.

31. Behm, "Glossa," *TDNT*, 1:724.

32. W. F. Moulton and A. S. Geden, *A Concordance to the Greek Testament* (Edinburgh: T. & T. Clark, 1963), 172–73.

33. William F. Arndt and F. Wilbur Gingrich, *A Greek-English Lexicon of the New Testament* (Chicago: University of Chicago Press, 1947), 184.

34. Gundry, "Ecstatic Utterance," 300.

35. R. Clyde McCone states that "these are not languages at all. Cappadocian was not a language at that time" ("The Phenomena of Pentecost," *Journal of the American Scientific Affiliation* 30 [September 1971]: 85). However, Luke does not state that they spoke Cappadocian, but that those from Cappadocia heard in whatever language they spoke. To state that someone from Texas heard speech in his own language is not a claim that he spoke Texan, but rather that he heard the language spoken in Texas, that is, English.

36. Charles R. Smith, *Tongues in Biblical Perspective* (Winona Lake, Ind.: BMH Books, 1972), 34–39.

37. Ibid., 39.
38. This is not an interpretation of the event by the crowd, but Luke's statement (written under inspiration of the Holy Spirit) describing what actually occurred. This statement alone (Acts 2:6) should be sufficient to settle the issue if the biblical testimony is accepted as valid.
39. Gundry, "Ecstatic Utterance," 304
40. Ibid.
41. See Arndt and Gingrich, *Lexicon*, 464–65. Liddell and Scott indicates that *laleo* is used in New Testament times just as *lego*, and that sometimes it is opposed to articulate speech (*Lexicon*, 1025–26).
42. Gundry, "Ecstatic Utterance," 304.
43. Liddell and Scott, *Lexicon*, 70, 702.
44. W. M. Ramsay, *A Historical Commentary on St. Paul's Epistle to the Galatians* (London: Hodder and Stoughton, 1899), 260–66.
45. Moulton and Milligan, *Vocabulary*, 257.
46. Behm, "Glossa," *TDNT*, 1:722–23.
47. Arndt and Gingrich, *Lexicon*, 101, 864.
48. Liddell and Scott, *Lexicon*, 226, 1927.
49. Arndt and Gingrich, *Lexicon*, 101.
50. In Acts 4:18 the disciples are told not to speak (*phtheggomai*) in the name of Jesus; 2 Pet. 2:16 refers to the speaking of Balaam's ass, which was intelligible; and 2 Pet. 2:18 refers to the speaking of false teachers.
51. Gundry, "Ecstatic Utterance," 303–4.
52. Smith, *Tongues in Biblical Perspective*, 39.
53. Smith (ibid., 29) argues that speaking in foreign languages would not be different in quality, since these languages are already spoken. The argument seems also to rule out ecstatic unintelligible utterance since pagans already spoke in this manner in their religious exercises. Continuing this same argument, the only difference (new quality) between pagan ecstasy and a gift of ecstatic tongues would be that one is genuinely from the Holy Spirit while the other is not. But the same would apply also to a miraculous ability to speak foreign languages contrasted with what is normal. The difference in quality in both cases would be that the New Testament gift was given by the Holy Spirit but the corresponding previously existing practice was not. To argue that "new" (*kainos*) implies "not previously existing" would also seem to rule out so-called angel language or heavenly language (unless it is assumed to be nonexistent prior to the day of Pentecost). If it was nonexistent until this time, then apparently angels did not use it. Why would it be called "angel language"? The logic of the argument for ecstatic speech based on the Greek word *kainos* is defective.

54. See, e.g., Moulton and Milligan, who show that the distinction between *kainos* and *neos* was losing ground in New Testament times (*Vocabulary*, 314–15).
55. See, e.g., Smith, *Tongues in Biblical Perspective*, 25–39.
56. See Behm, "Glossa," *TDNT*, 1:722; Arndt and Gingrich, *Lexicon*, 161; and numerous other authors.
57. Nichol, *Pentecostalism*, 12–13. In a bibliographic essay on Pentecostalism, Faupel feels that Nichol "has brought together the best of previous Pentecostal scholarship, and for this reason, his book serves as an excellent introduction to the Movement" (*The American Pentecostal Movement* [Wilmore, Ky.: Asbury Seminary, 1972], 11).
58. See, e.g., Carl Brumback, *What Meaneth This?* (Springfield, Mo.: Gospel Publishing House, 1947), 264ff.
59. Howard M. Ervin sees the significance of the term "speaking in the Spirit," but applies it only to speaking in tongues (*These Are Not Drunken, As Ye Suppose* [Plainfield, N.J.: Logos, 1968], 116–19). Although this is correct as far as he goes, there is no reason to exclude prophecy. Ervin misunderstands the verse. He thinks it is a *reassurance* that tongues speaking will be sound (p. 120). It is clear, however, that it is not reassurance but a *warning* that different spirits may prompt speaking, and that they may be verified by the *content* of their speech.
60. F. W. Beare, "Speaking With Tongues," *Journal of Biblical Literature* 83 (September 1964): 241.
61. Archibald Robertson and Alfred Plummer, *A Critical and Exegetical Commentary on the First Epistle of St. Paul to the Corinthians*, ICC, 2d ed. (Edinburgh: T. & T. Clark, 1914), 288.
62. Gundry ("Ecstatic Utterance," 301) argues that Paul did not actually hand over all of his possessions. It seems that he did, however. If he did not, then both of these actions would be actions that Paul had not performed, thereby supporting our basic thesis.
63. The verb "hand over" is active and indicates that the person would "donate" his body for burning rather than being forcefully burned. Such an action is highly improbable for a Christian.
64. Zane C. Hodges, "The Purpose of Tongues," *Bibliotheca Sacra* 120 (July–September 1963): 231. We can use Hodges' words and state, adding our own, "The apostle no more implies that he expects the readers to use angel languages than that he expects them to know all mysteries and all knowledge." We can also add, "The apostle no more implies that he himself spoke angel languages than he implies that he knew all mysteries and all knowledge and had given his body to be burned."

65. Gundry, 301.
66. See, e.g., Robertson and Plummer, 306.
67. Anthony Hoekema, *What About Tongues Speaking?* (Grand Rapids: Eerdmans, 1966), 43.
68. Gundry, "Ecstatic Utterance," 302–3.
69. Franz Delitzsch, *Biblical Commentary on the Prophecies of Isaiah*, 2 vols., in *Biblical Commentary on the Old Testament*, by C. F. Keil and F. Delitzsch (Grand Rapids; Eerdmans, 1967), 2:7.
70. Francis Brown, S. R. Driver, and Charles A. Briggs, *A Hebrew and English Lexicon of the Old Testament* (Oxford: Clarendon Press, 1962), 541. See also, Delitzsch, *Isaiah*, 2:7.
71. W. Gesenius and E. Kautzsch, *Gesenius' Hebrew Grammar*, trans. A. E. Cowley, 2d ed. (Oxford: Clarendon Press, 1963), 356. This view is also held by Delitzsch, *Isaiah*, 2:7; and Brown, Driver, and Briggs, *Lexicon*, 541. Numerous others regard Isaiah 28:11 as referring to language. The word *strange* in the expression "strange tongue" means "another," "different," "strange," or "alien" (Brown, Driver, and Briggs, *Lexicon*, 29), and the term for tongue has the meanings "tongue," "language," or "tongue-shaped" (ibid., 546). The two expressions "stammering in speech (barbarous language)" and "strange tongue (alien or strange language)" seem to be parallel concepts which both refer to the foreign language spoken by those who invaded Israel as a judgment from God. The Septuagint translation (*phaulismon cheileon dia glosses heteras*) changes the words to the plural, but otherwise seems close to the Hebrew (*Septuaginta*, ed. Alfred Rahlfs, 2 vols. [Stuttgart: Württembergische Bibelanstalt, 1935], 2:601). Paul's quotation of Isaiah 28:11 retains the plural but reverses the words "lip" and "tongue" (the variant readings make no difference in the discussion), indicating that he saw no significant difference between the terms as they were used in Isaiah 28:11. They both refer to language.
72. Compare Gundry's statement: "Without the translation the tongue might appear to be meaningless gibberish. The effectiveness of glossolalia as an authenticating sign (as well as its effectiveness in conveying a divine message—see xiv. 6–12, 16–18, and especially 23) depended on its difference from the ecstatic gobbledegook in Hellenistic religion! On the other hand, the amazement factor on the day of Pentecost consisted in the recognition by non-Palestinians of their native languages as they were being spoken by Galileans who ordinarily could not have spoken them" ("Ecstatic Utterance," 303).
73. Hans Windisch, "*Barbaros*," *TDNT*, 1:546–47. See also the standard lexicons.

74. Ervin, *These Are Not Drunken*, 124–25. Ervin, a well-known charismatic and professor at several charismatic schools, argues strongly for the concept that the speaker is in control of his speaking, not in a trancelike state, and that tongues are not ecstatic.
75. Robertson and Plummer, *First Epistle of St. Paul to the Corinthians*, 306. See also Behm, "Glossa," *TDNT*, 1:722; Frederick Dale Bruner, *Theology of the Holy Spirit* (Grand Rapids: Eerdmans, 1970), 145; and numerous others.
76. Robertson and Plummer, *First Epistle of St. Paul to the Corinthians*, 306.
77. See also Gundry's statement: "The fear of Paul that untranslated tongues might impress unbelievers as symptomatic of madness does not imply that normative Christian glossolalia took place in a frenzied state of mind. For Paul thanks God that he himself speaks in tongues more than all the Corinthians (xiv.18). He also implies that tongues with translation are as valuable as prophecy: 'He who prophesies is greater than he who speaks in tongues, unless someone interprets' (xiv. 5). Moreover, Paul prohibits the banning of glossolalia properly practiced (xiv.39). If the normative practice were ecstatic, Paul's concern to avoid the charge of madness would have caused him to ban the practice outright, and he never would have pointed to his own surpassing ability to speak in tongues. Nor would he have been so careful to leave the door open for tongues, even elevating them to the level of prophecy when combined with translation. The fear that unbelievers will think glossolalists are mad stems solely from the Corinthians' failure to require accompanying translation at all times, with the result that what Paul regarded as genuine human languages sounded to unbelievers like meaningless successions of syllables similar to the ecstatic speech in Hellenistic religions familiar to the hearers and thus led to an equation Paul did not want to be drawn" ("Ecstatic Utterance," 305).
78. The references in the New Testament show that this word is a common word for "translate" (see Moulton and Geden, *Concordance*, 216, 380). See, e.g., Acts 9:36 and the use of the uncompounded verb in John 1:38. Gundry says the same thing: "The term interpretation *(diermeneuo)*, used frequently in connexion with glossolalia in 1 Corinthians, normally refers to translating a language when used in such a context. Although the verb might refer to the explaining of mysterious utterances, its usage in Biblical Greek militates against that understanding. For Davies showed that out of twenty-one cases of *hermeneuo* and its cognates in the *Septuagint* and New Testament (again apart from the seven occurrences in question in 1 Corinthians xii–xiv), one refers to satire or

a figurative saying, two refer to explanation and eighteen to translation" ("Ecstatic Utterance," 301).

79. Smith argues to the effect that tongues must always be interpreted since 1 Cor. 14:2 states that no one understands. He continues that if tongues were languages, God could communicate by having the speaker speak the language of the hearers, thus obviating the need for interpretation. He sees no need for the interpreter if tongues are languages. His reasoning is based on two assumptions. The first is the assumption that the gift of tongues was primarily for communication. The Bible (1 Cor. 14:22) states clearly that it is a sign to unbelievers. The second assumption is a misunderstanding of 1 Cor. 14:2 (*Biblical Perspective*, 31–32). As we will show, this verse cannot possibly be an absolute statement describing tongues, but refers to their use in the assembly when no one understands, the situation Paul is addressing in Corinth.

80. The New Testament gives very little information regarding the gift of interpretation. It can only be surmised. It is clear from 1 Cor. 14 that tongues are not designed for use in the assembly but are a sign to unbelievers. Therefore the gift of interpretation is not intended to interpret messages to believers (although it may be used in the assembly as Paul allows in Corinth). Tongues (languages) used properly as a sign outside the assembly communicate only to the hearers since the speaker does not understand. The gift of interpretation would allow for mutual (two-way) communication when the occasion demanded or for explanation to the speaker and his party who did not understand.

81. C. K. Barrett, *A Commentary on the Second Epistle to the Corinthians* (London: Adam and Charles Black, 1973), 166–67.

82. Arndt and Gingrich, *Lexicon*, 276.

83. Philip E. Hughes, *Paul's Second Epistle to the Corinthians*, NICNT (Grand Rapids: Eerdmans, 1962), 190–92.

84. Ibid., 192.

85. Charles Hodge, *An Exposition of the Second Epistle to the Corinthians* (Grand Rapids: Eerdmans, n.d.), 132.

86. This has been previously mentioned. See lexical authorities such as Arndt and Gingrich, *Lexicon*, 161; Behm, "Glossa," *TDNT*, 1:722.

87. F. F. Bruce, *The Acts of the Apostles* (London: Tyndale, 1951), 82.

88. A. C. Thistleton argues from Philo and Josephus that the word *interpret* means "to put into words" rather than "to translate." However, he states that his article is "tentatively to suggest the possibility of a third alternative," indicating the tenuous nature of his conclusions. He does not demonstrate that *diermeneuo* or cognates means "put into

words" from ecstatic or nonlanguage utterance. Since he does not disprove the common meanings, "translate" or "interpret," for *hermeneuo*, his article adds little of any significance. The examples are largely from Philo, an allegorizing interpreter who can hardly be considered the ideal person to examine for the usage of the term *hermeneuo*. Few, if any, of the examples hold up under scrutiny. Rather than merely mean "put into words," as Thistleton claims, the examples have the idea "to express more clearly or accurately." Neither this idea nor Thistleton's concept can be considered any new insight that is particularly significant to the use of *hermeneuo* in 1 Cor. 14 (see Thistleton's, "The Interpretation of Tongues: A New Suggestion in the Light of Greek Usage in Philo and Josephus," *Journal of Theological Studies* 30 (April 1979): 15–36).

89. John Williams, *The Holy Spirit: Lord and Life-Giver* (Neptune, N.J.: Loizeaux, 1980), 213.
90. Peter states that they are the same (Acts 11:15–17).
91. Ervin also argues that all the tongues are the same experience, that is, language (*These Are Not Drunken*, 126–28).
92. Arndt and Gingrich, *Lexicon*, 161.
93. Behm, "Glossa," *TDNT*, 1:719–26.
94. Arndt and Gingrich, *Lexicon*, 161.
95. Behm, "Glossa," *TDNT*, 1:725–26.
96. A study of various Greek lexicons reveals the same thing. In addition to those referred to in this study, such lexicons as *A Manual Greek Lexicon of the New Testament* by Abbott-Smith, *A Greek-English Lexicon of the New Testament* by Joseph Henry Thayer, *A New Greek and English Lexicon* by James Donnegan, *Greek-English Lexicon of the New Testament* by Edward Robinson, and *Greek Lexicon of the Roman and Byzantine Periods* by E. A. Sophocles, either do not directly state that tongues are ecstatic unintelligible speech or else only refer to the disputed New Testament passages as evidence. They all reveal that ecstatic utterance is not a meaning of *glossa* supported by Greek usage.
97. William J. Samarin, *Tongues of Men and Angels* (New York: Macmillan, 1970), 211.
98. Ibid., 227–28.
99. Felicitas D. Goodman, *Speaking in Tongues* (Chicago: University of Chicago Press, 1972), vii, xi. As far as Goodman is concerned, Paul's tongues were not from the Holy Spirit, but may have had a common source with glossolalia of witch doctors and shamans.
100. Joseph Dillow, *Speaking in Tongues* (Grand Rapids: Zondervan, 1975), 15.

CHAPTER 7

Tongues: The Purpose for the Gift

WE MUST DETERMINE the purpose for which God gave the miraculous ability to speak normal human languages foreign to the speaker. As we might expect, there are different opinions regarding the proper purpose.

Devotional Use of the Gift of Tongues

Although the Pentecostal movement originally stressed the use of tongues in the public assembly, many charismatics today stress the private or devotional use of the gift of tongues.[1] Some state that this enables them to communicate better with God in prayer. Some profess to be edified by speaking in tongues privately.

Private tongues speaking does not involve one in the public manifestation normally associated with Pentecostalism. This makes it much more acceptable to many individuals. This also avoids the numerous biblical restrictions placed upon the use of tongues in the assembly (1 Cor. 14), which restrictions, if they are observed, make it impossible to emphasize the gift of tongues. The private "speaking in tongues" allows the tongues speaker to avoid calling attention to his activities. This private use of tongues, therefore, has made much greater penetration into the non-Pentecostal churches than the older mainline Pentecostal approach was able to do.

The term "devotional tongues" as used herein includes all uses of tongues speaking which may he classified as personal, private, or devotional. Tongues speaking as individual prayer and praise to

God or as self-edification will be included even if done in public since these are personal in nature.

Evidence for Devotional Tongues Only Inferential

The most obvious objection to the concept that the gift of tongues was for devotional or private use is often overlooked. There is no statement in the Bible that the gift of tongues is for devotional or private use. Neither are any of the New Testament instances of tongues speaking described as devotional, private, or for prayer. Such a concept is derived solely from alleged inferences in the New Testament.

Devotional Tongues Contrary to the Purpose for Gifts

Another obvious objection to devotional tongues is that such a gift would be in basic opposition to the purpose for all spiritual gifts. It would be in a category all by itself. Gifts are given in order to minister to others. The other gifts are clearly given for this purpose. Not only are there direct statements to this effect but the very names of the gifts demonstrate that they are for ministry. Devotional tongues would of necessity be a self-centered purpose for the gift of tongues. It is claimed that such devotional use edifies the speaker, brings him closer to God, and enables him to pray better. No matter how beneficial such claims sound, a private use of tongues cannot be anything but self-centered. No other gift is given to enhance the gifted one. It is improbable that tongues is different in this aspect from all other gifts. This would also mean that a small percentage of believers would have an advantage in prayer and communication with God. If tongues are to edify the individual speaker or provide better communication with God, one would expect such to be given to *all* believers, since God desires all to be edified and all to pray. The Bible clearly says, however, that all do *not* speak in tongues (1 Cor. 12:30). This statement is not made as a denunciation of those who do not; it is a statement in conclusion to the chapter showing that God did not *intend* for all to speak in tongues. Not everyone is expected to speak in tongues any more than they are all expected to exercise the other gifts in the passage, such as apostle or prophet.

First Corinthians 13:1–4 supports the concept that gifts are given to minister to others. It specifically signifies this regarding the gift of tongues by stating, "If I speak with the tongues of men and of angels, and do not have love, I am resounding brass or a clanging cymbal." Love *(agape)* in the New Testament is not merely an emotion but is concern for the welfare of others.[2] Paul describes the love to which he refers in verses 4–7:

> Love is longsuffering, love is kind, is not jealous, does not vaunt itself, is not puffed up; is not unseemly, does not seek its own, is not easily provoked, does not calculate evil; does not rejoice in unrighteousness, but rejoices in the truth; bears all things, believes all things, hopes all things, endures all things. (1 Cor. 13:4–7)

Paul refers to love as an attitude which is concerned for others. In this context it is on the plane of one's fellowmen rather than an attitude toward God.[3] This is the same love that Paul refers to in chapters 8–10 of this very Epistle and in Romans 14. This love governs one's actions toward others. The expression "have not love" must in this context (1 Cor. 13:1–4) mean to exercise the gift apart from love. It can hardly mean that a failure to possess love, as an abstract factor, nullifies whatever one does. Nor can it mean that a failure to love at any time nullifies ministry at some other time. Paul's argument is clear in the context: although one exercises gifts from the Holy Spirit, apart from love they do not profit the gifted person (see 13:1; 14:1).[4] The gifts must be used with the proper motive. They must be exercised as a ministry to benefit others. If exercised to exalt oneself, they may profit the recipients of the ministry, but apart from love they do not benefit the minister ("*I* am nothing," v. 2; "*I* am profited nothing," v. 3).[5]

Paul states very clearly that if he speaks in tongues apart from love, it is merely a noise. Two aspects in this verse are against devotional tongues. If tongues (as well as all gifts) are to be exercised in love, then obviously they cannot be for personal use. No one can exercise personal, private tongues as a ministry in love to others. Therefore, since Paul says tongues are to be exercised in love, he cannot regard tongues as devotional. In addition, if tongues exercised apart from love are valueless, especially to the speaker, then devotional tongues (since they cannot be exercised in love) are worthless to the speaker. Since no one else is present, they cannot be of value to others; therefore, they are of no value at all.

Devotional Tongues Contrary to the Purpose for Tongues

When Jesus instructed the disciples in Mark 16:15–17, he said,

> Go ye into all the world, and preach the gospel to every creature. He

that believeth and is baptized shall be saved; but he that believeth not shall be damned. And these signs shall accompany them that believe; In my name shall they cast out devils; they shall speak with new tongues.

Jesus commanded the disciples to evangelize, and he stated that certain signs would go along with them. One of the signs was "speaking with new tongues." Paul also states very explicitly that tongues are for the purpose of a "sign to unbelievers" (1 Cor. 14:22). The Greek construction involved is *eis semeion*, "for a sign"; the preposition *eis* with the accusative case is an expression of purpose.[6] Both passages (Mark 16:17; 1 Cor. 14:22) state that tongues are a sign; but they also indicate that they are a sign to unbelievers. The clearest description of tongues (Acts 2:4–11) describes an instance where they function as a sign to unbelievers. The only other occurrences of tongues speaking in the Bible are the events related in Acts 10:46 and 19:6. In every case the tongues functioned as a sign. The speaking was public.

In the latter two cases the reaction of unbelievers is not mentioned. The tongues speaking was by those who responded to the gospel and demonstrated to the disciples that these new groups were genuinely received into the body of Christ. The first instance, Acts 10:46, convinced the hitherto Jewish church that Gentiles were also to be converted. This of course did not need to be repeated since from that time on the Gentiles were accepted on this basis. The second instance, Acts 19:6, signified that disciples of John the Baptist, those who were righteous before Calvary, still needed to believe in Christ in order to be in the body of Christ. Disciples of John the Baptist who had not heard the gospel no longer exist of course. Therefore, the cases in Acts 10:46 and 19:6 were unusual onetime occurrences and not to be repeated. Even in these unusual cases tongues served as a publicly demonstrated sign to those present.

The gift of interpretation of tongues is another implication that God did not intend for the gift of tongues to be used devotionally. God does not need an interpreter in order to understand what is said. Interpretation is only needed to communicate to men. There is no need for an interpreter in order to pray to God, or praise him, or for any other use of devotional tongues. The statements of 1 Corinthians 14:22 and Mark 16:17, the example of Acts 2:4–11, the fact that tongues are human languages, and God's provision of the gift of interpretation all show that the gift of tongues was never intended by God to be used devotionally.

Tongues Not Intended as a Sign to the Speaker

What is the alleged purpose for or benefit of a private or devotional use of tongues? Ervin, as well as others, feels that they are for "prayer and praise addressed to God."[7] Since ministry to others is not possible, the purpose of necessity must be related solely to the speaker. Based on the statements of proponents and on logic, it seems that there are four possibilities.[8] Devotional tongues can be used for prayer, praise, self-edification, or a sign. The idea that devotional tongues are to be a sign is the easiest to rule out. A sign is to signify something. What can devotional tongues signify? The only possibility is that they signify to the speaker that he has a gift, that he has this particular gift (tongues), or that the Spirit is dealing with him. All of these have been suggested by tongues proponents. But none of these could be considered a purpose for a gift. Every gift can indicate to the possessor that he has a gift or that the Spirit is using him; therefore, this cannot be the purpose for which the gift of tongues was intended. God would hardly give a gift is merely to show that the possessor has the gift. The gift itself would be purposeless. There are other gifts of which the possessor may be aware, but they all have a purpose.

Tongues Not for Self-Edification

The opinion that tongues are for self-edification (and therefore private or devotional) is derived from 1 Corinthians 14:3–4, which states, "But he that prophesies speaks to men for edification, and exhortation, and comfort. He that speaks in a tongue edifies himself; but he that prophesies edifies the assembly."[9] But in this context, the statement "he that speaks in a tongue edifies himself" is not a statement lauding tongues as a gift for self-edification; rather, it is the reason why tongues are to give way to prophecy. It is a negative factor concerning tongues which is against their use in the assembly. Although prophecy edifies all the hearers, tongues only edify self.

This negative aspect is not a God-intended purpose for tongues (i.e., self-edification). It is a handicap of noninterpreted tongues when used in the assembly. It is the reason noninterpreted tongues are not allowed in the assembly. We must keep in mind that 1 Corinthians 14 discusses the use of prophecy and tongues *in the assembly*. "He that speaks in a tongue edifies himself" is a statement of the result of the misuse in the assembly when no one understands; it is not a description of the purpose for tongues since tongues, when properly used, do edify others. When men understand the tongues, they *are* edified. This is the express reason why Paul allows them to be used in the assembly when someone interprets. The hearers who understood were edified at Pentecost. Some may contend that although self-edification is a misuse and not the intended purpose of tongues, it is nevertheless profitable. This needs further examination.

There are two possible basic meanings for the expression "he that speaks in a tongue edifies himself." The verb "edify," *oikodomeo*, means "to build up."[10] Although this verb normally has a beneficial meaning, in 1 Corinthians 8:10 Paul uses the same verb to refer to a negative aspect of building up. He refers to a strong brother who may lead the weaker brother to an action which violates his conscience. This building up of the weak brother's conscience is not positive edification but a negative building up or hardening that results in sin. The direction of the edification, positive or negative, must be derived from the context. There are several indications that to "edify oneself" in 1 Corinthians 14:4 may have the negative connotation to build oneself up in the eyes of others. One of the basic problems Paul addresses in the letter to the Corinthians is the exaltation or building up of self. There were divisions apparently based on pride and self-glory (1:26–29; 3:3–7, 18, 21). Statements such as 1 Corinthians 4:6–7 make it probable that some were puffed up in regard to their gifts, particularly the gift of tongues. Thus, a negative self-exaltation was one of the problems at Corinth.

Verses in 1 Corinthians 14 are against the concept that one can be positively edified through a tongue which he does not understand. Verse 5 says that the congregation cannot be edified apart from understanding, and verse 6 states that there is no profit to the hearer unless he understands. If it is necessary for the hearers to understand in order to be positively edified, it seems to follow that the speaker must also understand in order to be edified. Paul also states that someone who speaks in a tongue when no one understands "speaks into air" (1 Cor. 14:9). He mentions this as a negative concept, not a desirable one. It gives no profit (or edification). In addition, the hearer's mind cannot respond to speech he does not understand. The hearer cannot say "amen" when someone gives thanks in tongues since "he does not know what you say" (v. 16). This is Paul's evidence that the hearer is not edified, as he explains in the next line, "For you give thanks well, but the other is not edified" (v. 17). There is no edification apart from understanding or knowing what is said.

Referring to tongues speaking which the speaker does not understand, Paul says that the speaker's mind is "unfruitful" (1 Cor. 14:14). This is the reason why the speaker is to pray that he can interpret.[11] This passage teaches that there is no edification for either speaker or hearer unless the meaning of the tongue is understood. Paul specifically includes prayer to God as speaking without fruit or edification for the one praying or any hearers unless the words are understood (1 Cor. 14:13–14). The reason Paul tells the Corinthians not to indulge in such prayer (or any nonunderstood tongues speaking) is because no one profits. There is no edification[12] (the mind is fruitless). First Corinthians 14:15–16 makes it clear that the hearer cannot know what is said unless the tongue is interpreted. This lack of understanding is the same as "not being edified" in verse 17.

Therefore, there can be no beneficial self-edification from devotional tongues which the speaker does not understand. The speaker's mind is fruitless. To Paul such speech is useless. He states twice regarding the assembly (vv. 5, 17) that edification cannot take place apart from understanding. These verses make it exceedingly doubtful that the self edification referred to in verse 4 is of a beneficial nature. What does the statement "edifies himself" (1 Cor. 14:4) imply if it is beneficial? Satisfactory explanations have not been produced.[13] It is difficult to conceive how anyone can edify himself, especially when the edification must be in alleged "tongues" apart from one's understanding. The expression "build himself up (edify himself)," in English, refers to training oneself with the help of outside aids such as books and observation of others, not solely on oneself. One cannot have the resources to build himself beyond his own knowledge unless some outside knowledge is obtained. But without understanding and use of the mind no knowledge can he obtained. The suggested ways in which one may beneficially edify himself by speaking in tongues do not bear up under examination. The most obvious explanation is that the speaker can learn spiritual truths through this means and thereby be edified. This is ruled out immediately by the fact that he understands nothing and his mind does not produce any benefit (it is fruitless; see v. 14) due to this very lack of understanding. The devotional tongues speaker can receive no spiritual truth or exhortation or encouragement from his speaking, since he does not understand what he says.

Another explanation commonly advanced is that the speaker's realization that God has given him a gift and is speaking through him is a blessing. This "blessing" is then considered to be edification. Godet, who was not a charismatic, feels that

> From his intimate communion with God, the glossolalate derives a blessing which even though it is not transformed into precise notions by the exercise of the understanding, makes itself felt as a power in the depths of the soul.[14]

This emotion or feeling ("power in the depths of the soul") is often directly equated with edification. Since it is impossible for the self-edification to be anything in the area of instruction, encouragement, or exhortation (due to the fact that no understanding occurs), the only remaining possibilities are those just stated. This "self-edification" must be based either on the knowledge that one is engaged in a spiritual exercise or on a spiritual thrill or "glow" (blessing).

But this cannot be the intended purpose for the gift of tongues, even if such knowledge or blessing were considered edification. For example, the purpose for the gift of prophet is not for self-edification through this knowledge that one is being used by God. The prophet can also derive an emotional blessing through his experience, but this is not the purpose for the gift. The same can be said for all of the gifts: one may be blessed from the knowledge that God is using him, and he may have a deep inner or emotional blessing. However, this is not the purpose for the gifts. Neither is the knowledge that one is speaking in tongues the intended purpose for tongues; nor is the feeling (blessing). This would mean that God gave a spiritual gift for the purpose that men would realize they have the gift. This is a gift of no value. If God desires someone to know he has a gift and is used of God, he can give him a gift which also has a use. The person can then know they have the gift from its use. The biblical concepts of spiritually building up believers depend on the Word of God, on understanding and knowledge, on exhortation and encouragement. Apostles, prophets, teachers, pastors, and evangelists are all given to communicate the gospel and to build up or edify the church (Eph. 4:7–12). The New Testament abounds with information. Believers are exhorted to act on the basis of those truths. In Paul's Epistles we find the pattern of establishing the truth (Rom. 1–11; Eph. 1–3) and afterward exhorting the recipients to act on the basis of that knowledge (Rom. 12:1–2ff.; Eph. 4:1ff.). Nowhere is anyone exhorted to experience a feeling or to act or grow spiritually on the basis of such emotion. To consider feeling (blessing) or the knowledge that one is being used as edification or spiritually beneficial and an end in itself is not a Christian concept. A feeling of blessing can come upon the Christian in many ways, but it cannot be considered as the purpose for giving a spiritual gift.

There are additional considerations which call into question the concept that tongues are for self-edification. God gave apostles, prophets, teachers, and evangelists in order to edify the believers. He also gave gifts, such as the word of knowledge and the word of wisdom, in addition to his written Word. All of these gifts depend upon understanding. A gift of tongues which self-edifies apart from understanding cannot possibly edify to the same extent that these edifying gifts are able to do. Self-edifying tongues would of necessity be an extraneous gift. It would be a gift which could never reach the level of edification possible from these other gifts. It would mean that God gave a gift of speech not understood by the speaker and which cannot possibly edify the speaker as much as the edification available through the other gifts and the Bible. It would also appear that a higher level of self-edification would be possible through a gift such as the gift of prophet or the gift of teaching, which can communicate many spiritual truths and provide every aspect of self-edification possible through speaking in tongues. No one can be edified more highly apart from his understanding than through his understanding. To consider tongues as designed for self-edification is to say that God gave a gift which cannot accomplish what the individual can accomplish apart from the gift.

Another factor to consider is that believers are not encouraged to grow spiritually through self-edification of tongues. There are numerous passages and exhortations for the believer to be spiritual and to grow in Christ, but not one of them mentions tongues. If tongues were for self-edification, one would expect them to be mentioned and in fact promoted. Ephesians 4:11 lists gifts given to edify the body of Christ, but tongues are not listed. If they were intended to edify, we should see them in this passage.

God did not intend for the gift of tongues to be used for self-edification. This is not the purpose for tongues. They are stated to be a sign to unbelievers. First Corinthians 14:4 is not giving the purpose for tongues but the reason not to exercise them when they are not understood. There are also implications that the expression "edifies himself" (1 Cor. 14:4) does not refer to beneficial edification. Several verses in the context state that there can be no edification apart from understanding. No satisfactory explanation has or can be given to show how tongues are able to edify self. Other gifts (and the Bible) are available that can edify more than any ability to speak unintelligibly.

Tongues Not for Prayer or Praise
The two remaining possibilities for a private or devotional purpose for tongues are based on the statements "for the one speaking in tongues speaks not to men, but to God" (1 Cor. 14:2) and "Let him speak to himself, and to God" (14:28). Both verses refer to "speaking to God." First Corinthians 14:14–17 is also often included as proof that tongues are for prayer to God. The two possibilities are that tongues are for praise or for prayer (communication) to God. Since there is no example in the Bible where tongues are used to communicate to God, this position depends solely upon the few verses above. An examination of the verses involved will determine if these verses support tongues for prayer and praise to God.

First Corinthians 14:2 is not a description of the gift of tongues, exalting it as a means of communication with God. Rather, it is the reason why prophecy is preferred. A wording of verses 1–3 that shows the main thrust will make this clear: "Be zealous that you prophesy because the tongues speaker does not speak to men, but to God. . . . but the prophet speaks edification to men." The Corinthians were to prefer prophesying (because it edifies men) over tongues because they are only spoken to God. In the assembly, "speaking to men" has the preference over "speaking to God," as it is meant in this verse. Paul would not say that speaking to God in prayer or as praise is a reason why tongues are not preferred. He states elsewhere that prayer and praise are essential in the assembly (see 1 Cor. 14:15–16, Eph. 6:18; Phil. 4:4–6; Col. 4:2; 1 Thess. 5:17; 1 Tim. 2:1, 8). Hence, 1 Corinthians 14:2 does not concern speaking to God in prayer or praise. The verse itself states the situation. The statement introduced by "for," *gar*, "for no man understands," gives the reason for the preceding statement, "he speaks . . . unto God." The reason he speaks to God is not because he is in prayer but because no one understands. The "speaking unto God" is equivalent to "only God understands." The reason why prophecy is preferred to tongues is because everyone understands prophecy, but if tongues are spoken when no one understands, only God is left to understand. The flow of thought shows that this is the same as "speaking into air" (v. 9). Hence, the phrase "speaks unto God" (14:2) is not speaking of

Tongues: The Purpose for the Gift

prayer or praise but of the fact that no human understands; therefore, only God can. There are other indications that 1 Corinthians 14:2 does not mean that tongues are intended as a means of prayer or praise to God. The reason someone "speaks unto God" is because "no one understands." Therefore, when someone understands, this is not so. Then, the speaker is not speaking to God but to men. Thus, this verse cannot refer to prayer to God, because prayer would still be to God even if someone did understand; but 1 Corinthians 14:2 does not hold true when someone understands. The tongues were understood on the day of Pentecost; therefore, the statement "he speaks to God" did not hold true in that situation. It does not hold true when the tongues are interpreted. God gave tongues as a sign to unbelievers (1 Cor. 14:22); therefore they were *intended* to be understood by men at Pentecost. God also gave the gift of interpretation; therefore, "tongues" were intended to be understood by men. The stated purpose for tongues (1 Cor. 14:22) is that they were intended for men. Therefore, 1 Corinthians 14:2 is not referring to an aspect of tongues that always holds true. "Speaking to God" in 1 Corinthians 14:2 holds true only when men are present but do not understand.

This is precisely the situation Paul attempts to correct in the Corinthian Epistle, namely, the use of tongues in the assembly when no one understands. This passage is not to exalt tongues as a means of communication with God but to show their limitation, that is, why they are less satisfactory than prophecy. Paul does not say, "Prefer prophecy because tongues are intended for prayer and praise to God." This would be no reason to suppress tongues. Instead, Paul says, "Prefer prophecy because, due to the fact that no one else understands, the tongues speaker cannot speak to men; only God can understand what he says." This verse is not intended to build up tongues as communication with God, but to suppress their use in the assembly when no one understands them (i.e., when only God understands).

Verse 2, "speaks to God," applies only in a situation where someone speaks in a tongue and the people present do not understand. This occurred in the Corinthian assembly where members spoke in tongues merely to indulge in the gift and with no useful purpose in mind. It did not occur in Acts 2:4–11 where the hearers understood the languages and it could not occur in any assembly obeying the biblical command to exercise tongues in the assembly only when an interpreter is present.

The next verse is similar: "But if there is no interpreter, he must keep silent in the assembly; and he should speak to himself, and to God" (1 Cor. 14:28). As in 14:2, this is not a description lauding tongues as a gift for communion with God. Neither is it an encouragement to use tongues privately. Rather, it is a discouragement to their use in the assembly. The statement "he should speak to himself, and to God" is parallel in the structure of the verse and in meaning to the statement, "he must keep silent in the assembly." If there is no one to interpret, the tongues speaker is to keep silent. This is equivalent to speaking to himself and to God. This verse, like verse 2, refers to the Corinthian situation, where no one interprets and, therefore, no one understands. In that situation, the tongues speaker is to keep silent in the assembly; that is, he is to "speak to himself, and to God." One cannot, of course, speak to himself if he does not understand; there is no communication. In this context the idea of speaking to oneself cannot mean anything but "speak away from others where only the speaker can hear and do not bother others." Can we actually think this verse means that tongues were given by God so that someone can talk to himself? No one needs a spiritual gift for this purpose.

But, if this verse supports devotional tongues (prayer or praise to God), it also supports talking to oneself. If the words "let him speak . . . to God" mean "pray or talk to God," then "he is to speak to himself" means "pray or talk to himself." In the one sentence "he is to speak to himself and to God," both "to himself" and "to God" must involve the same thing. If it means that tongues are directed toward God, it also means they are directed toward self. If this shows that tongues are for prayer or praise to God, it also shows that they are for prayer or praise to oneself. It cannot mean this; therefore, it cannot mean that tongues are for prayer or praise to God. So this verse means speak where only self and God can hear; that is, do not bother the assembly with speaking which no one understands.

This is similar in concept to the statement "Do you have faith? Have it to yourself before God" (Rom. 14:22). This statement in Romans certainly does not mean to direct faith toward self, nor is it encouraging private, devotional faith only. It refers to the believer who has faith that he may eat anything or faith that he does not need to observe any one day in a special manner. Paul tells him, "Rather than display your freedom (faith) in these areas by actually doing these things in front of the brother and so offending his conscience, on the contrary give up your freedom for his sake and keep it to yourself." So it is with tongues in 1 Corinthians 14:28. The man with the gift of tongues is not required to display it. When no interpreter is present, he is to keep it to himself and God. First Corinthians 14:28 no more urges the speaker to devotional tongues than the statement "Do not sing or play a guitar during the church meeting because it disturbs the assembly, but rather sing or play to yourself and to God" urges people to devotional singing and guitar-playing. Rather, it means, "Don't bother others with your tongues speaking; if you are not going to use it properly to minister to others, do not bother the assembly." Paul has already stated in verse 9 that speaking into the air is profitless. First Corinthians 14:2 and 14:28 give no support to the idea that tongues are designed for prayer and praise to God. They are negative in thrust, suppressing tongues in the assembly rather than promoting private tongues.

Verses 14–16 likewise are not promoting tongues as prayer vehicles. They state that it is better to pray with understanding. Paul testifies that rather than pray in the spirit without his understanding (that is, in nonunderstood tongues), he prefers to pray both in the spirit and at the same time with his mind (understanding), he prefers to pray in a language he understands. Paul is not saying, "I will at some times speak in the spirit and at other times speak with the mind." He states that, in contrast to speaking only in the spirit (v. 14) apart from his mind (understanding), he prefers to speak with both; namely, in a language he understands. Verses 14–16 state, "For if I pray in a tongue, my spirit prays, but my mind is unfruitful. What then? I will pray with the spirit, and I will pray with the mind also." This is not an argument for prayer in tongues but the reason why tongues need to be interpreted; that is, "the spirit prays, but the mind is fruitless," unless the tongues are interpreted. This does not describe the fruitless aspect of the hearer's minds, but of the speaker's mind. It is a deficiency or negative act for someone to pray in a tongue he does not understand and thus, it is a reason for not praying in an uninterpreted tongue. Paul desires that both his mind and his spirit be involved in prayer. This is impossible when praying in a tongue which the speaker does not understand.

Paul not only argues for the need to understand prayer, but in the following verses (vv. 16–17) he says the same thing concerning blessing and thanksgiving. But if private blessing, thanksgiving, and prayer are not proper uses of tongues, then how can they be used to praise God? Praising God to others is not an option since devotional tongues are private. In addition, others would not understand the praise. Speaking *to God* and also *for God* to others are ruled out. How can he be praised? There are additional reasons to question the concept of prayer-or-praise tongues.

First, it is improbable that God would give a gift of speaking foreign languages, which are intended for people, in order to praise or to pray to him. It is less probable that he would give a gift of speaking unintelligible speech (or any speech not understood by the speaker) to communicate to God in prayer since Jesus himself spoke against such practice. He said, "But when ye pray, use not vain repetitions, as the heathen do: for they think that they shall be heard for their much speaking. Be not ye therefore like unto them" (Matt. 6:7–8a). Jesus then gave the intelligible Lord's Prayer as a proper example to follow. The word translated "use vain repetitions" is the Greek verb *battalogeo*. It is parallel in meaning, in this verse, to "much speaking," *polulogia*.[15] There is general agreement that the idea of babbling or stammering is meant in Matthew 6:7. We may conclude that Jesus spoke against prayer which consisted of unintelligible speech or babbling, similar to the pagan prayers. In contrast, Jesus gave a clear, rational prayer which is to the point and understandable. He said to pray "in this way." He said nothing regarding the use of tongues in order to pray. Thus, it is improbable that God would give a gift of unintelligible prayer to believers. Jesus also said not to pray "as the heathen do." Glossolalia (ecstatic unintelligible speech) is common in pagan communication with their gods but was not common in the church until modern times.

Some have attempted to read the concept of prayer glossolalia into the expression "the Spirit itself intercedes for us with unuttered groanings" (Rom. 8:26). However, this verse applies to *all* Christians, as the entire chapter shows. The preceding verses referred to "we who have the firstfruits of the Spirit groan within ourselves, anxiously waiting for our adoption" (Rom. 8:23). The following verses refer to aspects such as foreknowledge, predestination, calling, justification, and the permanence of Christ's love, aspects that pertain to every believer. The statement of Romans 8:26 is true for every believer, without any conditions. The words translated as in the King James version, "groanings which cannot be uttered" *(stenagmois alaletois)*, do not mean speaking in tongues. The word *alaletos* has the idea of "unexpressed," "wordless,"[16] or "unutterable."[17] Cranfield feels that the choice lies between "ineffable," "that cannot be expressed in ordinary speech," or "unspoken," with the next verse suggesting the latter.[18] The *a* in *alaletos* is similar to the English prefix "un-" (*a-laletos* = un-spoken); the expression means "unspoken" or "inaudible." Since it is in combination with the word "groanings," there is little possibility that any audible utterance is meant in this verse. Cranfield also argues that

> *Stenagmois alaletois* must refer to the Spirit's own *stenagmoi*, and it is highly unlikely that Paul would think of the ecstatic utterances of certain Christians, inspired by the Spirit though these utterances might be, as being the Spirit's own *stenagmoi*. It is surely much more probable that the reference is to groanings imperceptible to the Christians themselves.[19]

It seems that the Spirit makes the groanings rather than the individual in prayer. In addition, since tongues are languages, it is even less likely that this verse refers to tongues speaking in prayer. Languages, angelic included, would hardly be classified as inaudible groanings. Thus, Romans 8:26 lends no support to the use of tongues for prayer.

The concept of a special gift for prayer and praise to God also seems to violate basic Christian teaching. The New Testament teaches that every Christian has full access to God through Jesus Christ. This access was obtained for every Christian by Christ's death on the cross (John 14:13–14; Eph. 2:18; 3:12). Every Christian is instructed to pray continually, but there is no implication anywhere in the New Testament that certain individuals have greater access to God or greater prayer ability. To state that a special gift is necessary or better for prayer implies that ordinary prayer is deficient and that those without the gift do not have complete access to God the Father. This view of tongues amounts to the allegation that in some mystical sense the speaker can better communicate with or praise God by speaking apart from his understanding than by speaking words which have meaning to him. There needs to be some biblical explanation showing why this is better; however, none has been produced. It is sometimes claimed that prayer in tongues allows greater freedom in prayer, but this can only be due to a psychological "letting go" since we are already free in prayer. There are no restrictions from God's side; therefore, the only restrictions would be in the individual's emotions. Yet such emotional release in prayer apart from rationality is not biblical prayer. Biblical prayer is prayer based on knowledge. In addition, since tongues have been demonstrated to be foreign languages, this position amounts to the claim that an Englishman, for example, can pray and praise God better in Chinese than he can in his own language, or even more to the point, "he can pray better or praise God better in Chinese than the Chinese can in Chinese." The basic assumption underlying this view is that rational participation, knowledge, or understanding somehow hinders communication with God, and that a state of ecstasy is more in tune with God. This, of course, is not a Christian perspective but is typical of pagan religions.

Romans 8:26 teaches that the Holy Spirit helps all believers in prayer. Every believer has full access to God upon the basis of Christ's death, and every believer is told to pray and that he will be heard. Hence, there is no need for a special language in which to pray to God. There is not the slightest possibility that the believer's communication with God can be improved by speaking in tongues. The New Testament is replete with statements that lack of understanding and knowledge are hindrances and deficiencies in the believer's life. They are not benefits for spirituality. Tongues are never used in the biblical examples of prayer directed to God.

The need for a gift to praise God in a tongue also needs an explanation. There must be some explanation showing why God would prefer to be praised in German, for example, by an Englishman, but would not consider the same praise by a German to be adequate. It is even more difficult to explain why God would deem praise in unintelligible, heavenly, or angelic language (i.e., speaking apart from the understanding) to be better than praise which the speaker understands; in fact, so much better that he gave a miraculous gift for this purpose. No passage implies that the praise of angels is better than the praise of men (see Rev. 4:11–5:14). The biblical examples of praise and prayer in heaven, as well as on earth, are all intelligible to those around them. First Corinthians 13:8 states that tongues will cease, but there is no apparent reason for the cessation of a gift which supplies a supernatural ability to praise God.[20] This would seem as permanent as love. We know that believers will continue to praise God throughout eternity.

The statement in Acts 10:46, "For they heard them speak with tongues, and magnify God," does not necessarily mean that the speaker magnified God by tongues; instead, it probably describes two separate actions, since apparently the words which magnified

God were understood. Even if we assume that they did magnify God in their tongues speaking, certainly magnifying God was not the purpose for the speaking in Acts 10:46. The tongues in this instance were to prove that the speakers had been placed into the body of Christ. Any speaking which is intelligible, including tongues, must have some content. This content may magnify God, but it is not the purpose for tongues.

There is no basis upon which to assume that tongues are for private or personal use. The possessor of every other gift can be aware of his gift and that God is using him, but this is not the purpose for his gift. The possessors of other gifts can pray and praise God but this is not the purpose for their gift. The fact that tongues are languages militates further against private use. There is no reason for foreign languages to be used privately. The devotional use of tongues is also in outright opposition to the stated purpose for tongues in 1 Corinthians 14:22 ("a sign to unbelievers"). The devotional use of tongues is not found in the Bible, and the concept is contrary to basic Christian truths.

Tongues for Ministry to Unbelievers

The entire context of 1 Corinthians 14 is against tongues as a gift designed by God for use in the assembly.[21] The practice of speaking in tongues is restricted in almost every verse. This tone of suppression was so strong that Paul felt the need to warn the Corinthians not to prohibit tongues altogether. Paul had no desire to speak in tongues in the assembly (1 Cor. 14:19). Tongues were not intended to edify the assembly. Paul merely allowed them to be so used with certain restrictions such as the need that an interpreter be present, that one person speak at a time, and that no women were to speak. This is so clear that many have argued that since tongues are not really for use in the assembly, they must be intended for personal, private use. This, however, ignores the large arena consisting of public use outside the assembly.

Tongues Intended for One Purpose

There is no basis upon which to see a difference in the nature or kind of tongues referred to in Acts and Corinthians. There are many, however, who see the basic sameness in the nature of tongues but argue for a distinction in purpose and operation.[22] This distinction is standard in Pentecostal circles.[23] The "Statement of Fundamental Truths" of the Assemblies of God" refers to "the initial physical sign of speaking with other tongues (Acts 2:4)" and concludes that it is "the same in essence as the gift of tongues (1 Cor. 12:4–10, 28), but different in purpose and use."[24] Brumback, in a work which is "perhaps the best apology for the Pentecostal distinctives,"[25] feels that this distinction is "perhaps the decisive point in the entire controversy."[26] This "standard" Pentecostal view does not argue so much for a difference in the nature of tongues in Acts and Corinthians as it does for a difference in purpose. The tongues in 1 Corinthians are stated to be the gift of tongues given for public and personal edification, but the tongues in Acts (esp. Acts 2:4–11) are a sign. This sign is that one has received the so-called baptism of the Spirit.

A study of the passages, however, makes it very clear that this distinction cannot be upheld. Not only are all the tongues in the New Testament the same in nature (languages), but they are also given for the same purpose. The concept that the tongues in Acts are a sign but that the tongues in Corinthians refer to the gift is contrary to the explicit statement of 1 Corinthians 14:22 where the tongues in Corinth are specifically said to be for a sign to unbelievers. Tongues are called a sign *(semeion)* in both Mark 16:17, 20 and 1 Corinthians 14:22. They function as a sign in Acts 2:4–11, 10:44–46 (see 11:15–18), and 19:6. Although the "gift of the Holy Spirit" probably refers to the Spirit himself, the fact that this is closely connected in Acts 2:38 and 10:45–46 (see 11:17) with the tongues emphasizes that the tongues in these passages are in fact a gift. The speakers in no way earned, looked for, or expected to speak in tongues since in each case it is clear that they had never even heard of such a phenomenon. Although the term *charisma*, "gifts," is used five times in 1 Corinthians 12, it is never specifically referred to tongues. Three times it refers directly to "gifts of healings," and in the other two passages (12:4, 31) it is a general term. Therefore, there is no more stress in 1 Corinthians on the fact that tongues are a gift than there is in Mark or Acts. To state that the tongues in Acts are a sign in contrast to those in 1 Corinthians not only is without basis but is contrary to the express statement that the tongues in Corinthians are given by God in order to be a sign (1 Cor. 14:22).

We have seen that the tongues speaking in Acts and Corinthians refers to the same phenomenon, that is, speaking in previously unlearned foreign languages. The same terms are used and no difference is implied. The artificial distinction that the tongues in Acts are a sign and those in Corinth refer to the gift is seen to be an erroneous distinction. Those in Corinth are stated to be a sign. They are all gifts of the Holy Spirit; those in Corinth are no more emphasized as gifts than those in Acts. One other aspect should be noted. The tongues in Corinthians are stated to be for use other than in the assembly. Those in Mark are also for use outside the assembly. This agrees with all three (the only three) historical instances described in Acts (2:4–11, 10:44–46, 19:6). All three instances occurred outside the assembly. There is complete agreement in all passages, with no conflict. There is no distinction in purpose and operation; rather, tongues were given by God for one purpose.

Tongues as a Sign to Unbelievers

The purpose for the other gifts is readily apparent and usually, if not always, revealed in the name. The gift of tongues is actually no exception to this. The word "tongue," *glossa*, normally means language. If we recognize that this gift is the gift of languages, then the purpose is obvious. It is the miraculous ability to speak to foreigners in their own language.[27] This view alone is supported by direct statements of Scripture. It alone has no problems. And yet it has been opposed most consistently by those who do not accept the testimony of the Bible. They offer no evidence but merely scoff at such a position. This is due to the fact that such a gift requires a miracle. However, speaking unintelligibly requires no miracle and in fact is a common occurrence apart from Christianity.

No purpose consistent with the New Testament is apparent for ecstatic unintelligible speech. Neither is any biblically oriented purpose obvious for angelic or heavenly language. There is no purpose for devotional tongues, no matter what their nature might be, which cannot be better fulfilled by some other gift or the Word of God. Therefore, it is logical to doubt that any of these assumed purposes are correct. Since tongues are languages, we would logically expect the gift of tongues to have a purpose which requires the ability to speak foreign languages. This fact must be consistent with any conclusion as to the purpose of tongues.

Another fact which must be consistent with the purpose for tongues is that God gave tongues to be used outside the assembly; they are not for use in church. Prophecy is always valid in the assembly and is in fact designed for it. By contrast, tongues by themselves are not valid for the assembly. Another gift, that of interpretation, is also needed before tongues can be used. First Corinthians 14 shows that the two gifts do not always go together;

therefore, tongues must be designed for a purpose where they can also function alone. This, however, is not in the assembly. In 1 Corinthians 14:18–19 Paul makes a direct statement that tongues are not for use in the assembly. The expression "in the assembly I would rather speak five words with my understanding, . . . than ten thousand words in a tongue" is equivalent to "not at all." This may be seen in a similar expression: "I would rather have five dogs than ten thousand cats." The speaker means that he has no desire at all for cats. Paul says that he used tongues often, but he also adds that he did not at all desire to speak in tongues in the assembly. There is only one solution: Paul spoke somewhere outside the assembly. Tongues are not for use in the assembly of believers. This is why Paul discourages this use and restricts it so greatly.

First Corinthians 14:22, the only verse which specifically states the purpose for tongues, says "Wherefore tongues are for a sign, not for those who believe, but to the unbelievers: but prophesying is not to the unbelievers, but to those who believe." This comes immediately after an exhortation not to be children in thinking, but to be mature. In effect the passage says, "Stop being childish; be mature. Tongues are not for believers (in the assembly), but are a sign to unbelievers." Using tongues among believers is childish. This purpose, as a sign to unbelievers, fits perfectly with use outside the assembly. It necessarily must be outside the assembly.

However, the same expression "sign to unbelievers" makes it impossible to regard the purpose of tongues as devotional or for private prayer and praise to God. The following verse (14:23) does not conflict with this view. The unbeliever does not accept the tongues speaking as a sign in the Corinthian type of situation because he enters an assembly where all speak in tongues, and obviously no one understands. This appears to be madness. But when properly used, as at Pentecost, tongues are a sign to unbelievers.

Tongues a Sign Not Only to Unbelieving Jews

Some have agreed that tongues are intended as a sign to unbelievers, but they have restricted this only to unbelieving Jews.[28] Dillow regards it as a sign of judgment on Israel.[29] This opinion is based on Paul's citation of Isaiah 28:11 in 1 Corinthians 14:21, from which Paul draws the conclusion (14:22) that tongues are a "sign to unbelievers." The major arguments for restricting this sign to Jews are that the quotation (Isa. 28:11) states that the tongues which Isaiah referred to shall be a sign to this people and that Jews were present during each of the instances of tongues speaking described in Acts. This second argument, however, is without any weight, since there is no incident at all in the book of Acts where Jews are not present. Acts describes the establishing of the church, which began at Jerusalem and was spread by the Jewish Christians to the rest of the world. Since Acts describes this ministry, no point can be made of the fact that Jews were present. It would be strange if no Jews were present in Jerusalem on the day of Pentecost (Acts 2:4–11), on the first outreach to Gentiles (10:46), or in outreach to those who had previously received John the Baptist's baptism (19:3–6). Neither does the first point establish that the New Testament gift of tongues is a sign to unbelieving Jews. Isaiah 28:11 states, "For with stammering lips and another tongue will he speak to this people." This quotation is generally regarded as a prophecy of the Assyrian invasion. The prophecy is to Israel concerning judgment due to their unbelief. Paul draws the conclusion from this that tongues are a sign to unbelievers (1 Cor. 14:22). Paul does not state that the gift of tongues is a fulfillment of this prophecy. Few would say that the gift of tongues is prophesied in Isaiah 28:11. But if it is not a fulfillment of this prophecy, then Paul is using the quotation to draw a principle and not to state that the details are fulfilled. Therefore "this people" and the aspect of judgment may or may not be included in the principle. Apparently they are not since Paul concludes only that tongues are a sign to unbelievers and says nothing regarding Jews or judgment. Since Paul is writing to a largely Gentile church regarding a New Testament gift, he would certainly explain if his statement concerned only Jews.

The view that tongues are a sign of judgment to unbelieving Israel is also inconsistent with the other gifts. Mark 16:17–20 regards tongues as a sign to confirm the gospel; they so functioned in Acts 2:4–11. The reaction in Acts 2:4–11 is, What does it mean? This agrees with the other gifts and with 1 Corinthians 14:22. None of the other gifts, however, are a sign of judgment or only for Jews. The other gifts are all for the benefit of those to whom they minister. The other gifts are related primarily to the church. If tongues are a sign of judgment to unbelieving Israel, they are not related directly to the church. It is not only safer but preferable to agree with Paul that the principle of God's action in Isaiah 28:11 reveals that tongues are a sign to *unbelievers* and not to read in "Jews." If such a procedure were followed consistently, then

Paul's statement in 1 Corinthians 9:14, "Even so hath the Lord ordained that they which preach the gospel should live of the gospel," applies only to Jewish preachers since the argument is based on statements made to Israel. This thinking would also restrict the warning examples of 1 Corinthians 10:1–12 and the warning proper of 1 Corinthians 10:12 to Jews. However, Paul states that they are *our* examples (10:11).

In the Gospels Jesus stated (Matt. 12:39; 16:4; Mark 8:12) that no sign would be given to Israel ("this generation") except the resurrection. As late as the time of the Epistle to the Corinthians, it is implied that although the Jews "seek a sign" (1 Cor. 1:22–23) they received none. Statements such as these seem to be against the idea that the Jews received a special sign during the apostolic age, a sign consisting of speaking in tongues.

Tongues Not a Sign of a Postconversion Baptism of the Spirit

Pentecostals not only make a distinction in purpose between the tongues in Acts and those in Corinthians, but they also consider tongues as the initial evidence of a baptism of the Spirit which occurs after conversion. This evidence shows that the individual has received "the baptism." This is the "distinct" Pentecostal doctrine.[30] Brumback feels that this distinction in purpose and the issue of tongues as evidence of Spirit baptism are "perhaps the decisive point of the entire controversy."[31] He admits that if the distinction cannot be maintained, "then the Pentecostal theology on the evidence teaching suffers a severe blow."[32] We have already discussed this distinction in purpose and have shown that there is no basis in the Bible for such a distinction in purpose. Tongues are one in nature and in purpose. There are also many reasons to reject the idea that tongues are a sign of postconversion Spirit baptism.[33]

One primary reason to reject such a concept is that the purpose of tongues is specifically stated in 1 Corinthians 14:22 as a sign to unbelievers. This does not agree with the doctrine that they are a sign proving that a believer has received the "second blessing." There is no statement in the Bible to the effect that tongues are the initial evidence of such an event. Therefore, we have a stated purpose for tongues that disagrees with the "evidence" teaching, but no statement that the purpose is evidence of "the baptism."

When the passages mentioning tongues are studied, we find the following. Mark 16:17–20 refers to tongues as a sign to be used for evangelistic ministry to unbelievers. Acts 2:4–11 is a specific instance where tongues functioned as a sign to the unbelieving onlookers. Peter nowhere states on that occasion that this is the proof for a postconversion Spirit baptism. The next instance of tongues speaking occurred in Cornelius's house (Acts 10:46). There is no mention of any postconversion baptism of the Spirit in this passage. The Bible says in clear terms that this is the reception of the Spirit that occurs at salvation. Peter was preaching the basic evangelistic message about Jesus Christ when the event occurred. Cornelius had not heard of Jesus before, and therefore he was not a Christian. In addition the Holy Spirit came upon all who heard the Word, not upon Cornelius only. There is no suggestion that the others were believers prior to this. The issue is clearly stated in Acts 11:14–18, where Peter explains the ministry he had to those in Cornelius's house (10:1–48), beginning with a report of the statement that an angel made to Cornelius that Peter "shall tell thee words, whereby thou and all thy house shall be saved" (11:14). The angel said that Peter would tell Cornelius and his house how to be saved. Peter then states,

> And as I began to speak, the Holy Ghost fell on them, as on us at the beginning. Then remembered I the word of the Lord, how that he said, John indeed baptized with water; but ye shall be baptized with the Holy Ghost. Forasmuch then as God gave them the like gift as he did unto us, who believed on the Lord Jesus Christ; what was I, that I could withstand God? (Acts 11:15–17)

Peter states that the Spirit fell on Cornelius's household as on the apostles and others in Jerusalem at the beginning. He refers to the beginning, that is, Pentecost. Since he overlooks the events in between, such as the conversion of the Samaritans (Acts 8:5–25), it seems clear that tongues had not occurred since Pentecost. If they had, this would have been additional and ideal evidence to vindicate Peter's ministry to the Gentiles, a ministry for which he was on trial. It would have helped immensely if Peter could have said it happened to them as it always has at Pentecost and Samaria. It is implied, therefore, that this had not happened since Pentecost. No instance is recorded. Peter's audience, consisting of apostles and brethren in Judaea (Acts 11:1), understood the event to be salvation. They replied, "Then hath God also to the Gentiles granted repentance unto life" (11:18). This could not be stated more clearly. It concerned "repentance unto life."

Acts 19:1–6 is the final event in Acts referring to speaking in tongues. The individuals concerned had never heard of Jesus Christ nor of the Holy Spirit. They had received only John's baptism (v. 3).[34] Paul then told them of Jesus Christ, and they heard (believed) and were baptized. When Paul immediately placed his hands on them, they spoke in tongues. Prior to this they had not heard of the Spirit nor of Christ, so obviously they had not believed in the gospel nor had they received any of the Spirit. This is conversion, not a postconversion baptism of the Spirit.

The final passage mentioning tongues is 1 Corinthians 12–14. There is nothing that even remotely resembles a teaching or incident of postconversion baptism of the Spirit. Tongues as evidence of Spirit baptism can meet none of the basic aspects, such as the fact that gifts are for ministry, which are true of all gifts.

A final blow is the realization that tongues as a sign that a believer has received a postconversion baptism of the Spirit would be especially appropriate in the assembly. Therefore, the arguments of 1 Corinthians 14 could not apply. It would be as acceptable as prophecy. There would be no need for an interpreter. Why would it be restricted to one at a time or to three at the most? Why couldn't women speak if it were evidence of "the baptism"? If it were evidence of "the baptism," why did Paul speak more than they all? Why continue speaking once the evidence was given? The Pentecostal doctrine must of necessity make a distinction in tongues or else all of these questions show the falsity of the claim that tongues demonstrate a postconversion baptism of the Spirit. Yet we have seen that no such distinction exists. Tongues are not evidence for an alleged postconversion baptism of the Spirit.

Conclusion on the Intended Purpose of Tongues

It is certain that tongues are foreign languages, are a sign to unbelievers, and are for use outside the assembly. These principles do not fit devotional tongues, ecstatic tongues, tongues as the sign of an alleged Spirit baptism, or tongues exercised in a church meeting. There are two other facts to be mentioned. All gifts are to be used in order to minister to others. This has been demonstrated previously. Secondly, the gift of interpretation means that God intended for there to be communication with others, for understanding to occur. All of these principles add up to one clear purpose which is completely biblical in perspective and also logical. Tongues are the miraculous ability to speak foreign languages in order to be a sign to unbelievers and thus gain a hearing for the gospel. They may be used to communicate the gospel itself although that is not expressly delineated. Whether they are used to communicate the gospel itself or whether they are used only to attract attention to the messengers is inconsequential. Their purpose in either case is evangelistic. They are evangelistic, and they function in the same way as the gifts of miracles and healing which were demonstrated earlier to be signs to unbelievers and not for the benefit of believers. This purpose fits all the principles for spiritual gifts, supplies a simple, straightforward purpose which is positively in line with God's purposes, and fits all of the specific statements regarding the gift of tongues. It does not agree with any of the present-day uses for alleged tongues.

This is the only view in which the gift of interpretation appears to have its proper sphere. If tongues are for private devotional use, then the gift of interpretation becomes extraneous. If tongues are ecstatic unintelligible utterance, then of necessity an interpreter is needed, but the question arises, Why did God give a gift of unintelligible speech, a second gift of making the utterance intelligible, and when these two gifts of necessity are used together they accomplish no more than one person speaking so he can be understood? Why two gifts to accomplish no more than one? It is hard to believe that God gives one man the gift of unintelligible utterance and another man the gift of making it sensible. Some may object that this applies to foreign language as well, but this is not true. Mere unintelligible utterance serves no purpose of any kind unless interpreted. However, the ability to speak foreign language to unbelievers who speak that language provides a valid purpose for both the gift of tongues and the gift of interpretation individually. One may speak a foreign language to those who speak the language, and no interpreter is needed. The hearers are the interpreters, as on the day of Pentecost. Therefore, the gift of tongues may be useful and stand independently. The gift of interpretation can also function apart from the gift of tongues since the interpreter can interpret languages spoken by those who normally speak them.

The purpose for tongues that has just been set forth explains why only some have this gift. It is not primarily for the individual; therefore, it is similar to all other gifts, and only those intended by God to minister with tongues have it. The other purposes commonly alleged for tongues are primarily for the benefit of the speaker; therefore, the question arises, "Why do only a few have this extra benefit?" This problem disappears with the above solution. God gave a useful gift which functioned in a similar way to the other gifts (for ministry to others) and which was clearly miraculous and honoring to Him.

Tongues and Spiritual Vitality

The proponents of today's tongues often assert that the experience and the results connected with it are bringing a revival of spiritual vitality to the church. We are then faced with the question, Does the biblical gift of tongues produce spiritual vitality in a church or individual? The answer is clear and easy to find. First Corinthians shows that the genuine gift of tongues will not in itself increase the spiritual vitality of a church or an individual. The Corinthian church, which was the only church in the New Testament specifically stated to have engaged in tongues speaking, was the most carnal church in the New Testament. Paul told them they were carnal and not spiritual (1 Cor. 3:1–3). They were divided, condoned gross immorality, lacked love, dragged each other before heathen judges, had disorderly services, had doctrinal problems, misunderstood spiritual gifts (including both their purpose and use), and were making a drunken party out of the Lord's table. Their improper emphasis on tongues possibly led to some of these problems. Paul was interested in the spiritual vitality of the churches, but he said specifically that he would much rather speak in church in a language he could understand than in tongues. If tongues add to a church's vitality, why did Paul prefer not to use them in the church? When Paul mentioned the gifts which edify and build the church spiritually (Eph. 4:11), why didn't he include tongues?

Not only is it clear from the example of the Corinthian church that tongues will not increase the spiritual vitality of the church or the individual, but it is also clear from the purpose for which tongues were given. A gift given as a sign to unbelievers is not designed to build up believers. Gifts such as prophet and teacher are for this purpose. The Corinthians, however, were emphasizing a gift intended to be a sign to unbelievers rather than the edifying gifts, such as prophet and teacher.

The Priority of the Gift of Tongues

More is said in the New Testament regarding the priority of the gift of tongues than that of any other gift.[35] This is due to the misplaced emphasis upon this gift by the Corinthian church. Although many contend that tongues are a gift of high priority and a necessary evidence of Spirit baptism, the New Testament teaches otherwise.[36] There is very little emphasis given to tongues in the New Testament. Only a few cases of tongues speaking are described in the book of Acts although Acts covers a span of many years. Each of the cases described (Acts 2, 10, 19) is a special occasion, and the tongues speaking is only incidental to the purpose for describing the occasion. Paul states that he spoke in tongues "more than you all" (1 Cor. 14:18), but this is the only evidence that we have concerning tongues in Paul's life. So little emphasis is placed on it that, although Paul presumably spoke in tongues frequently, no occasion is described. Apparently it was not considered to be significant. Paul only mentions tongues in one passage, 1 Corinthians 12–14, and that discussion is to deemphasize them. This is the only mention of tongues in the Epistles, and it restricts tongues. No passage states that any church other than the Corinthian church practiced tongues speaking in New Testament times. Three out of the four passages in the Epistles dealing with spiritual gifts (Rom. 12:4–8; Eph. 4:11; 1 Pet. 4:10–11) do not even mention tongues. There is no encouragement anywhere in the New Testament for a believer to speak in tongues; instead, they are discouraged in 1 Corinthians.[37] Although believers are exhorted concerning many aspects of the spiritual life, they are never exhorted to seek or speak in tongues.

Tongues was only one of many gifts given to the church and was not given to all believers. In 1 Corinthians 12:29–30 Paul asks rhetorically, "Are all apostles? Are all prophets? Are all teachers? Are all workers of miracles? Do all have the gifts of healing? Do all speak in tongues? Do all interpret?" The answer to each one of these questions is No![38] Paul explains that all gifts are necessary, and that the gifts are varied among the believers in order that the whole body of Christ may function properly (1 Cor. 12:4–31). Genuine tongues speakers were only a small portion of the believers.

First Corinthians 12:28 gives a specific statement concerning the priority of tongues: "God has set some in the church, first apostles, secondly prophets, thirdly teachers, then miracles, then gifts of healings, helps, governments, kinds of tongues."

The order expressed in the terms "first," "second," and "third" is not one of time since the gifts were not given in this order of time. Tongues were given at the beginning, on the day of Pentecost, and yet are below many gifts in this list. In the New Testament, "apostle" is the gift of highest priority, and "prophet" is second. Therefore, the order expressed in this verse is one of priority. In order of priority, apostles come first, then prophets, then teachers. (Paul does not include every gift. "Evangelist" is one of the gifts that is not included; however, he includes enough to convey his point that tongues are low in priority relative to the other spiritual gifts.) Note that the gift of governments, which of necessity involves some function of prominence, is lower in priority than the spiritually edifying gifts. Tongues is the lowest gift in this list, below miracles, helps, and governments. It is grammatically possible that all of those in the latter part of the list are somewhat on a par and are referred to as a group since the numerical designations "first," "second," "third," and the term "then" or "next" *(epeita)* are not continued. Tongues, healings, and miracles are all lower in priority than teaching.

This aspect of the low priority of tongues is the background for the entire discussion in 1 Corinthians 12 and 14. After referring to the high priority of gifts such as apostle, prophet, and teacher, and then the relatively low priority of miracles, healings, and especially tongues (and stating that none of these gifts are possessed by every believer), Paul states in the next verse (12:31), "But be zealous for the greater gifts." There can be no doubt in the context that Paul means to be zealous for the higher priority gifts, specifically in contrast to the gift of tongues.[39] In 1 Corinthians 14:12 he again specifically refers to the desirability of the gift of prophecy in contrast to the gift of tongues. This emphasis on the higher priority of prophecy over tongues continues throughout the chapter. At the end of the chapter he says, "Be zealous for prohesying." He has so clearly set forth the low priority of tongues and the completely useless nature of this gift when no one understands what is said that he realizes the obvious response by the Corinthians would be to rule out tongues altogether. Therefore, in contrast to urging the Corinthians to have zeal for prophecy, he merely states, "Do not forbid tongues" (14:39).

The New Testament states that Christians should emphasize the gifts that are of higher priority and that edify. When misunderstood, tongues are of no value and as a gift are of relatively low priority.[40] Paul wrote to correct the Corinthians because of their misplaced emphasis on the gift of tongues. In 1 Corinthians 12 he refutes the idea, which they apparently held, that the gift of tongues is to be emphasized and that all should desire it. It can be stated with complete certainty that any individual, group, or church that emphasizes tongues is in error on this point. Even if today's tongues were genuine gifts of the Holy Spirit, such an emphasis is wrong. Any individual, group, or church that claims that all believers should seek tongues and speak in tongues is making a claim contrary to Scripture.

Seeking the Gift of Tongues

The idea of seeking certain spiritual gifts has been discussed in detail. It was shown that God gives the gifts according to his own will, and that there is no proof in the Bible that anyone ever obtained a gift by seeking it. Furthermore, it was shown that the passages often used to prove that one should seek gifts do not teach such an idea. This section will briefly discuss the idea of seeking the gift of tongues, since this concept is so prevalent today.

There are only three passages which describe incidents of tongues speaking. These are Acts 2:4–11; 10:46; and 19:6. In each of these instances the tongues speaking is the initial instance for the speakers involved. Not one of the verses suggests that any of the speakers sought the gift of tongues. On the contrary, they did not seek to speak in tongues. Those who spoke in tongues on the day of Pentecost had never heard of this gift and had no idea that it was coming upon them or that it was a gift for the church. How could they, therefore, seek it? Even in the unlikely event that Cornelius and his household (Acts 10:46) had heard of the events at Pentecost, they had no concept of gifts to the church; they certainly had no reason to be informed sufficiently to expect to receive the gift of tongues when they had not even heard the gospel.

Peter and the believing Jews who were with him definitely did not expect these Gentiles to speak in tongues since they were amazed when it happened (Acts 10:45). The Jews were not only amazed at this but were surprised that Gentiles could be saved at all. Therefore, to postulate that these Gentiles were seeking to speak in tongues is contrary to the evidence. Since they were converted at this time, such a theory also requires that they be seeking the gift of tongues before they heard the gospel and before salvation. It is also clear that those who spoke in tongues in Acts 19:6 were not aware that the gift existed, nor did they seek it. Paul asked them if they had received the Holy Spirit. They answered, "We have not heard if there is a Holy Spirit," or, as it is usually interpreted, "We did not hear if the Holy Spirit was given" (Acts 19:2). It is certain that they had not heard of Pentecost, of the reception of the Holy Spirit by believers, or of spiritual gifts from the Holy Spirit. As is stated in verse 4, they had not even heard of Jesus Christ. Who will assert contrary to all this evidence that these were seeking the gift of tongues? These three instances are the *only* biblical descriptions of receiving this gift and of exercising it. The only information we have reveals that this gift did not come by seeking it or by believing that it was available, nor by any knowledge of or attitude toward spiritual gifts. They received the gift purely according to God's will.

This should make it clear that the gift of tongues, if given today, would come upon genuine believers of every persuasion. It would not come just on those who believe in tongues or upon only those in Pentecostal groups. It would come upon believers even though they did not seek or even desire it.[41] The Pentecostal explanation for the absence of tongues throughout church history is that men did not have faith in the gifts or believe in the gift of tongues, and therefore they did not receive it. This does not agree with the biblical accounts and is merely an attempt to explain away what is an all-but-impossible obstacle to the view that genuine tongues are given today, that is, if tongues did not cease, why were there seventeen hundred or more years with no plausible claims?

The Bible contains no exhortation to seek or desire the gift of tongues. On the contrary, it includes specific statements that believers should emphasize and have a zeal for gifts other than the gift of tongues (1 Cor. 12:31; 14:1, 39). Even if one seeks certain spiritual gifts, despite all the proof that gifts do not come by seeking, it is clear that one should not seek tongues.

Restrictions on the Use of Tongues

If tongues are designed to be a miraculous ability to speak languages as a sign to unbelievers, then any private use of tongues or speaking in the assembly is not the best use. Although tongues were allowed in the assembly in Corinth, apparently no one in the first century ever imagined such a thing as devotional tongues. Use of the gift of tongues in the assembly is discouraged, but it may be used with certain restrictions. The first restriction is based on the general theme of 1 Corinthians 14, "Let all things be done unto edifying" (14:26). The first restriction is that no one may speak in tongues at any time in the assembly unless an interpreter is present (14:28). Another restriction is that only a limited number are to speak, and then they may speak only one at a time. Two, perhaps three, are permitted to speak, one by one. A third restriction states that women are not to speak in the assembly (14:34–35). At the least this restriction includes speaking in tongues. Finally, all of the assembly are to behave in an orderly manner (14:33, 40). These restrictions, it must be remembered, apply to the genuine gift of tongues.

Summary of the Biblical Teaching on the Gift of Tongues

The gift of tongues is the ability to miraculously speak foreign language. The translation "language" is the most natural interpretation of the word *glossa* in the passages concerning the gift of tongues. This is supported by the fact that Acts 2:4–11, the only description of tongues speaking in the Bible, explicitly states that real human language was spoken. First Corinthians 13:1 shows that the tongues or languages of men are what is involved in the gift of tongues in 1 Corinthians also. Since the conclusion of 1 Corinthians 14:21–22 regarding the gift of tongues is based on an Old Testament reference to foreign invaders, this passage definitely implies that normal human languages are what is meant by "tongues" in this passage. There is no proof that *glossa* can mean ecstatic speech, nor is there any evidence that it was used this way. Until recent times, the church has always considered this gift to be the ability to speak foreign languages.

The New Testament gives no intimation that the gift of tongues was "ecstatic" in the normal sense of the term. The speaker was in control of the gift and was able to stop it. The tongues speaking was no more under the Spirit's control than were other spiritual gifts, such as prophecy. Therefore, there is no basis to assume an ecstatic state, nor any accompanying physical phenomena, such as jerking, convulsions, foaming at the mouth, shouting, abnormal voice tone or pitch, or unusual rate of speech.

Tongues are specifically stated to be designed as a sign to unbelievers (1 Cor. 14:22). Such a purpose does not fit devotional or angel language. There is no apparent purpose for ecstatic or angel tongues. The ability to miraculously speak foreign language has a definite purpose that is in agreement with the purpose for all spiritual gifts and is in harmony with the New Testament. Tongues are foreign languages used to gain a hearing for the gospel message. This allows for the normal use of *glossa* as foreign language and for the statement that tongues are a sign to unbelievers. It allows for Paul's statement that tongues are not designed to be used in church. It is also in harmony with the needs of the church, especially at the beginning.

It is also certain that the gift of tongues is of low priority. Teaching and other gifts are to be preferred. According to 1 Corinthians 12–14 there should be no emphasis on the gift of tongues. Although the passages often cited do not imply that anyone should seek any gift, if someone desires a specific gift, it should be something other than tongues. There is no statement in the Bible about private or devotional use of the gift of tongues. Such a use is contrary to the purpose for spiritual gifts since it is purely for the benefit of the speaker. This cannot be exercised in love. Such a use raises the question, Why are some benefited in their devotional life and others not? Why does anyone need such a gift since Romans 8:26 declares that all believers have the Holy Spirit's help in prayer? The belief in devotional tongues is an implicit denial of the sufficiency of justification in Christ and implicit advocacy of the view that some additional step is necessary for perfect communion with God. The provision by God of the gift of interpretation of tongues also shows that tongues were not meant for private use. Tongues, whether personal or public, do not add to spiritual vitality, as is evident from the Corinthian church. They are like all other gifts; that is, they were given for ministry to others.

* * *

1. Walter J. Hollenweger, *The Pentecostals* (London: SCM, 1972), 342–43. Many procharismatics espouse these claims; see Josephine Massyngberde Ford, "The Charismatic Gifts in Worship," in *The Charismatic Movement*, ed. Michael Hamilton (Grand Rapids: Eerdmans, 1975), 115–16.
2. See John 3:16; Gal. 5:13; Phil. 2:1–8; and numerous other passages. See also Ethelbert Stauffer, "Agapao," in *Theological Dictionary of the New Testament*, ed. Gerhard Kittel, Gerhard Friedrich, and Geoffrey W. Bromiley, trans. Geoffrey W. Bromiley (Grand Rapids: Eerdmans, 1964-1976), 1:49–55.
3. Archibald Robertson and Alfred Plummer note that this is "specially in reference to its manifestation to men" (*A Critical and Exegetical Commentary on the First Epistle of St. Paul to the Corinthians*, ICC, 2d ed. [Edinburgh: T. & T. Clark, 1914], 285). However, they ignore the context and vv. 4–7 when they fail to realize that love in this passage refers solely to love toward people.
4. F. L. Godet, *The First Epistle to the Corinthians* 2 vols. (Grand Rapids: Zondervan, 1971), 2:235, 240.
5. If tongues or the other gifts are exercised in love, they do profit the user in that there is future profit in the sense of rewards due to any

service for Christ. However, this is not profit in the sense that the gift is used to minister to or edify oneself.
6. Wayne A. Grudem tries to build an argument that prophecy is a sign to believers and in the process states that 1 Cor. 14:22 is not a purpose construction (*The Gift of Prophecy in the New Testament and Today* [Westchester, Ill.: Crossway, 1988], 174–77). However, this construction is commonly a purpose construction and this sense fits perfectly in this passage. Grudem's problem is that he has failed to consider that both the prophesying and the tongues described in this verse are spoken to an assembly of believers. The fact that an unbeliever comes into the assembly does not change this. The prophecy is addressed to believers, and since it is understandable, the unbeliever understands what is said to the believers. Thus, Grudem's reason for interpreting the verse as he does is invalid.
7. Howard M. Ervin, *These Are Not Drunken, As Ye Suppose* (Plainfield, N.J.: Logos, 1968), 107.
8. Carl Brumback, *What Meaneth This?* (Springfield, Mo.: Gospel Publishing House, 1947), 291–98. He argues that tongues are for praise, and he states that they were used for praise to God at Pentecost before the crowd gathered (pp. 35ff.). This is contrary to the passage which says that the crowd was present and heard the speaking in tongues. See also Earl P. Paulk, *Your Pentecostal Neighbor* (Cleveland, Tenn.: Pathway, 1958), 67; Hollenweger, *Pentecostals*, 342–43; Ford, "Gifts," 115.
9. Along with v. 2, vv. 3–4 contain arguments explaining why Paul made the statement in v. 1 that prophecy is to be preferred over tongues.
10. William F. Arndt and F. Wilbur Gingrich, *A Greek-English Lexicon of the New Testament* (Chicago: University of Chicago Press, 1947), 560–61.
11. The word for *mind* may mean "mind" or "the capacity to understand." Note that the mind is unfruitful. The verse does not say that the speaking or communication is unfruitful. Therefore, the mind of the speaker himself is unfruitful; that is, there is no understanding or edification. Some have interpreted the expression *my mind is unfruitful* to mean "my mind does not produce fruit in others," that is, the speaker does not communicate to others. This view requires a certain amount of understanding on the part of the speaker which, however, he cannot communicate to others. However, vv. 15 and 19 show that the mind (*nous*) is not involved at all when someone speaks in tongues. The statement "my mind is unfruitful" is equivalent to the expression "apart from my mind" in the following verses. The mind, since it is not involved, produces no fruit in the speaker; therefore, he cannot communicate to others. The reason the speaker cannot communicate

the message is because there is no understanding or else he could communicate that which he understood. Even if the position is held that "my mind is unfruitful" refers to a lack of communicating to others, it is only because there is no understanding on the part of the speaker. In either view the speaker does not understand. "Unfruitful," however, clearly means "apart from my mind." Therefore, there is no edification of self and so none of others.

12. If the speaker is edified apart from his own understanding, the obvious question arises, "If he is spiritually stimulated by hearing himself utter sounds which he does not understand, why cannot others be spiritually stimulated by hearing the same sounds?" (James D. Bales, *Pat Boone and the Gift of Tongues* [Searcy, Ark., 1970], 109–10). The hearer is not spiritually stimulated, nor can the speaker be in any profitable way.

13. Robertson and Plummer state that the speaker "built up himself," but they do not say how this is done or what it means (*First Corinthians*, 367). None of the numerous uses of *oikodomeo* in the Septuagint parallel this concept. See Hatch and Redpath, *Concordance*, 970–72. *Oikodomeo* does not appear to be used in the sense of personal edification in the Septuagint. See also Otto Michel, "Oikodomeo," *TDNT*, 5:137–38. *The Exhaustive Concordance of the Bible*, by James Strong, shows that the English translators did not translate any Old Testament verb by the word "edify." Eph. 4:16 does not use the verb but the noun "edification." The body of Christ as a group is self-edified by the ministry of the members to each other.

14. F. L. Godet, *First Corinthians*, 2:268.

15. The word *battalogeo* does not occur in the Septuagint and occurs only in this passage in the New Testament. Arndt and Gingrich define it as "babble, to speak without thinking" (*Lexicon*, 137). Moulton and Milligan see a connection between *battalogeo*, *battogeo*, and *battalos*, the nickname of Demosthenes who was so called "because of the torrent of words at his command, which made envious rivals call him "the gabbler" (*Vocabulary*, 107). Liddell and Scott refer to similar words, all meaning to stammer, and define *battologeo* as "speak stammeringly, say the same thing over and over" (*Lexicon*, 311). Beare feels that Jesus' meaning in this passage is that the disciples are not to "babble meaningless sounds" ("Speaking with Tongues," *Journal of Biblical Literature* 83 [September 1964]: 229). Delling agrees that it means "babble" in this verse ("Battalogeo," *TDNT*, 1:597). Lampe defines the term as it was used shortly after New Testament times (*Patristic Greek Lexicon*, 294). One example is clearly speech apart from understanding (Damasus *Trophaea* 2.4.4., which states, "*me epistamenos alla battologeon*, not understanding,

but babbling"). Another example from an early church father refers to unintelligible utterance (Gregory Nyssa).
16. Arndt and Gingrich, *Lexicon*, 34.
17. Liddell and Scott, *Lexicon*, 60.
18. C. E. B. Cranfield, *The Epistle to the Romans*, ICC, 2 vols. (Edinburgh: T. & T. Clark, 1975-1979), 1:423-24.
19. Ibid.
20. Nor is there any reason why angel languages would cease. This is further implication that tongues are not heavenly or angelic language.
21. Carl Brumback, *What Meaneth This?*, pp. 299ff. Brumback believes that the purpose of tongues is twofold: "individual and collective edification" (*What Meaneth This?* 265)
22. Ibid., 261-72.
23. See Hollenweger, *The Pentecostals*, 342; Erling Jorstad, *The Holy Spirit in Today's Church* (New York: Abingdon, 1973), 81; Nichol, *Pentecostalism*, 12-13.
24. Article 8, "The Evidence of the Baptism in the Holy Ghost," as recorded in the Appendix to William W. Menzies, *Anointed to Serve* (Springfield, Mo.: Gospel Publishing House, 1971), 388. Menzies is the "historian par excellence in the Assemblies of God," according to David Faupel in his *The American Pentecostal Movement* (Wilmore, Ky.: Asbury Seminary, 1972), 22.
25. Faupel, 33.
26. Brumback, *What Meaneth This?* 261-62. Frederick Dale Bruner states that this is the unique doctrine for Pentecostalism (*A Theology of the Holy Spirit* [Grand Rapids: Eerdmans, 1970], 76-77).
27. The other proposed uses for tongues depend largely on the opinion that tongues are ecstatic utterance. Once it is realized that tongues are languages, the purpose is self-evident. The evidence could hardly be stronger or stated more explicitly, and the nature of tongues fits this view alone.
28. See, e.g., Joseph Dillow, *Speaking in Tongues* (Grand Rapids: Zondervan, 1975), 26-27. Dillow's entire discussion is based on this concept and falls with it (see pp. 95-107). See also B. F. Cate, *The Nine Gifts of the Spirit* (Des Plaines, Ill.: Regular Baptist Press, 1965), 17; and C. Norman Sellers, *Biblical Conclusions Concerning Tongues* (N.p., 1970), 10.
29. Dillow, *Tongues*, 26-27.
30. Bruner, *A Theology of the Holy Spirit*, 76-77.
31. Brumback, *What Meaneth This?* 261-62.
32. Ibid.
33. There is no evidence for an alleged "baptism of the Spirit" ("second blessing") which occurs after salvation. It is not the purpose of this work to refute this concept, which has been dealt with adequately in

works such as Bruner's *A Theology of the Holy Spirit*, referred to in footnote 26. Suffice it to say that a "second blessing" is contrary to basic Christian doctrine that the believer has everything he needs for the spiritual life immediately upon salvation.

34. As Bruner shows, Paul's question (Acts 19:3) when these disciples showed ignorance of the Holy Spirit was based on the assumption that they could not have been baptized into Christ (saved). When they showed that they were unaware of the Spirit, Paul said, "Into what then were you baptized?" (Bruner, *Theology of the Spirit*, 207–12).

35. Ford, "Charismatic Gifts," 114, recognizes that tongues is not the most important gift and states, "On the other hand there is little evidence to say that it is the least gift." There may not be enough evidence to prove tongues is the least of all gifts but there is a quantity of material with implications for deciding on the priority of tongues.

36. It should be clarified that priority does not necessarily mean inferiority, although it may be implied. Ervin argues that subordination is not necessarily inferiority (*These Are Not Drunken*, 140). However, subordination, although it may not require inherent inferiority, does indicate relative importance. This section is not explicitly dealing with inferiority but priority or importance.

37. Although they are not completely ruled out when interpreted, the rules that Paul gives will suppress their practice, and the statements that they are not designed for the assembly will discourage their use. This discouragement was so obvious that Paul felt constrained to conclude the discussion by telling them not to do what seems obvious, that is, forbid tongues altogether.

38. The questions are introduced by the Greek negative *me*, "no." There are two negatives used in questions in New Testament Greek. This one calls for the answer "No!" This answer is clear from both the argument of the passage and Greek grammar.

39. Ervin's argument that there is no implied opposition or antithesis between tongues and prophecy in this passage (14:1, 5) is based on one interpretation of "rather" *(mallon de)* and is contrary to the entire context (Ervin, *These Are Not Drunken*, 159–60). No matter how these words are rendered (Ervin, "more than that"), the basic point is that prophecy is to be preferred over tongues in the assembly. This is spelled out in v. 24 and is the reason for the basic statement in v. 1 (see the connective "for," *gar*).

40. The low priority is not on evangelism. The gift of evangelist accomplishes this. Tongues as a sign were a helping adjunct to this ministry, but evangelism can and did function apart from this gift.

41. The examples from Acts are the very instances used by Pentecostals to prove that *all* should speak in tongues as a sign of "spirit baptism." But in each case none of the recipients had ever heard of, much less sought, to speak in tongues.

CHAPTER 8

The Gifts in History

PROOF THAT TONGUES speaking and miracles have not occurred or occurred only sporadically throughout church history would show that these gifts are not normal for the church. In this case, the charismatics must explain why the genuine church has not experienced such phenomena over many centuries. On the other hand, proof that there has been a continuous occurrence throughout church history of phenomena similar to today's charismatic phenomena would be an implication in its favor.

Alleged Occurrences of Tongues in the Church

The Encyclopaedia Britannica mentions the instances of tongues speaking described in the New Testament, refers to the adherents of Montanus in the early church, and then jumps to the thirteenth century.

During later church history, glossolalia occurred among the mendicant friars of the thirteenth century, the little prophets of Cevennes, the Camisards, the Jansenists, and the Irvingites. Tradition has it that the gift of tongues was found also among the early Quakers and Shakers, as well as among the converts of John Wesley and George Whitefield. St. Francis Xavier and St. Vincent Ferrer are said to have possessed it. In modern times glossolalia has been found chiefly among Holiness and Pentecostal groups, though in the 1960s there was an upsurge of the practice among the more orthodox branches of Protestantism.[1]

Nichol refers to Donald Gee's quotation from an earlier edition of the *Encyclopaedia*, which up to the reference to Whitefield is similar to the above quotation except the earlier edition does not mention the Camisards. In a footnote Nichol says,

> It must be noted that when one checks the primary sources, there are few data to support the contention of the *Britannica* or Gee who repeats the claim. Except for a clear-cut evidence that *glossolalia* had manifested itself among the Irvingites and, perhaps, sporadically among the Camisards, there is little else that the writer has been able to document.[2]

Hinson, a professor of church history at Southern Baptist Theological Seminary, wrote an article on the history of glossolalia in a larger book of that title.[3] He states,

> Glossolalia has not enjoyed wide currency until recent times. The first sixteen centuries of its history were lean ones indeed. Although we find several references in the early Fathers, they leave us in little doubt about the apparent insignificance of tongues in their day. Some contemporary scholars even doubt whether the Montanists, often cited as the ancient prototype for the Pentecostals, actually practiced glossolalia. Then, if the first five centuries were lean, the next were starvation years for the practice in Western Christendom and doubtful ones in Eastern Christendom. The few scattered references to it are dubious in themselves and made even more dubious by the characteristic credulity of the Middle Ages.
>
> A tongues movement began to bud again during the mid-seventeenth century, first among the English dissenters and then among the Cevenols in France. For the next two centuries, we can discern new bursts sprouting here and there like prairie grass after a spring shower.
>
> Only in the twentieth century has glossolalia prospered.[4]

Hinson states that possible instances of glossolalia are connected with Montanus, were referred to by Irenaeus, and were considered a thing of the past by the time of Chrysostom and Augustine. He refers to the testimony that certain Catholic saints spoke in tongues and shows that the information is doubtful, particularly in the case of Francis Xavier who had great difficulty communicating to tribes.[5] He refers to the Cevenols, Irvingites, Ranters, Quakers, Wesley's meetings, Shakers, Mormons, and Jansenists as those who possibly exercised glossolalia during the seventeenth to nineteenth centuries.[6]

We will now examine these instances, remembering that Nichol and others were unable to document glossolalia among most of these groups.

In the Early Church
Montanus (ca. A.D. 160). Montanus and his followers were characterized as prophets rather than tongues speakers.[7] In fact, there is no clear statement that Montanus and his followers spoke in tongues. Cutten states,

> The Montanists, however, while characterized by the same ecstatic seizures as those who spoke with tongues, must be thought of rather as prophets, for they neither attempted to speak foreign languages nor the unintelligible prattle known in the Corinthian church.[8]

Apparently there is no extant evidence that Montanus claimed to speak in tongues, nor did his opponents regard him as claiming to have the gift of tongues. The use of terms like *raving* to describe Montanus does not require that his speech be unintelligible. Irenaeus (ca. 170) uses the term *raving* to describe intelligible speech by a false teacher (i.e., one who teaches false doctrine).[9] Whatever Montanus and his followers did was not associated by the early church with the gift of tongues but with prophecy. Schaff describes Montanus and the two women who followed him.

> All three went forth as prophets and reformers of the Christian life, and proclaimed the near approach of the age of the Holy Spirit and of the millennial reign in Pepuza, a small village of Phrygia, upon which the new Jerusalem was to come down.[10]

If Montanus and the two women spoke or prophesied these things, which did not come true, then their prophecies were false. In addition, Schaff refers to a statement of Maximilla, one of the two prophetesses, who said, "After me there is no more prophecy, but only the end of the world."[11] These are false prophecies; therefore, they are not prophecies from the Holy Spirit. According to Deuteronomy 18:20–22, prophecies that do not come true are a sign of a false prophet. Montanus claimed to be a prophet, and those who argued against him argued on the basis of his claim to be a prophet.[12] In addition, he deviated from apostolic doctrine.[13] He cannot be used as evidence for glossolalia of any kind, nor do he and his followers constitute testimony for any genuine gift of tongues or prophecy in the early church.

Celsus, an enemy of Christianity in the second century, may refer to Montanists' claims when he speaks of prophets who claim to be God, the Son of God, or the Divine Spirit.[14] Celsus also says the following in regard to these prophets:

> To these promises are added strange, fanatical, and quite unintelligible words, of which no rational person can find the meaning: for so dark are they, as to have no meaning at all; but they give occasion to every fool or imposter to apply them to suit his own purposes.[15]

It is doubtful that Celsus means that the words spoken were not spoken in normal language. He apparently means that the sayings were difficult to comprehend. It would be difficult for imposters to apply unintelligible speech to their purposes. Origen considers the prophecies spoken of to be understandable, since he says regarding Celsus, "If he were dealing honestly in his accusations, he ought to have given the exact terms of the prophecies."[16] Of course this would be impossible if the prophecies were not in normal speech. Referring to the quotation above from Celsus, Origen says, "This statement of Celsus seems ingeniously designed to dissuade readers from attempting any inquiry or careful search into their meaning."[17] Origen not only regards the statements of the prophets in question as understandable but accuses Celsus of dishonesty in his statement that they are dark and without meaning. Origen continues, "And Celsus is not to be believed when he says that he has heard such men prophesy; for no prophets bearing any resemblance to the ancient prophets have appeared in the time of Celsus."[18]

Origen says that in his day (ca. 254) there were no prophets in the church bearing any resemblance to the ancient prophets. He follows this with remarks concerning true and false prophets. Therefore, Origen apparently did not believe that genuine prophets were around in his day, nor did he believe that the individuals referred to by Celsus spoke in unintelligible utterance. This is one of the very few instances Kydd found that he regards as examples of tongues speaking in the early church.[19] Yet if Origen's remarks made at that time are accepted, this is not a reference to tongues.

Montanus' ecstatic utterance is described as follows: "He was carried away in spirit and wrought up into a certain kind of frenzy and irregular ecstasy, raving, and speaking, and uttering strange things, and proclaiming what was contrary to the institutions that had prevailed in the church. . . ."[20] Notice that it is not stated that he spoke in an unintelligible manner. Apparently Montanus abandoned any self-control and use of his own will when in his ecstasy.

Montanus is a clear witness for the existence in the early church of false claims to possess ecstatic spiritual gifts. This false movement gained a large number of adherents and greatly perplexed the church. Many apparently sincere believers, such as Tertullian, were caught up in this movement and defended it. In many ways this early movement parallels that of today.

Irenaeus (ca. A.D. 175). Hinson describes three instances where Irenaeus, Bishop of Lyon in the second century, refers to tongues speaking.[21] The first refers to Acts 2 but does not describe tongues or refer to occurrences in Irenaeus's own day.[22] In the second quotation Irenaeus states:

> For this reason does the apostle declare, "We speak wisdom among them that are perfect" who have received the Spirit of God, and who through the Spirit of God do speak in all languages, as he used himself also to speak. In like manner we do also hear many brethren in the church, who possess prophetic gifts, and who through the spirit speak all kinds of languages and bring to light for the general benefit the hidden things of men and declare the mysteries of God whom also the apostle terms "spiritual."[23]

Hoekema demonstrates that it is not clear whether Irenaeus refers to some who speak foreign languages or to ecstatic speech, nor is it clear whether he states that such occurred in his day.[24] The expression "in all languages" seems to refer to actual foreign languages, which as shown previously is descriptive of the genuine gift of tongues. The statement "whom also the apostle terms spiritual," most probably refers to incidents occurring in the apostle Paul's day since it refers to persons described by him. Therefore, it is unlikely that Irenaeus actually heard such speech or is saying that this occurred in his day. He apparently refers to the church in the apostolic times as described in the New Testament. This is the second of the few alleged instances of tongues in the early church.[25] Just like the other instance, it does not appear to support that claim.

The third reference in Irenaeus says nothing in regard to speaking in tongues. It does refer to a woman deceived by a charlatan who appears to be an agnostic false prophet. She utters nonsense at his bidding, although even in this patently false case of prophecy there is no suggestion that the speech is other than her normal language.

The alleged evidence for the existence of the gift of tongues in the second century is based on only one statement of Irenaeus, which in actuality appears to refer to New Testament times. Irenaeus's statement not only refers to New Testament instances rather than to postapostolic times, but it does not refer to unintelligible utterance but to actual languages. Irenaeus does, however, reveal that false miracle workers existed in his day.[26]

Additional Evidence in the Early Church. As Hoekema points out, Tertullian's statement in *Against Marcion*, V, 8, is no proof for the genuine gift of tongues in his age. Tertullian was a Montanist and probably referred to Montanist activities, which as we have seen are not from the Holy Spirit. He does not mention tongues speaking but does refer to the interpretation of tongues. Neither does he imply that the speaking referred to is unintelligible.[27]

> Let Marcion then exhibit, as gifts of his god, some prophets, such as have not spoken by human sense, but with the Spirit of God, such as have both predicted things to come and have made manifest the secrets of the heart; let him produce a psalm, a vision, a prayer; only let it be by the Spirit in an ecstasy, that is in a rapture, whenever an interpretation of tongues has occurred to him; . . . Now all these signs [of spiritual gifts] are forthcoming from my side.[28]

Since Tertullian in this discussion contrasts Marcion's god with his own God, it is probable that Tertullian refers to the miraculous workings of his God as described in the Bible, rather than affirming that such occurred in his day. Tertullian also links the gift of tongues with knowledge.[29]

Novatian (ca. 250) is referred to by Kydd as evidence for all the charismata. However, the use of the present tense does not prove that Novatian is referring to practices in his day, although it is a possibility. The way the charismata are described and the fact that the present tense gives a description of the Spirit involved makes it probable that he is referring to the New Testament.[30]

Chrysostom (ca. 345–407), patriarch of Constantinople, regarded the genuine gift of tongues as the ability to speak in various foreign languages.[31] He also states that tongues are a thing of the past. He refers specifically to 1 Corinthians 12:1–2, but it is clear from his following remarks that he actually is considering chapters 12–14. The gift of tongues as well as prophecy is not only included in his thinking but prominent when he says,

> This whole place is very obscure: but the obscurity is produced by our ignorance of the facts referred to and by their cessation, being such as then used to occur but now no longer take place. And why do they not happen now? Why look now, the cause too of the obscurity hath produced us again another question; namely, why did they then happen, and now do so no more?[32]

This is an unambiguous statement by a leader in the fourth-century church (who would have knowledge of a large geographical area) that tongues, prophecy, and probably certain other gifts had ceased. They no longer occurred in the church, and they had not occurred for a sufficient length of time. The facts regarding them had dropped from available knowledge so that the passage is considered obscure by the time of this homily.

Augustine (354–430), bishop of Hippo in Africa, is another church leader from the fourth century who represents a different geographical area. Augustine says,

> In the earliest times "the Holy Ghost fell upon them that believed: and they spoke with tongues," which they had not learned, "as the Spirit gave them utterance." These were signs adapted to the time. For there behooved to be that betokening of the Holy Spirit in all tongues, to shew that the gospel of God was to run through all tongues over the whole earth. That thing was done for a betokening and it passed away.[33]

Note that Augustine declares that tongues speaking is past, that it belonged to the earliest times. He refers to the past and states, "these were signs adapted to the times," but he also adds that they had passed away. In addition, it seems certain that he regarded tongues as normal human languages since he describes them as "tongues which they had not learned" and as a betokening "in all tongues" to "run through all tongues over the whole earth." As Hoekema says,

> It would seem, therefore, that by the time of Chrysostom there is no evidence of glossolalia in the eastern church, and that by the time of Augustine there is no trace of tongue-speaking in the western church. A question we are moved to ask already at this point is this: if glossolalia is as important a gift of the Spirit as present-day Pentecostals and Neo-Pentecostals say it is, why did God allow it simply to disappear from the church?[34]

Notice that neither Augustine nor Chrysostom regarded glossolalia as something that had ceased in their recent past. The facts are "obscure" to Chrysostom since they are so far removed in time. To Augustine, tongues were for the "earliest times," that is, the apostolic age. Therefore, as far as these two early church leaders are concerned, tongues had ceased "long ago." Due to their position of leadership, neither of these men would have been ignorant of instances of tongues speaking occurring in their respective areas. It seems safe to assume that by the end of the fourth century biblical tongues in the church had long ceased.

In the Medieval, Reformation, and Postreformation Church

After a gap of about a thousand years, there are several examples of reputed tongues speaking. Hinson cites several from J. J. Gorres, *Die Christliche Mystik*, and one from G. B. Cutten, *Speaking with Tongues*.[35] Hoekema also cites from Cutten.[36] All of the instances cited concern canonized saints of the Catholic church. Apparently Xavier, one of the saints mentioned, had no miraculous ability to speak other languages as he is reported to have done. In fact, he had difficulty speaking to diverse foreign groups.[37] Hoekema's analysis seems appropriate.

> When we see how the process of embellishing the history of saints with fantastic legends was operative in the case of Xavier, we learn to take with more than a grain of salt other medieval claims for the miraculous gift of tongues.[38]

Warfield also demonstrates that medieval claims of miracle working by saints are not reliable.[39] As Hinson says, "The surprising thing in view of the general credulity of the medieval era is that there are so few reports."[40] The cases cited, referring to certain Catholic saints, are not supported by fact. However, all of the claims cited concern speaking in actual foreign languages to people who speak that language. Therefore, even if the claims were true, none of these instances even remotely supports present-day tongues phenomena. Since they are not factual, neither are they testimony for the occurrence of the genuine gift of tongues. Thus, the gap in the occurrences of genuine instances of tongues speaking and other charismatic phenomena among believers lengthens to the seventeenth century. This is a very difficult gap to explain according to the theories of modern charismatic proponents. Furthermore, apparently unintelligible or "heavenly" utterance was not equated with the biblical gift of tongues throughout this time. It was understood as the ability to speak known languages.

The Camisards and Cevenols. According to the *Encyclopaedia Britannica*, the Camisards were prominent around 1702–1705. Their spiritual manifestations consisted of violent physical agitation that eventually was accompanied by alleged speaking in the French of the Huguenot Bible. All kinds of miracles were claimed, including lights in the sky, voices singing to them, shots and wounds rendered harmless, shedding tears of blood, and others.[41] It is doubtful that this movement was spontaneous, since Pierre Jurieus's book apparently stimulated the people to expect such, and the enthusiasm was communicated to the young by men such as DuSerre.[42] This movement, which had many instances of ecstatic utterance, considered their utterances as prophecy. A large number of their prophets were children. The prophecies were often accompanied by physical agitation, including foaming at the mouth and convulsions.

Cutten describes the Cevenols rather thoroughly. He states that initially they emphasized mysterious sounds in the air.[43] One of the prophets was a baby at the breast, and numerous children from three to twelve years old prophesied.[44] The prophecies were reported to be in Latin, Hebrew, and French, as well as in the native language. The term "celestial language," which Cutten uses, does not imply unintelligible utterance as is clear from his statement describing "celestial language through those who were normally unable to express such thought or use such language."[45] The thought was intelligible. Although Mackie disagrees with others when he states that the French was bad,[46] the testimony is consistent that the so-called glossolalia was reputed to be in normal languages and connected with prophecy rather than the gift of tongues. Samarin says,

> About earlier groups, the Camisards and Jansenists of seventeenth-century France and the Anabaptists and the Waldenses in the sixteenth century, all frequently cited as having been glossolalists, linguistic information becomes scarcer and very unreliable. We cannot be certain at all that their verbal behavior was like modern glossolalia.[47]

The phenomena coincided with strong persecution. One province was reported to have eight thousand prophets, and on one occasion all the women and girls in an entire city quaked and "prophesied" publicly. There were claims that harps were heard in the sky and stars guided people to worship.[48] One eyewitness reported

> They turn's round with great violence till being quite giddy they fell upon the floor. When so fallen, they roll'd their eyes frightfully, look'd wild and ghostly, worked their lips in divers figures, druil'd and foam'd at the mouth, held their breath, heav'd their breasts, puff'd and swell'd their throats and sometimes lay as if they were in a trance. Then on a sudden they would start up, shake their heads, gulp and hiccup strangely, clap their hands, move their feet oddly, shake their whole bodies into contortions, in the nature of convulsion. Then they would quake, groan, laugh, belch, sigh, sing, shriek hideously; and at last stretching their mouth open, in a yawning, distorted dreadful manner, in a doleful tone, and as loud as they were able, would utter their prophecies.[49]

Several things should be noted. Many of the claimed miracles, such as lights, harps, and psalms in the sky are entirely without biblical precedent. Therefore, there was a propensity among these people for miraculous manifestations that are nonbiblical. The professed glossolalia are apparently in languages or were asserted to be. The incidence of prophecy among children mitigates against its biblical genuineness as well as the nonbiblical convulsions and foaming at the mouth that accompanied it. Apparently they also prophesied things that failed to take place, as Hoekema indicates.[50] The presence of eight thousand prophets in one province and an entire city of women and girls prophesying is contrary to the entire tenor of the New Testament teaching on spiritual gifts.

Therefore, as late as 1700 Christians did not equate unintelligible utterance with the New Testament gift of tongues. The claims all refer to actual languages. None of the groups studied thus far placed any real emphasis on tongues speaking or expected all believers to do so. The stress of Montanus and the Camisards was in the area of prophecy where they claimed to give additional revelation, which proved to be false. The Camisards's or Cevenols's experiences cannot be considered as genuine manifestations of the Holy Spirit. They provide no evidence for the presence of tongues similar to those present in charismatic groups today since their claims to tongues and the emphases are dissimilar. However, their emphasis on the miraculous gifts, the presence of physical agitation, and claims that all gifts are to be expected are all similar to today's thrust.

Another item is similar to present-day charismatic claims. The Cevenols in the 1700s predicted, "The speedy coming of the Lord, and the setting up of His personal reign on earth, of which, they explained, the present diffusion of the spiritual gifts among them was the preparation and the sign."[51] This is equivalent to the latter-rain theory of Pentecostals today. A little less than three hundred years ago the Cevenols or their theological defenders apparently claimed that the miraculous manifestations were a special diffusion of the Spirit and gifts for the latter-days or end of the age. This explanation for the sudden outburst of a phenomenon without historical precedent is, of course, used today also. It was false then, as history has proved, and it is certainly not demonstrated as biblical today.

The Jansenists. The *Encyclopedia Americana* does not mention glossolalia or miraculous happenings in connection with Jansen or Jansenism.[52] The article in the *Encyclopaedia Britannica* shows that the Jansenists were confirmed Roman Catholics who left the Roman Catholic Church due to physical persecution.[53] Referring to the differences between Jansen's view and that of Protestants, this article states:

> He vehemently rejected their doctrine of justification by faith; conversion might be instantaneous, but it was only the beginning of a long and gradual process of justification. Secondly, although the one thing necessary in religion was a personal relation of the human soul to its maker, Jansen held that such a relation was only possible in and through the Roman Church.[54]

A movement with such antecedents in doctrine and perspective will not commend itself to sound believers as a probable group for manifestations of the Holy Spirit.

Regarding glossolalia, this same article states:

> The Jansenists who remained in France had meanwhile fallen on evil days. Persecution usually begets hysteria in its victims; and the more extravagant members of the party were far advanced on the road which leads to apocalyptic prophecy and "speaking with tongues."[55]

The article does not say that these individuals actually spoke with tongues or prophesied. It does imply that only a few became involved, and they were rejected by the other Jansenists.

A more detailed description of what was involved states,

A young Jansenist clergyman, François de Paris, had died in 1727 as a result of his ascetic practices, with his "appeal" in his hand, and some miraculous cures performed at his grave were looked upon as a divine confirmation of the cause of the Appellants; even children fell into convulsions and trances on his grave, prophesying and testifying against the bull. Infidels were carried away by the fanaticism of the thousands who knelt at the grave of Paris in the churchyard of St. Medard. In 1732 the king ordered the graveyard to be closed; but portions of earth . . . were equally efficacious, and the number of convulsionary prophets of coming ruin to church and state continued to increase until the movement ended in strife, and sometimes in moral disorder, after giving occasion to the skeptics to draw conclusions unfavorable to the miracles of Christianity.[56]

This description, which includes "efficacious" earth, convulsions, prophesying by children and moral disorder certainly does not commend such experiences as from the Holy Spirit. Cutten states,

Some people while visiting that tomb experienced ecstasy and convulsive movements that became contagious and many who were thus seized prophesied and uttered unintelligible expressions in an unconscious "state."[57]

Regarding the prophecies,

[They] even prayed against its coming and the closing of the mouth with the hand did not prevent its appearance. Inarticulate sounds alternated with unconscious singing of hymns and afterward there was rarely any recollection of what had been said.[58]

One of their leaders writes, "In every true conversion God speaks at least once to the soul as distinctly as on the Damascus road he spoke to St. Paul."[59] Another leader felt that, "Conversion is no affair of a moment; it was a slow and gradual process, involving a long course of discipline."[60]

Some of the miraculous happenings connected with Jansenism include the "miracle of the Holy Thorn" when a young girl was cured of an "ulcerated eye by touching a relic from the crown of thorns in the convent chapel at Port Royal,"[61] and the above-mentioned miracles of Saint Medard which were "a series of astonishing cures—mostly of nervous diseases—effected at the tomb of Francois de Paris."[62] The article further observes that

It was but a step to apocalyptic prophecy and speaking with tongues. The so-called *Convulsionnaires* worked themselves up, by means of frightful self-torture, into a state of ecstasy, in which they prophesied and cured diseases.[63]

Analyzing the information enables us to see that the Jansenists had no intention of leaving the Roman Catholic Church but were ardent Roman Catholics. The group in Holland that calls itself the old Roman Catholic Church "adheres strictly to Catholic beliefs and practices—the practices of two hundred years ago," except for rejecting the papal bull against them and the infallibility of the pope.[64] They were doctrinally unsound regarding justification. The miracles of healing referred to were effected by such things as touching relics or were effected at a tomb. Even "efficacious" earth was involved in the healings. Convulsions and other nonbiblical manifestations were present. Those prophesying were often unable to control themselves. This is not true of gifts from the Holy Spirit that 1 Corinthians 14:27–33 specifically shows are under the speakers' control. The Jansenists' emphasis was on miraculous cures and prophesying rather than on tongues. They apparently used unscriptural means such as self-torture to work themselves into a state of ecstasy.

The Radical Anabaptists. Nichol states that the radical Anabaptists in Germany as well as the Jansenists displayed glossolalia.[65] However, the article in the *Encyclopaedia of Religion and Ethics* makes no mention of glossolalia, miracles, or anything similar to these in connection with Anabaptists.[66] The same is true of the *Encyclopaedia Britannica* and Broadbent.[67] *The New Schaff-Herzog Encyclopedia of Religious Knowledge* divides Anabaptists into two main groups: the sober Anabaptists and the fanatical Anabaptists.[68]

Although one of the fanatical Anabaptists, Melchior Hoffman, declared that he was one of the two witnesses of Revelation 11:3 and that Strasbourg, France, was to be the New Jerusalem and the seat of universal dominion, the Schaff-Herzog article makes no reference at all to tongues speaking or miracles.[69] Another Anabaptist leader claimed to be the other witness, transferred the "capital of the kingdom of the saints to Munster" and advocated force in maintaining it.[70] The next leader, John of Leyden, proclaimed himself king and announced polygamy as the law of the kingdom.[71] If these leaders and the Munster group be considered typical, then these radical Anabaptists were unquestionably involved in false prophecy concerning the second advent and the New Jerusalem and were advocating various immoral practices. The radical Anabaptists, however, do not provide evidence for a genuine occurrence of the gift of tongues. The sober Anabaptists were apparently genuine believers noted for their piety. Yet we have no indication that tongues speaking or miracle working was emphasized by either the radical or the sober Anabaptists, if it even occurred at all.

The Irvingites. Many discussions concerning the tongues phenomena are connected with Irving in the eighteenth century. As is characteristic of today's movement, the tongues speakers in that day were told to seek tongues.[72] Irving's church eventually had apostles, prophets, and tongues speakers, as well as other gifts. However, before long the alleged prophets contradicted their own statements and claimed that other prophets spoke by an evil spirit. Some "were convicted of having framed their own message."[73] One of the leading prophets admitted that he was deluded and had spoken by an evil spirit.[74] Those with the gifts in Scotland called those in London "deceitful workers."[75] Many admitted that their gifts were not genuine. Contrary to 1 Corinthians 14:32, the tongues speakers apparently lost all control of their actions while speaking. The citations of eyewitnesses render questionable the entire movement and even the sincerity of Irving.[76] Many women were involved in the actual speaking, especially in the assembly.

Initially people believed that the tongues, which often seemed to be merely a long yell, were genuine language. Observers describing the speaking reveal that there was no edifying content to the utterance; the experience itself was the main emphasis. Cutten cites an instance of Irving's meetings as "swoons, shrieking, bedlam, laughing, and groaning."[77] The prophets humiliated Irving, the "angel" of the church, and exercised control over him through their prophecies. He "was not allowed to baptize a child, but was told to wait until, on the bidding of the prophets, he should again be ordained by an apostle."[78]

The nature of this movement is not only attested to by the above but by the resulting drift into Catholic doctrine. The group eventually became the Catholic Apostolic Church, complete with altars, clerical vestments, extreme unction, transubstantiation, as well as candles, incense, and holy water.[79] Eventually, some of the people associated with this movement admitted that their utterance was not from God. Thus the experiences of the eighteenth-century Irvingites do not provide evidence for a genuine gift of tongues or prophecy.

The Shakers, Ranters, and Quakers. Another group often cited as evidence for glossolalia are the Shakers. However, this group can hardly be classified as Christian. This fact alone precludes the possibility that their actions were prompted by the Spirit of God. Ann Lee, the woman acknowledged as their leader, considered herself to be the second incarnation of Christ and was "acknowledged by the society as mother in Christ."[80] Some of their unsound doctrines are as follows:

> They reject the doctrine of the Trinity, of the bodily resurrection, and of an atonement for sin. They do not worship either Jesus or Ann Lee, holding both to be honored and loved. They believe that it is possible to communicate with the spirit world, and that the special gifts of the spirit have not ceased. They believe that sinlessness of life is not only a possibility, but an obligation. They hold that the world will have the opportunity of salvation in the next life.[81]

Cutten cites an instance where the spirit of a departed Indian is supposed to be the spirit speaking through a Shaker.[82] This is, of course, contrary to the Bible (e.g., Deut. 18:11). Those holding such doctrines are definitely not empowered by God's spirit. Mackie also gives evidence that at times some Shakers danced naked.[83]

Although the Shakers cannot be considered as evidence for genuine gifts of the Holy Spirit, they are evidence for phenomena similar to today's charismatic movement. According to Cutten, in times past Shakers spoke in unintelligible tongues, and their meetings were accompanied by stamping, jumping, and turning.[84] Hinson states that they regarded tongues, dancing, and diverse ecstatic states as the highest expressions of worship.[85]

Some scholars presume that the Ranters provide support for the occurrence of the gift of tongues. But the facts regarding this group that appeared in seventeenth-century England do not bear out the claim. The *Encyclopedia of Religion and Ethics* cites from their own writers as well as from others to show that they were pantheistic and antinomian. Their antinomianism resulted in moral problems since they felt they were above the "usual moral distinctions of right and wrong."[86] This article cites George Fox's experiences in which Ranters claimed to be God. Richard Baxter also testified to the immorality of the Ranters. The facts show that the Ranters were not a Christian group but were pantheistic and often immoral, exalting their own inner light above the Scripture.[87] Another source states that the Ranters made open professions of lewdness and irreligion and that they believed that God, angels, devils, heaven, and hell are fiction and false.[88] Such a group provides no evidence for the genuine gift of tongues.

Another sect often cited as practicing glossolalia are the Quakers. To become a Quaker one does not have to be converted since everyone born into a Quaker family is a member; others become members merely upon request.[89] Divided into two main groups, at least one of them is liberal in theology, denying such doctrines as the full deity of Christ, the imputation of Adam's sin, and the vicarious atonement.[90] Neither the early Quakers nor those of today seem to place any emphasis on glossolalia. Encyclopedia articles on Quakers, some written by Quakers, do not mention any of the miraculous gifts except for the mention of prophecy. Whereas Gromacki states, "It is reported that speaking in tongues took place among the Quakers,"[91] neither Hoekema[92] nor Nichol[93] include them as examples of tongues speakers. Hinson states, "The early Quakers probably witnessed tongue-speaking as one of the many expressions of the Spirit's power in their lives."[94] Cutten states that the early Quakers made no claim to possess the gift of tongues.[95] Yet, as he says, this would not be unexpected from people who would "march through the Streets naked and exhume bodies with the expectation of restoring them to life."[96]

Neither the Shakers nor Ranters were Christian in a biblical sense as their doctrines preclude them from this category. Whether the Quakers engaged in tongues speaking is uncertain so they are not definite evidence for it.

Wesley's Ministry and Revival Ministries. Scholars often point out that John Wesley's meetings were sometimes accompanied by physical manifestations. Referring to a meeting by an early Methodist preacher, Hinson says,

> Both adults and children fell under the power of the Spirit. They shrieked, swooned, fell to the floor as if dead, babbled senselessly, cried out in praise of God, and so on.[97]

Nothing in the New Testament resembles this, not even the day of Pentecost. There is, therefore, ample reason to doubt that such phenomena are from God. Referring to physical manifestations, Wesley says,

> Whereas the truth is 1) God suddenly and strongly convinced many

that they were lost sinners; the natural consequences whereof were sudden outcries and bodily convulsions; 2) to strengthen and encourage them that believed, and to make His work more apparent, He favored several of them with trances and visions; 3) in some of these instances, after a time, nature mixed with grace; 4) Satan likewise mimicked this work of God in order to discredit the whole work.[98]

The people affected in this case were not believers, but unregenerate. Therefore, these manifestations were not spiritual gifts. The only thing comparable in the New Testament accounts is the violence caused by demons when they were cast out. There is no statement here that tongues speaking or prophecy were involved, and Wesley himself doubted that all the phenomena were genuine. Wesley also describes trances that occurred.[99] However, no glossolalia were involved nor were the utterances edifying.

Sweet refers to frontier revivals in America where "sinners" or unbelievers jerked and became involved in convulsive movements[100] and where there were sobs, shrieks, shouts, and spasms, dashing scores to the ground.[101] However, we have no evidence that these were spiritual gifts or that tongues speaking occurred or that believers were involved in such actions. In his study of the Holiness-Pentecostal movement, Synan refers to falling, jerking, barking, trances, holy laughs, and wild dances. He states that after "praying through," some "would crawl on all fours and bark like dogs."[102] Even unbelieving students at the University of Georgia fell, jerked, shouted, and talked in tongues.[103] These manifestations were not restricted to believers and therefore were not spiritual gifts. Some were so ridiculous that it is blasphemous to associate them with the Spirit of God. Does the New Testament give any basis to claim that actions such as these come from the Holy Spirit?

In the Modern Church

The Modern Pentecostal Movement. The history of the modern tongues movement has been traced thoroughly by several recent authors. All agree on the fact that the modern-day movement has its roots in the holiness movement of the last century. Referring to a holiness theologian of that time, Dayton states,

> The first of Mahan's books is fairly typical of the development given to holiness theology until about the time of the Civil War,

while the second book indicates a new theological development of the doctrine that gained acceptance in the years after the Civil War and by the turn of the century had become widely accepted not only in holiness circles but to a certain extent beyond them. The new element is the use of the term "baptism of the Holy Ghost" and the model of Pentecost in Acts 2 in explicating the meaning of "entire sanctification."[104]

Dayton says that this is more than a mere shift in terminology, since "when 'Christian perfection' becomes 'baptism of the Holy Ghost' there is a major theological transformation." A few of the changes he mentions are "a shift from Christocentrism to an emphasis on the Holy Spirit that is really quite radical in character," "a new emphasis on power," and a shift from "emphasis on the goal and nature of the 'holy' life to an event in which this takes place."[105]

Some attempt to trace Pentecostalism further back in time, connecting it with Wesley and the revivals.[106] However, this is questionable, since Wesley's doctrine of the Christian life apparently places the emphasis on Christ and little on the work of the Holy Spirit.[107] Dollar traces Pentecostalism to the Mormons and the Shakers.[108] The many charismatic and neo-Pentecostal groups present in our day are all rooted in the Pentecostal movement either by direct physical or ideological connection. In effect they are merely modifications of it. There is little doubt that Pentecostals, neo-Pentecostals, and other charismatic groups are merely different aspects of one movement that has its roots in the holiness movement but entailed a theological departure from the standard holiness thinking.

Tongues in Church History: A Summary

Phenomena such as those that occur in the present-day tongues movement were not equated with the spiritual gift of tongues in the early church or even through medieval times. We have no testimony for the gift of tongues in the church from the time of the apostles except for one questionable statement by Irenaeus. This means that we have no evidence of any kind from the second century onward. Irenaeus may well have referred to New Testament times rather than his own. The overall testimony of history supports the conclusion that no genuine gift of tongues occurred during his times.

Alleged Occurrences of Tongues Among Non-Christian Groups

The *Encyclopaedia Britannica* states,

> The gift of tongues and of their interpretation was not peculiar to the Christian church, but was a repetition in it of a phase common to ancient religions. Virgil (Aen. vi. 46, 98) draws a life like picture of the ancient prophetess "speaking with tongues." He depicts her quick changes of color, her dishevelled hair, her panting breast, her apparent increase of stature as the god draws nigh and fills her with his divine afflatus. Then her voice loses its mortal's ring. . . .
> Oracular possession of the kind above described is also common among savages and people of lower cultures; and Dr. Tylor, in his *Primitive Culture*, ii. 14 gives examples of ecstatic utterance interpreted by the sane. Thus in the Sandwich Islands the god Oro gave his oracles through a priest who "ceased to act, or speak as a voluntary agent, but with limbs convulsed, his features distorted and terrific, his eyes wild and strained, he would roll on the ground foaming at the mouth, and reveal the will of God in shrill cries and sounds violent and distinct which the attending priests duly interpreted to the people."[109]

It is interesting to note that recent editions of this encyclopedia, possibly out of deference to our present historical context, play down the fact that glossolalia occur in non-Christian circles, although this was pointed out in the earlier editions. This article refers to the fact that ecstatic utterance similar to that in the charismatic movement was common in ancient religions. However, these were not gifts of the Holy Spirit; rather, they had another origin.

The reference above to Virgil describes an ancient Greek pagan priestess of Sibyl. The passage shows that her actions were not considered unusual but religious.[110] The priestess tried to shake off the influence, but "he [the god] so much the rather plies her raving mouth."[111]

> In such words from the shrine doth Cumae's Sibyl chant her awful riddles, and echo through the cave in darkness shrouding truth; so shakes the reins Apollo in her raving mouth, and plies deep in her breast the goad. Soon as had ebbed her frenzy, and the frantic lips were still.[112]

Behm refers to similar phenomena in Greek pagan religion, such as the Thracian Dionysus, the Delphic Phrygia, and the Sibyls.[113] Plato states that men attain prophetic truth only when the "intelligence is enthralled in sleep, or he is demented by some distemper or possession."[114] In order to understand what he has said, the man must first recover his wits," or else he "cannot judge of the visions which he sees or the words which he utters."[115]

Tylor refers to incidents that are common in animism or primitive religions where an individual pours "forth wild incoherent raving, or with thought and eloquence beyond his sober faculties to command, to counsel, to foretell."[116] Tylor discusses convulsive ecstasy among Indian tribes of the past and then refers to the seizure or overcoming of the individual.

> Thus in the religion of uncultured races, the phenomenon of being "struck" holds so recognized a position that imposters will even counterfeit it. In its morbid nature, its genuine cases at least plainly correspond with the fits which history records among the convulsionnaires of St. Medard and the enthusiasts of the Cevennes.[117]

Tylor then refers to similar phenomena during the revivals in England, Ireland, and America.

The shamans of Eskimo religion and of Siberia experience ecstatic states. Lommel describes the ecstatic state of these shamans. In one case the shaman makes "unintelligible mutterings and hiccoughs," and eventually changes to wild shouts, animal calls, a "whole cascade of sounds," and chanting.[118] Eliade refers to those being initiated into the position of shaman among the Tungus of Manchuria. After an initial hysterical experience, the candidate begins babbling "incoherent words."[119] Eliade also refers to the "secret language" used by shamans and says,

> Even where a secret language is not directly concerned, traces of it are to be found in the incomprehensible refrains that are repeated during seances, as, for example, among the Altaians.
> This phenomenon is not exclusively North Asian and Artic; it occurs almost everywhere. During the seance the Semang Pygmy *hala* talks with the Cenoi (celestial spirits) in their language. . . . The Batak shaman uses the "language of the spirits" during seances; and the shamanic chants of the Dusun (North Borneo) are in secret language.[120]

Gromacki refers to instances of glossolalia or frenzied speech among the early Phoenecians, the ancient Greek religions and oracles, the Greco-Roman mystery religions, Mohammedanism, pagan Eskimos, and pagans in Tibet and China.[121] Regarding tongues speaking among the Mormons, Synan states,

> Even the Mormon church experienced much the same motor phenomena that characterized the early Methodists and later Pentecostals. Shouting, jerks, and dancing were common in their services, and Brigham Young not only spoke in unknown tongues but interpreted his own messages to his hearers.[122]

Goodman refers to Trobiand Islanders who spoke to spirits. One was a respectable and quiet man who when speaking to the spirits spoke in a loud and high-pitched tone, and afterward was exhausted.[123] By comparing the utterance of the spiritualist Umbanda cult and Pentecostal groups, Goodman shows that glossolalia, similar to that among Pentecostals, is prevalent in paganism and the world. It is interesting to note that, although Goodman is apparently not certain that there is a personal God, she did experience involuntarily some of the phenomena associated with one Pentecostal group that she was studying.[124] Certainly, hers was not one of the New Testament spiritual gifts! She also concluded that glossolalia fits a pattern and becomes stereotyped in the individual and that the utterance "mirrors that of the person who guided the glossolalist into the behavior. There is little variation of sound patterns within the group arising around a particular guide."[125]

Speaking in incoherent fashion or unknown language is a common factor in pagan religions. It is much more characteristic of non-Christian religions than it is of Christianity. There is a history of glossolalia among religious groups that are in no way under the influence of the Holy Spirit. Certain characteristics tend to be common in pagan glossolalia when the speaker is in a trancelike, ecstatic state. There is usually a routine or procedure to bring on the experience. The tongues speaker's voice pattern and intonation are abnormal, and the utterance is usually unintelligible, although some claim to speak in intelligible languages. The speaker often is unaware of his own statements or actions. There are usually other physical manifestations such as increased breathing rate and distension. Foaming at the mouth and convulsions occur sometimes. During the experience the speaker often experiences an inner glow or "high" that is followed by an emotional letdown. Whereas the first experience is often the most difficult or crucial, subsequent experiences are easier to initiate.

Several things need to be clarified. It is clear that glossolalia or tongues speaking has occurred among many non-Christian groups. This, however, is not proof for the spiritual gift of tongues given by the Holy Spirit but is evidence that ecstatic utterance has occurred under other influences. The average investigator has too frequently equated all glossolalia with the spiritual gift of tongues, but there is no valid reason to make such an equation.

Goodman takes theologians to task because they do not discuss the question with the same presuppositions and beliefs that she has. She assumes that the glossolalia of the Pentecostal movement are the same as those of the New Testament.[126] Like many others, she mistakenly assumes that the tongues speaking in the modern tongues movement is the same phenomenon as the spiritual gift of tongues in the New Testament. Therefore, her demonstration that the glossolalia of the Pentecostal groups are similar to that of pagan religion is valid, but her assumption that this similarity includes the New Testament gift of tongues is contrary to the New Testament.

Today's tongue speaking resembles that found in pagan religions, but it is unlike the biblical gift of tongues. The gift of tongues in the Bible is not unintelligible speech; rather, it is intelligible language. There is no evidence that the biblical tongues speaker spoke in an ecstatic, trancelike, or dissociated state, or that he experienced an exalted feeling while exercising his gift, or was "carried away" or in any way not completely aware of what was happening, and able to control it, much as a teacher or evangelist can control his gift.

In fact the New Testament reveals that none of these characteristics of modern tongues speaking were involved in the genuine spiritual gift of tongues. It is contrary to the evidence to believe that other phenomena, such as jerks, quaking, laughing, crying, dancing, shrieking, and barking occurred in conjunction with this gift or the gift of prophecy, nor was it tolerated in the assembly. In 1 Corinthians 14:23 Paul states that a church where all speak in tongues presents the appearance of a madhouse. He certainly would have mentioned these other phenomena if they occurred in the assembly in conjunction with tongues speaking. The one genuinely possessing the biblical gift of tongues had no difficulty in acquiring the gift initially or using it. The initial gift of tongues speaking on the day of Pentecost required no effort on the part of the speakers to initiate the experience, nor did any other tongues speaking described in the Bible; neither did the individual seek tongues or expect to speak in tongues.

Healing, Miracles, and Other Gifts

The lack of evidence in the history of the church for the miraculous gifts, despite recent claims to the contrary, is so conspicuous that several theories have been invented in order to explain it. This is the reason for ideas such as the "latter-rain" theory and the speculation that the gifts dropped out of existence due to a lack of faith. We have just seen that there is no evidence for the continuance of the gift of tongues. In fact the evidence is against their continuance. The continuance of the other miraculous gifts is also questionable. Kydd, a charismatic, made a study of the gifts during the first three centuries of the church. He states that "there is no example of a non-Montanist Christian prophet coming from the second half of the second century."[127] This statement should be considered in conjunction with the fact that Montanus was apparently a false prophet whose prophecies did not come to pass. Kydd's conclusion may be summarized in his statement that "following about A.D. 260 evidence for the presence of spiritual gifts is nonexistent."[128] Even the evidence that Kydd produces for the gifts prior to A.D. 260 is sketchy at best. Also, it is questionable whether most of the scant available evidence is actually speaking of the miraculous gifts. In many cases it is also questionable whether the testimony concerns incidents contemporary to the writer or to incidents during the apostolic times.

Writing around the close of the first century, Ignatius groups prophets with the apostles and regards them as past.[129] Origen, writing around A.D. 250, notes that the miraculous gifts including miracles had diminished so that only a few traces remained.[130] He differentiates these from those in the New Testament. Origen also states that in the time of Celsus no prophets had appeared "bearing any resemblance to the ancient prophets."[131] As we have already mentioned, Chrysostom, patriarch of Constantinople, describes the gifts in 1 Corinthians 12–14 as no longer occurring in his day.[132] He states that they were so far in the past as to be obscure. Warfield mentions several statements of Chrysostom such as "miracles do not happen now," and "of miraculous powers, not even a vestige is left." He also asks, "Why are there not those now who raise the dead and perform cures?"[133] Augustine, bishop of Hippo, agrees by testifying that the presence of the Spirit was not given in his time by miracles.[134] There is little question that these miraculous gifts did not continue until the present time.

At the same time, however, there is an apparent paradox that Warfield pointed out years ago. Some of these same Fathers who state that miracles ceased in some sense with the apostolic age mention miracles contemporary with themselves.[135] Deere gives the misleading implication that Augustine did not believe in miracles but as he grew more mature he came to believe in them.[136] However, this is not the case since Augustine states that he was aware of miracles before he became a clergyman.[137] Therefore, there must be some other solution.

First, we must remember that these early church fathers were widely acquainted and familiar with the practices of the churches in their time. They all give specific and clear testimony that miracles such as occurred during the apostolic age did not occur in their day. In addition, those who have studied this issue historically agree that there is very little evidence that any of the sign gifts continued. We have seen that even that little amount of evidence is itself questionable. Thus, it seems that these Fathers did not see nor were they aware of any miracles that conformed to or were equivalent to the biblical miracles and signs. The alleged miracles during their day are healings and often of the most bizarre type, including healing by relics and by proximity to dead believers' graves.[138] It is revealing that Deere, rather than admitting this lack of evidence, argues for the validity of healing by relics and dead men's bones, bringing up the case of Elisha's bones.[139] But Elisha's bones were definitely an unusual occurrence even in Scripture and are presented as unusual. Nor did people go to Elisha's bones for healing. Does Deere have any evidence that dead believers today can be placed in the graves of dead Christians and be raised? If he does not, then how is his reference to Elisha's bones relevant to the subject of New Testament gifts? Furthermore, how is the incident with Elisha's bones evidence for spiritual gifts at any time? Is Deere claiming that this Old Testament prophet was exercising spiritual gifts after he was dead? The fact overlooked in this entire discussion is that healing by relics and by proximity to gravesites is no evidence for the continuance of spiritual gifts exercised by living believers who possess the respective gifts. Bones and graves do not possess spiritual gifts, and even if they did, this proves nothing regarding whether Christians have these gifts. If not bizarre, the contemporary miracles referred to by the early Fathers are usually described as answers to prayers by the believers. But this is evidence for the validity of James 5:14, not for the presence of gifts. Another factor must not be overlooked. The biblical miracles were so convincing that the recipients could not restrain themselves from publicizing this even when admonished not to do so. However, as Augustine asserts, those healed during his day usually kept it quiet even when urged to publicize it. This is in total contrast to the biblical healings and reveals that the recipients of these contemporary miracles must have lacked the conviction that a miracle had occurred, a conviction that those healed in the New Testament definitely had.

Thus, we can see that there is consistent and clear testimony that the biblical miracles did not continue. The alleged miracles contemporary to the early church fathers were questionable even at that time and are not incidents of people exercising gifts of healings or miracles. Rather, the alleged incidents are answers to prayer or healing by relics. We do see, however, that the early church, including the leaders, was very willing to accept miracles and healings and was not reluctant to accept the miraculous. The consistent testimony of the early church fathers that the biblical miracles had ceased was not due to a reluctance to believe in miracles but because biblical miracles were not occurring in their day.

A Note of Caution

A study of church history calls for caution in regard to the continuance of miraculous gifts. Glossolalia, not in the sense of speaking actual languages but in the sense of ecstatic utterance, have occurred and continue to occur among some non-Christian groups. These manifestations, however, cannot be from the Holy Spirit. The Old Testament includes examples of miracles that were not produced by the Holy Spirit such as the magicians who opposed Moses. Again, in the New Testament one reads of the "miracles" of Simon Magus, the sons of Sceva, Elymas the sorcerer, and the mantic girl in Phillippi, none of whom represent the Holy Spirit. The early church fathers also testify to apparently miraculous workings in the non-Christian world of their day. Therefore, "miracles" that differ from those recorded in the New Testament should be viewed with scepticism.

The modern-day phenomena do not resemble the biblical gifts. There is no definite evidence in church history for any manifestation of the genuine gift of tongues, prophecy or miracles since the time of the original apostles. However, there is evidence in history for ecstatic phenomena connected with incoherent utterance, physical manifestations, and claims to prophecy wherein the participants were connected with non-Christian pagan religions, thereby precluding them as genuine gifts of the Holy Spirit. History refutes the idea that the modern charismatic phenomena are gifts given by the Holy Spirit and dismisses the idea that the present movement is linked with the early church.

※ ※ ※

1. *Encyclopaedia Britannica*, 14th ed., s.v. "Tongues, Gift of."
2. John Thomas Nichol, *Pentecostalism* (New York: Harper and Row, 1966), 11.
3. Frank Stagg, E. Glenn Hinson, and Wayne E. Oates, *Glossolalia*, 45–75.
4. Ibid., 45–46.
5. Ibid., 56–57.
6. Ibid., 59–66.
7. Ibid., 47–48.
8. George B. Cutten, *Speaking With Tongues* (New Haven, Conn.: Yale University Press, 1927), 35.
9. Irenaeus, *Against Heresies*, in *The Ante-Nicene Fathers*, 8 vols. (Buffalo: Christian Literature, 1885), 1:15.4.
10. Philip Schaff, *History of the Christian Church*, 8 vols. (Grand Rapids: Eerdmans, 1952), 2:418.
11. Ibid., 425.
12. Eusebius, *Ecclesiastical History*, in *The Nicene and Post-Nicene Fathers*, 2d series, 14 vols. (Grand Rapids, Eerdmans, 1952), 1:V.16–19.
13. Adolph Harnack, *History of Dogma*, 7 vols. (New York: Russell and Russell, 1958), 2:98.
14. Origen, *Against Celsus*, in *The Ante-Nicene Fathers*, 8 vols. (Buffalo: Christian Literature, 1887), 4:VIII, 9.
15. Ibid.
16. Ibid., VII, 10.
17. Ibid.
18. Ibid., VII, 11.
19. Ronald A. N. Kydd, *Charismatic Gifts in the Early Church* (Peabody, Mass.: Hendrickson, 1984), 36–39, 45.
20. Eusebius, *Ecclesiastical History*, V, 16.
21. Stagg, Hinson, Oates, *Glossolalia*, 48–49.

22. Irenaeus, *Against Heresies*, III, 12.
23. Ibid., V, 6.
24. Anthony A. Hoekema, *What About Tongues Speaking?* (Grand Rapids: Eerdmans, 1966), 12–15. See also S. D. Currie, "Speaking in Tongues," *Interpretation* 19 (July 1965): 277.
25. Kydd, *Charismatic Gifts*, 45.
26. Irenaeus, *Against Heresies*, II, 31.3.
27. Hoekema, *Tongues Speaking?* 16.
28. Tertullian, *Against Marcion*, vol. 3 in *The Ante-Nicene Fathers* (Buffalo: Christian Literature, 1885), V, 8.
29. Ibid.
30. Ronald A. N. Kydd tries to show that Novatian is evidence for the charismata around A.D. 250. A careful study of the evidence shows that Novatian refers to activities of the Holy Spirit as described in the New Testament and does not state that the charismatic gifts occurred in his day. See Kydd's "Novatian's *De Trinitate*, 29: Evidence of the Charismatic?" *Scottish Journal of Theology* 30 (1977): 313–18; and his *Charismatic Gifts*, 60–64.
31. Chrysostom, *Homilies in First Corinthians*. Homily XXIX and XXXVI, in *The Nicene and Post-Nicene Fathers*, 13 vols. (Grand Rapids: Eerdmans, 1956), 12:168, 218.
32. Ibid., 168.
33. Augustine, *The Epistle of St. John*, VI, 10, in *The Nicene and Post-Nicene Fathers*, 13 vols. (Grand Rapids: Eerdmans, 1956), 7:497–98.
34. Hoekema, *Tongues Speaking*, 17–18.
35. Stagg, Hinson, and Oates, *Glossolalia*, 56–57.
36. Hoekema, *Tongues Speaking*, 18–19.
37. Stagg, Hinson, and Oates, *Glossolalia*, 57; and Hoekema, *Tongues Speaking*, 19, citing Cutten.
38. Hoekema, *Tongues Speaking*, 19.
39. B. B. Warfield, *Counterfeit Miracles* (1918; reprint, London: Banner of Truth, 1972), 248.
40. Stagg, Hinson, and Oates, *Glossolalia*, 56.
41. *Encyclopaedia Britannica*, 14th ed., s.v. "Camisards."
42. Ibid.
43. Cutten, *Speaking With Tongues*, 51.
44. Ibid., 58.
45. Ibid., 51.
46. Alexander Mackie, *The Gift of Tongues* (New York: Doran, 1921), 79.
47. William J. Samarin, *Tongues of Men and Angels* (New York: Macmillan, 1970), 13.
48. Cutten, *Speaking With Tongues*, 54–57.

49. Cited by Mackie, *The Gift of Tongues*, 71–72.
50. Hoekema, *Tongues Speaking*, 20.
51. Warfield, *Counterfeit Miracles*, 130.
52. *Encyclopedia Americana* (1962), 15:615–16.
53. *Encyclopaedia Britannica*, 14th ed., 12:892.
54. Ibid.
55. Ibid.
56. *The New Schaff-Herzog Encyclopedia of Religious Knowledge* (1967), s.v. "Jansen."
57. Cutten, *Speaking With Tongues*, 67.
58. Ibid., 68.
59. James Hastings, ed., *Encyclopedia of Religion and Ethics* (New York: Charles Scribner's Sons, n.d.), 7:477.
60. Ibid., 478.
61. Ibid.
62. Ibid., 480.
63. Ibid.
64. Ibid., 481.
65. Nichol, *Pentecostalism*, 22.
66. Hastings, *Encyclopedia of Religion and Ethics*, 1:406–12.
67. E. H. Broadbent, *The Pilgrim Church* (London: Pickering and Inglis, 1963), 153–85.
68. *The New Schaff-Herzog Religious Encyclopedia*, Vol. 1, 161–63.
69. Ibid., 163.
70. Ibid.
71. Ibid.
72. Warfield, *Counterfeit Miracles*, 138–40.
73. Ibid., 142.
74. Ibid., 143.
75. Ibid., 145.
76. Ibid., 149–152, 296–299.
77. Cutten, *Speaking With Tongues*, 98–99.
78. *The New Schaff-Herzog Encyclopedia*, Vol. 6, 34.
79. Ibid., Vol. 2, 457–459.
80. Hastings, *Encyclopedia of Religion and Ethics*, 3:782.
81. Ibid.
82. Cutten, *Speaking With Tongues*, 81.
83. Mackie, *The Gift of Tongues*, 94–99.
84. Cutten, *Speaking With Tongues*, 76ff.
85. Stagg, Hinson, Oates, 66.
86. Hastings, *Encyclopedia of Religion and Ethics*, 10:579.
87. Ibid.

88. M'Clintoch, John and James Strong, eds. *Cyclopaedia of Biblical, Theological, and Ecclesiastical Literature*, 12 vols. (1887; reprint, Grand Rapids: Baker, 1970), 8:908.
89. *Encyclopaedia Britannica*, 14th ed., s.v. "Friends, Society of."
90. M'Clintoch, Strong, *Cyclopaedia*, 3:667–73.
91. Gromacki, 21.
92. Hoekema, *Tongues Speaking*, 10–23.
93. Nichol, *Pentecostalism*, 18–24.
94. Stagg, Hinson, and Oates, *Glossolalia*, 63.
95. Cutten, *Speaking With Tongues*, 68.
96. Ibid.
97. Stagg, Hinson, and Oates, *Glossolalia*, 64.
98. John Wesley, *The Journal of John Wesley* (Chicago: Moody, n.d.), 239.
99. Ibid., 234–35.
100. W. W. Sweet, *The Story of Religion in America* (New York: Harper and Brothers, 1930), 230.
101. Ibid., 229.
102. Vinson Synan, *The Holiness Pentecostal Movement in the United States* (Grand Rapids: Eerdmans, 1971), 24.
103. Ibid., 25.
104. Donald W. Dayton, "Asa Mahan and the Development of American Holiness Theology," *Wesleyan Theological Journal* 9 (Spring 1974): 61.
105. Ibid., 64–66.
106. Frederick Dale Bruner, *A Theology of the Holy Spirit* (Grand Rapids: Eerdmans, 1970), 42, 47.
107. Herbert McGonigle, "Pneumatological Nomenclature in Early Methodism," *Wesleyan Theological Journal* 8 (Spring 1973): 64.
108. George W. Dollar, "Church History and the Tongues Movement," *Bibliotheca Sacra* 120 (October 1963): 320.
109. *Encyclopaedia Britannica*, 14th ed., Vol. 22, 282–83.
110. Virgil, *The Aeneid*, VI, 32–102, in *Great Books of the Western World*, trans. James Rhoades (Chicago: Encyclopaedia Britannica, 195?).
111. Ibid., VI, 78–79.
112. Ibid., VI, 96–102.
113. Behm, "Glossa," *TDNT*, 1:722.
114. Plato, *Timaeus*, 71–72.
115. Ibid.
116. Sir E. B. Tylor, *Religion in Primitive Culture*, 2 vols. (New York: Harper and Brothers, 1958), 2:210.
117. Ibid., 506.
118. Andreas Lommel, *Shamanism* (New York: McGraw Hill, 1967), 69.

119. Mircea Eliade, *Shamanism* (New York: Bollinger Foundation, 1964), 18.
120. Ibid., 96–97.
121. Robert G. Gromacki, *The Modern Tongues Movement* (Philadelphia: Presbyterian and Reformed, 1967), 5–10.
122. Synan, *The Holiness Pentecostal Movement*, 25.
123. Felicitas D. Goodman, *Speaking in Tongues* (Chicago: University of Chicago Press), xvi.
124. Ibid., 506.
125. Ibid., 121–23.
126. Ibid., xvi–xx.
127. Kydd, *Charismatic Gifts*, 34.
128. Ibid., 57.
129. Ignatius, *To the Philadelphians*, 5. 1,2.
130. Origen, *Against Celsus*, 1,2; 2,8; 7,8.
131. Ibid., 7,11.
132. Chrysostom, *Hom.1 Cor, xxiv and xxxvi*.
133. Warfield, *Counterfeit Miracles*, 42.
134. Augustine, *The Epistle of Saint John*, vi,10.
135. Warfield, *Counterfeit Miracles*, 46f.
136. Deere, *Surprised by the Power of the Spirit* (Grand Rapids: Zondervan, 1993), 74.
137. Augustine, *City of God*, xx.
138. Ibid.
139. Deere, *Surprised*, 74.

CHAPTER 9

Cessation of Gifts: Are Some Gifts Temporary?

THE MAJORITY OF Christians have always believed that certain gifts were only for the first century. History raises serious doubts that manifestation of certain gifts has actually occurred since that time. The present-day alleged instances of tongues speaking, miracle working, and healing do not bear any similarity to the biblical descriptions of the respective gifts. Thus we are justified in questioning the theory that all of the spiritual gifts have continued throughout the church age.

One of the basic assumptions made by charismatic groups is that the Spirit operates the same way today as he did in the first century. But the Bible makes no statement that all gifts will continue throughout the church age. Before we examine the scriptural evidence, however, we will consider several other factors.

The General Opinion Regarding the Gift of Apostle

Most Christians agree that apostles are no longer present in the church. This admission denies the basic assumption that all gifts are permanently given to the church. Anyone who believes that apostles were present only in the early church has already admitted that at least one gift has ceased. To claim that the office but not the gift of apostle has ceased is not a solution since such a distinction between office and gift does not appear in the Bible. Any evidence that apostles do not exist today in the full sense of the New Testament apostle is evidence that the Spirit is not distributing gifts in the same way as in the early church. We cannot accept the claim that apostles are present today in some sense other than those in the New Testament. The only gift of apostle that can be accepted in this discussion is the one described in the New Testament. At least one gift was temporary according to the opinion of most believers and according to the biblical evidence

The fact that the gift of apostle ceased with the apostolic age is a devastating blow to the basic assumption underlying the entire charismatic perspective, namely, the assumption that all gifts are to be operative throughout the church age. We know that at least one gift ceased; therefore, their foundational assumption is incorrect. Nevertheless, Deere tries to nullify the fact that one of the spiritual gifts ceased in the first century by claiming that the gift of apostle is not a spiritual gift. As we examine this idea we must keep in mind that even if apostleship were not a spiritual gift, the fact that it ceased would still show that one of the functions given to the body of Christ did cease. Thus, all of the functions of the beginning church did not continue. Therefore, the church today should not expect to have all of the functions that the church had in the first century.

Deere argues that Paul never applies the term *charisma* to apostleship, nor does he speak of apostleship in the same way as the other gifts.[1] Thus, he concludes that apostleship is not a spiritual gift. However, Deere is wrong on every point. First, the definition of a spiritual gift is not "something that is described by the term *charisma*" as Deere implies; therefore, even if it were true that the gift of apostle is not described by the term *charisma*, this would not show that apostleship is not a spiritual gift. Perhaps Deere is confused in thinking that the modern term *charismatic* is determinative for spiritual gifts in the Bible, but the term is used more broadly. For example, *charisma* is used of salvation (Rom. 5:5, 10), of eternal life (Rom. 6:23), of the ability to remain single (1 Cor. 7:7), and of answer to prayer (2 Cor. 1:11). It is a general term rather than only a definitive term for spiritual gifts. A spiritual gift is a God-given ability to minister as a member of the body of Christ. Apostleship meets this criteria and has always been accepted as one of the spiritual gifts.

Furthermore, it is erroneous to claim that the term *charisma* is not used of the apostle. It is used of the apostle, and the gift of apostle is included in the lists of gifts that also include the gifts of tongues, miracles, and healing. First Corinthians 12:4–5 introduces the rest of the chapter using the term *charisma* but also using the terms "administrations" and "operations." The gifts in 1 Corinthians 12:8–10, which Deere argues are the *charismata*, are in fact introduced by the expression "manifestation of the Spirit" and not directly by *charismata*; however, it is clear from the flow of thought that they are also included under the term *charisma*. But it is also just as clear that this discussion is one flow of thought through the end of the chapter and thus apostles, prophets, teachers, miracles, healings, tongues, helps, and governments in verses 28–30 are also included under the term *charismata*. Verse 12 is joined to the previous discussion both by the word "for" and by content and refers to "members of the body." This discussion of the members of the body continues through verse 30. Verse 31, which continues the thought of verses 28–30, uses the term *charisma* to refer to the gifts mentioned in verses 28–30. These verses discuss the priority of the various gifts. In verse 31 the statement "Be zealous for the greater gifts *(charismata)*" definitely refers back to those gifts, including apostle, just discussed in verses 28–31. This is certain not only from the immediate context but also from the fact that 1 Corinthians 14 continues this discussion and stresses the priority of the gift of prophet over tongues, in accordance with the priority listed in verses 28–30.

Apostle is also listed along with miracles, healing, tongues, prophet, and the other gifts, revealing that Paul regards it as one of the same category. Furthermore, apostles, as well as prophets, evangelists, pastors and teachers, are stated to be gifts, using the Greek word *doma*, "gifts," in Ephesians 4:11. Two of these gifts, prophets and teachers, are included under the term *charisma* in Romans 12:6–8, but miracles, healing, and tongues are not included. In Romans 12 the term *charisma* is used to describe the people who exercise the abilities. Thus, apostles are included with the other spiritual gifts in such a way that it is clear that they are included among the spiritual gifts. The gifts and the persons who possess the gift cannot be separated as Deere attempts to do. His attempt to remove the apostle from the category of spiritual gifts not only fails, but it highlights an oversight common to charismatics, namely, that the primary purpose for spiritual gifts is for ministry not just for sporadic manifestations of power to amaze and strengthen weak Christians. Thus, apostleship is a gift for ministry par excellence, but it is still a spiritual gift.

Deere's argument that apostleship is not spoken of in the same way as the other gifts is also misleading. No gift is spoken of in the same way as the other gifts since they all differ. Tongues are not spoken of in the same way as teaching or giving, but they are all spiritual gifts. How many gifts are spoken of in any way other than to give their title? Using Deere's argument, there is no biblical or logical basis upon which to say that apostles or prophets are not spiritual gifts but that miracles and tongues are.

Other points made by Deere are also misleading. Since he is familiar with the literature on gifts, he must be aware that it is not "clear" that James, the Lord's brother, is an apostle, nor is it "clear" that Barnabas is an apostle in the sense of the apostolic gift, nor is it even probable that Silas is an apostle since there is definite evidence against it. There is sufficient evidence that "all the apostles" in 1 Corinthians 15:7 refers to the "twelve" that he certainly should give some evidence before making the improbable and misleading assertion that it may refer to others. Yet his own statements seem to ignore these issues.[2] For example, he maintains that according to 2 Corinthians 11:13 the number of apostles "could not have been fixed in New Testament times, or else there would be no possibility for these men to masquerade as apostles,"[3] but such a deduction does not follow. Whether a number is fixed has no logical relationship to what others may claim. The number of genuine apostles has no bearing on whether other men can claim to be apostles. What Deere apparently assumes is that if the number was fixed, then every Christian would know and accept it, and they would consistently refuse to accept any false apostles. Thus, all of those who would be tempted to make such a claim would be so discouraged that no one would ever pretend to be an apostle. The mere statement of these assumptions shows how illogical his argument really is. The number of genuine Messiahs is definitely fixed at one, yet according to the Bible there have been and will be many who will claim to be the Messiah. Deere's arguments do little to challenge the fact that at least one gift was temporary and ceased with the apostolic age. What about the other gifts?

The Absence of the Miraculous Gifts in History

As we discussed in the previous chapter, the isolated and sporadic occurrences alleged to be tongues is evidence in itself that the genuine gift did not occur. If God continued to give this gift, we have no reason to assume that it would not be given uniformly and regularly to the church. No one has maintained that other gifts such as evangelism, helps, government, and teaching occurred only in a few places separated by hundreds of years. Furthermore, when these few scattered instances of alleged tongues are examined, the evidence is against them as the genuine New Testament gift of tongues.

No instance of the gift of tongues has been demonstrated from the apostolic age until modern times. The church as a whole has always believed that the gift of tongues ceased with the apostles. Chrysostom (345–407) and Augustine (354–430) give clear statements that the gift of tongues ceased long before their time. The fact that tongues ceased is recognized by many who assume that this gift is present today. An attempt is made to solve this problem by admitting that the gift ceased but claiming that it is given again today. If the gift of tongues had continued normally in the church as it was given in the beginning, then there would be no question raised regarding its occurrence today. The issue is only raised today because it did in fact cease. This same argument from history applies to other gifts such as prophecy, healing, and miracles. There is not one certain occurrence of these gifts since apostolic times. If these gifts did continue through the history of the church, then why is there such a dearth of evidence for it? Because their cessation is so evident, even many Pentecostals regard today's phenomena as a "latter-day" outpouring of the Spirit.

A common attempt by charismatics to evade this fact of history is to claim that the early Christians came to disbelieve in the miraculous gifts, and therefore these gifts disappeared due to a lack of faith. As Deere states it, "when people stopped seeking spiritual gifts (*in direct disobedience to God's commands:* 1 Corinthians 12:39, 14:1, 39) and stopped making provision for their exercise within their churches, they ceased to experience the gifts."[4]

Before discussing this argument, it seems necessary to point out that anyone familiar with Greek would know that "seek" is not one of the more probable meanings for the verb used in 1 Corinthians 12:31, 14:1, and 14:39. The usual meaning, "zeal" fits perfectly in this passage. It is unlikely that the verb ever means "seek" and, in any case, it cannot have this meaning in this context. Therefore, his repeated insistence that these verses teach believers to seek the miraculous gifts seems intentionally designed to take advantage of the uninformed reader. However, even if the verb is interpreted as "seek," rather than teaching that believers should seek the miraculous gifts, these verses would teach just the opposite. They would teach that the believer should seek the edifying gifts such as prophet and teacher instead of seeking the miraculous gifts such as tongues, miracles, and healing. Whether the verb in question is translated "be zealous," "covet," or "seek," there is no question that it is for the edifying or "greater" gifts, not for the miraculous gifts. Thus, if the verb in these verses means "seek," as Deere translates it, then the church was biblically correct in not seeking the miraculous gifts but rather seeking the edifying gifts, such as teacher. Regardless of the translation followed in these verses, it does not in any way teach what Deere implies. It would be accurate to say that it teaches the opposite.

Regarding the argument that the miraculous gifts dropped out of existence because the church stopped believing in them, we should note that it is based on the assumption that gifts come only to those who believe in them and seek them. However, this is an unwarranted assumption since there is no biblical evidence for it. There is no instance in the Bible where anyone received a gift by seeking it or as a result of believing in that gift. On the contrary, those who are described as speaking in tongues had no idea such a gift existed until they spoke. Nowhere in the Bible are Christians told to seek any gifts or admonished to believe in the miraculous gifts. Several times 1 Corinthians 12 specifies that the gifts are given only on the basis of God's will. As a primary thrust this passage presents the concept that the individual has no say in this matter and must, therefore, be satisfied with and function with whatever gift God has given him.

The argument itself is faulty in all respects. Although it is often asserted that the early church, especially the leaders, became bureaucratic and led the church to disbelieve in gifts, no evidence is given to support this claim. It seems to be derived from a necessity to explain why the early church did not continue to function with all the same functions as in the book of Acts. It also conflicts with the facts. As we have seen, the early church and its leaders were very open and receptive to the "miraculous." They seemed to be willing to believe in even the most bizarre types of "miracles," such as healing by relics and at gravesides. Therefore, the credulity of the early church toward the miraculous shows that they would not at all disbelieve nor would their leaders encourage disbelief in the miraculous gifts if they were still occurring.

This brings up another aspect of this situation. The miraculous gifts in the book of Acts were so obvious that even the enemies of the gospel were unable to deny them. If these gifts were functioning, then how could believers deny that they existed? How could anyone in the church have come to the conclusion that they could not happen? If all of the gifts were functioning all around believers as a normal function of the church passed on directly from the beginning, is it reasonable to speculate that Christians would stop believing in them? Could any church leader convince believers that miracles did not occur while they were watching them take place? The only way that the church could stop believing in the miraculous gifts is if they no longer occurred. The only way that they would no longer occur is if God no longer gave them. Therefore, the fact that the church came to disbelieve in the miraculous gifts can only be explained due to the fact that God discontinued these gifts. The facts of history as well as 1 Corinthians 12–14 make it certain that the early church was too inclined toward the miraculous to disbelieve in the miraculous gifts as long as they were occurring.

Are we to take seriously the claim that in a nonscientific age, where the entire society believed in the supernatural and miraculous, while surrounded by the genuine miracles and miraculous gifts, that almost the entirety of Christianity disbelieved in miracles so that they ceased? Note that this charismatic argument requires that the miracles must be disbelieved while they are occurring and then they stop due to the disbelief. In addition, we are to accept the equally illogical corollary that in the most rationalistic of ages, after no miracles had occurred for nineteen hundred years, twentieth-century Christians believed in them to the extent that they recurred? Do modern Christians have more faith in these gifts than an early church surrounded by them?

If modern Christians, apart from any "concrete" evidence believed, how can we accept that the early Christians, immersed in miracles, could disbelieve irrefutable facts? Furthermore, if this "miraculous infusion" of the Holy Spirit gives power, joy, purpose, and revitalizes the church as modern charismatics claim, how could such a tremendous blessing be rejected by the early church? This entire concept is unreasonable.

The argument that the miraculous gifts ceased due to a lack of belief in these gifts is not an answer but an evasion of the facts of history and contrary to biblical evidence. It is equally illogical to compare the cessation of these gifts to the temporary loss in sections of Christianity of some doctrines such as justification by faith. These doctrinal errors were due to man's frailty or error and largely due to the presence of unbelievers in the church. Gifts, however, are given by God apart from human desire or doctrine. No gift in the Bible was a result of correct doctrine regarding gifts but often came on

Christians who were not even aware of gifts. The believers at Pentecost were not aware of tongues nor were the disciples in Acts 19:6. The Corinthian church was full of erroneous thinking regarding gifts; however, the gifts still functioned. The gifts of teaching, giving, helps, showing mercy, and evangelism apparently have always functioned even though most Christians have not been aware of them. The Bible is specific on the fact that the gifts are given solely on the basis of God's will. Even unbelievers were unable to refute and disbelieve in the genuine miracles.

The present charismatic phenomena lack any historical connection with the apostolic church. Therefore, it would be overly naive to accept the charismatic claims apart from some proof of a direct historical connection or solid biblical evidence that these phenomena are the same as those in the Scripture. However, the evidence is against them on both counts.

The Need for Miracles in the Beginning Church

The gospel message was unusual and astounding. A man executed in a very small country was presented as the Son of God who came to die for all men. For those who trusted in him, God would by grace forgive their sins. Few people outside Israel had ever heard of Jesus. He died before the church was established. He was executed after a brief career. These facts at least show the difficulty faced by early evangelists. The miraculous sign gifts put this whole message in a different perspective since the miracles were evidence that the message was from God. The need for confirmation at the beginning certainly seems greater than the need for this today.

To argue that there is as great a need today and thus there was no greater need at the beginning of the church is to be out of touch with both the Scripture and historical reality.[5] There was an initial need to establish the apostles as representatives of the crucified and resurrected Lord Jesus Christ and so to establish the apostolic doctrine. There was a necessity to establish the connection between Christ and the apostolic church. The apostles, the eyewitnesses of the resurrection, were to proclaim this fact and the gospel message. The initial promulgation of the resurrection and the establishment of the apostolic authority to proclaim, clarify, correct error, produce an ecclesiology and New Testament theology is a situation never faced since that time. Deere's assumption that there was no greater need at that time is both scripturally and historically inaccurate.

Cessation of Gifts: Are Some Gifts Temporary? 239

When Christians faced opposition and persecution during the Reformation period, there certainly was as much a need for miraculous confirmation as today, yet none was given. The same may be said of the Waldensians, the Huguenots, and various other groups in church history. Yet no miraculous confirmation was given. There is no reason to assume that a greater need exists today than in other times. There is no correlation between alleged occurrences of miraculous gifts in our times and seemingly areas of high spiritual need. In fact, the charismatic movement began in the so-called Christianized countries rather than in the more spiritually needy areas.

Biblical Indications of Change

Pentecost

There are additional implications in the New Testament that all things have not remained the same as in the beginning of the church. Regardless of assertions that another Pentecost has occurred in recent times, there has never been a duplication of the events that happened on the day of Pentecost. The number of people involved, the number of languages spoken, the presence of the twelve apostles, the number of people converted, the fact that none of these had ever heard of or looked for the gift of tongues, and the phenomena of the tongues of fire and the mighty rushing sound all combined to produce an event never duplicated.

Additional Events in Acts

Ananias and Sapphira dropped dead at Peter's word in front of the church (Acts 5:5, 10). The Holy Spirit has not worked this way throughout church history, nor does he today. Paul's conversion has not been duplicated today (9:1–9). Peter's vision of the sheet (10:10–15) and Paul's blinding of the sorcerer (13:11–12) have not been duplicated today. Direct appearances of angels, such as in Acts 12:6–11, do not occur today. There are numerous incidents that occurred through the power of the Holy Spirit that have not since occurred. It is clear that the Holy Spirit has not operated throughout the age of the church in all of the ways described in the book of Acts.

Biblical Evidence of the Temporary Nature of Certain Gifts

The only question remaining is, Which gifts are temporary? We have already shown biblically that apostles and prophets are no longer given. This is sufficient to prove the principle of temporary gifts; however, we will consider some additional statements of the New Testament.

Proponents of the charismatic movement have managed to shift the burden of proof regarding the temporary nature of some gifts to their opponents. They have done this by assuming that all things have remained the same throughout the church age, and they have demanded proof to the contrary. Since the facts of church history reveal that the Holy Spirit has not been functioning in all the ways that he did in the book of Acts, the basic assumption that all things have remained the same is incorrect. The burden of proof rests on those who insist that all the gifts are to be seen today. They should present indisputable proof from the Bible that their position is true. However, they cannot do this. The following sections will cover various passages that demonstrate the temporary nature of certain gifts.

Ephesians 2:20

This passage has been discussed in the chapter on apostles and prophets. There we demonstrated that the expression "of the apostles and prophets" is definitely an occurrence of the appositional genitive. This verse then states that the apostles and prophets are the foundation of the church and that Christ is the cornerstone. The passage refers to the universal church, not to a local church or mission field. Foundations are necessarily at the building of any structure. Although the building in Ephesians 2:20 is a figure of speech, it illustrates truth. Christ, the cornerstone, came first. The members of the church are actually "built upon" (Gk. *epoikodomeo*) the foundation. This passage strongly implies that apostles and prophets are of the past and were only at the beginning.

Someone may say, "We still need the foundation; therefore, apostles and prophets are still given." We still need Christ the cornerstone, but he has not been present physically since he ascended. Christ fulfilled his purpose on earth, and the church continues based on that. Likewise the apostles and prophets fulfilled their purpose, and the church builds on that.

Hebrews 2:3–4

This passage states that miraculous workings were used by God in order to confirm the initial preaching of the gospel. It says,

> How shall we escape, if we neglect so great salvation; which at the first began to be spoken by the Lord, and was confirmed unto us by them that heard him; God also bearing them witness, both with signs and wonders, and with divers miracles, and gifts of the Holy Ghost, according to his own will? (Heb. 2:3-4)

The signs and wonders and miracles spoken of here are the same terms used throughout the book of Acts to describe the miraculous workings and ministries of the apostles. These terms *dunamis, semeion,* and *teras* are also used in Romans 15:19 and 2 Corinthians 12:12 to describe Paul's ministry, and in 2 Thessalonians 2:9 to describe the false miracles of the man of sin. Therefore, there is no doubt that this passage refers to miraculous signs such as healing and raising the dead.

The subject discussed is the salvation that was confirmed to the addressees of Hebrews by those who actually heard the Lord. They were eyewitnesses of the Lord and were, therefore, the first generation of Christians. God bore witness together with them by means of the miraculous signs. This was a thing of the past by the time the Epistle was written. The verb "was confirmed" (Gk. *ebebaiothe*) is in the past tense (aorist). Apparently this confirmation was not going on at the time of writing. The present tense of the participle, "bearing witness," relates to the main verb, "was confirmed." God was not bearing witness at the time Hebrews was written, but he bore witness by the miracles at that past time while the eyewitnesses testified to the Hebrews.

This passage states explicitly that God gave miraculous signs to confirm the evangelistic preaching (to unbelievers) by the eyewitnesses of the Lord (those who heard), probably apostles. This confirmation was a thing of the past when the Epistle was written. It was not going on at the time but occurred in connection with the original eyewitness testimony.

Romans 15:18-20

In this passage Paul definitely refers to evangelistic ministry, that is, ministry to unbelievers.

> For I will not dare to speak of any of those things which Christ hath not wrought by me, to make the Gentiles obedient, by word and deed, through mighty signs and wonders, by the power of the Spirit of God; so that from Jerusalem, and round about to Illyricum, I have fully preached the gospel of Christ. Yea, so have I strived to preach the

gospel, not where Christ was named, lest I should build upon another man's foundation. (Rom. 15:18-20)

This passage refers to a ministry of "preaching the gospel not where Christ was named." It refers to ministry "to make the Gentiles obedient," and in verse 16 to "ministering the gospel of God." Paul states in verse 19 that he "fulfilled the gospel of Christ." He uses the verb *euaggelizo* and the noun *euaggelion*, from which we derive the English word "evangelize." This ministry was evangelistic ministry to *unbelievers*.

Although there are different interpretations of the expression, "I will not dare to speak of any of those things which Christ hath not wrought by me" (v. 18), the passage is clear that the "mighty signs and wonders" are concerned with this ministry to the unreached. The signs and wonders are agents bringing about the obedience of the Gentiles. Paul regards signs and wonders as signs that helped bring about gentile obedience to the gospel of Christ. As signs they were confirmatory. As the context reveals, this is related particularly to Paul's ministry as the apostle to the Gentiles.

Second Corinthians 12:12

This passage also has been discussed previously. Paul refers to his previous ministry to the Corinthians, probably the time when he first brought the gospel. He relates the miracle working to the apostles when he says, "For in nothing am I behind the very chiefest apostles, though I be nothing. Truly the signs of an apostle were wrought among you in all patience, in signs, and wonders, and mighty deeds" (2 Cor. 12:11-12). He was not behind the other apostles since he wrought miraculous works. This implies that all the apostles performed signs and wonders. Paul was an apostle, hence, he did the same. Miracle working appears to have been evidence of apostleship. Therefore, it must be mainly restricted to the apostles or else how could it prove that Paul was an apostle? The book of Acts bears out the fact that miracles were almost entirely restricted to the apostles. If restricted basically to the apostles, then miracle working was for the first century and was never widespread.

Mark 16:15-20

This passage definitely refers to evangelistic ministry to unbelievers. Verse 15 says, "And he said unto them, go ye into all the world, and preach the gospel to every creature." Miraculous signs, including speaking in tongues, healing, and casting out demons, would follow this ministry. The passage ends with, "And they went forth, and preached everywhere, the Lord working with them, and confirming the word by the signs which followed" (v. 20). These miraculous signs, including tongues, were used by the Lord to confirm the testimony of these eyewitnesses of the Lord. "Confirm" (Gk. *bebaioo*) is the same verb used in Hebrew 2:3–4, where it is stated that the testimony of the original eyewitnesses had been confirmed by miraculous signs, but this was now past. Mark 16:20 refers to eyewitnesses, and the perspective is past. They preached and the Lord confirmed it. The implication is that this was accomplished by them and was not going on at the time of the writing of Mark's Gospel.

The Book of Acts

There are several passages in Acts specifying that miraculous works were done by God through the apostles in order to confirm the early proclamation of the gospel. For example, Acts 14:3 says, "Therefore they continued for a long time to speak boldly concerning the Lord, who testified to the word of his grace by giving signs and wonders to be done by their hands." If some today desire to be as the early church in Acts, then why don't they use miraculous works in this way as a testimony to the word of God's grace to unbelievers? The many instances of miracle working in Acts have been discussed earlier and are consistent with this verse. The testimony of the entire New Testament is consistent with this verse.

First Corinthians 13:8–13

Although many use 1 Corinthians 13:8–13 as their main argument that tongues have ceased, the other verses discussed in this chapter and the other evidence given in this book show that belief in the cessation of some gifts does not stand or fall with this passage. First Corinthians 13:8–13 clearly states that tongues will cease and that knowledge and prophecy will be "done away." However, there is considerable dispute concerning the time when these events occur.

In this chapter Paul stresses the need to exercise spiritual gifts with the attitude of love. He states that none of the gifts (tongues, knowledge, prophecy) are anything in themselves and that they do not profit the one exercising the gift unless used with love (vv. 1–7). In the last part of the chapter (vv. 8–13) he writes that love remains, whereas prophecy, knowledge, and tongues do not. Paul says:

Love never fails: but whether prophecies, they shall be set aside; or tongues, they shall cease; or knowledge, it shall be set aside. For we know in part, and we prophesy in part. But when that which is complete *(to teleion)* comes, then that which is partial shall be set aside. When I was a child, I spoke like a child, I thought like a child, I reasoned like a child: but when I became a man, I put away childish things. For now we see in a mirror, indistinctly; but then face to face: now I know partially; but then shall I know fully even as also I am known. But now faith, hope, and love remain, these three; and the greatest of these is love. (1 Cor. 13:8–13)

Since the point at which this "setting aside" takes place is described as when "that which is perfect comes," many have discussed the meaning of "perfect" *(teleion)* in this passage, arriving at different conclusions. Although the word *teleion* is often translated "perfect," it can mean either "finished, complete, mature, or perfect." The "perfect" in this passage is specifically contrasted as the opposite to "that which is partial." Therefore, the meaning of "perfect" must be "complete." This not only is a common meaning for *teleion*, it is the only one that makes a sensible contrast with "partial."

The meaning "mature" is derived by some interpreters from the illustration in verse 11, but one possible interpretation of an illustrative statement that can be taken in several ways cannot dictate the meaning of a perfectly clear statement that can only be reasonably interpreted in one way. Thus, *teleion* must mean "complete." Just as an individual sets aside or replaces the things of childhood when he becomes mature (v. 11), so completed things set aside or replace their partial components when the partial are completed (v. 10).

The repetition of this idea shows that it is a major stress in this passage. Verse 9 states that the reason prophecies and knowledge will be set aside is that they are only partial. Verse 10 as we have just seen refers to "complete" replacing "partial." Verse 12 then begins to close the discussion by stating that, "Now we only know partially; but then (at the *teleion*), we will know completely." Thus, it is definite that the concept of "complete" replacing "partial" is the basic point in this passage, showing why love outlasts prophecies, knowledge, and tongues.

Notice that verse 10 is a general principle rather than a statement of specifics. It states a commonly recognized general principle and is used as a general principle in this passage. Paul gives it as a self-evident reason for his argument that prophecies and knowledge will be set aside due to the fact that they are partial. He apparently expects this to be a self-explanatory statement. The conclusive evidence that this is a general principle is the use of the neuter singulars "that which is partial" and "that which is complete." The neuter singular shows that these are used to refer to the general concepts of anything that is partial and anything that is complete. If it referred to the specifics of this passage, which would be partial prophecies and partial knowledge, then it would be feminine since both are feminine.

Therefore, the fact that *telcion* is neuter shows it is a general principle and tells us nothing about the gender of what is referred to in this discussion. This is the same as the fact that the neuter *to ek merous* ("that which is partial") tells us nothing about the gender of what is referred to as "partial" in the passage. According to the context, the "partial" are prophecies and knowledge, both of which are feminine.

The meaning of *teleion* is also unmistakable in this passage and, in fact, is specifically stated in verse 12. It is when partial knowledge is replaced by complete knowledge and partial prophecies are replaced by direct sight. Paul states this as an individual event—when the individual knows and sees—rather than as a group event such as the translation of the church to heaven. Yet a group event is a possibility if the individual aspect in verse 12 is deemphasized and the aspect of completed prophecy is put in its place. Paul seems to be saying, "Emphasize love, which lasts, instead of prophecies, knowledge, and tongues, which are only temporal and will one day be superseded."

One other significant aspect should be noted. The prophecies and knowledge in this passage are not the gifts themselves, as most interpreters seem to assume, but the content associated with the gifts. There are several reasons for understanding the passage in this way. The gifts are not partial, nor will there be a day when the partial gifts will be replaced by complete gifts. The stress in this passage is not on the gifts but on knowledge and prophecies, such as Agabus's prophecy regarding famine. The word "prophecies" used here does refer to the gift in a few passages. However, it usually refers to the prophecies themselves. Likewise, "knowledge" is not described anywhere as one of the spiritual gifts. The "word of knowledge" is the gift; however, this title is not used here. Finally, verse 12 refers not to gifts specifically but to unclear versus direct sight and partial versus complete knowledge. In the same way, "tongues" in this discussion must refer to language rather than to the gift. When the gift of tongues is being discussed, some qualifying addition such as "speak in" tongues or "the" tongues is used.[6] The apparent exception in 1 Corinthians 14:26 actually refers to the language spoken rather than the gift itself and is, therefore, no exception.

Someone will object that this entire section of 1 Corinthians discusses gifts; therefore, this must be the issue here. While Paul is still discussing gifts, in this particular section he is discussing the content resulting from the gifts and the basic element involved in the gift of tongues. He does this in order to show that the basic reason for these gifts is only temporal and the gifts are, therefore, less significant than love that lasts. Direct sight and complete knowledge will eventually be every Christian's privilege; therefore, the partial knowledge and prophecy resulting from the gifts will no longer be necessary.

The content resulting from these gifts goes on long after the gift was exercised to produce that content. For example, Isaiah prophesied many years ago and his prophecy still remains, although both Isaiah and his gift are long gone. Thus, whatever the *teleion* may be, it is only the content that continues, not necessarily the gift. It is only language that continues to that point, not necessarily the gift. If, as seems apparent in the passage, the *teleion* refers to the individual's presence with the Lord, this passage does not refer to some prophetic point in history. These factors mean that this passage does not teach when gifts will cease or how long they will last. It serves to remind the Corinthians of the abiding nature of love in contrast to the gifts, which by their inherent nature are only temporal, only for this life.

Summary

One incontrovertible fact solves the basic question, Are some gifts temporary? That fact is that the gift of New Testament apostle has ceased. According to 1 Corinthians 9:1–2, an apostle must have seen the resurrected Lord. Paul is the last one who qualified (1 Cor. 15:8); therefore, he was the last apostle. As we have previously discussed, other passages also support this. According to 2 Corinthians 12:12, an apostle had to be able to perform signs, miracles, and wonders. The examples given in the New Testament have not been duplicated. Paul says that such signs confirmed his evangelistic ministry as apostle to the Gentiles. The overwhelming consensus of the church since earliest times is that apostles were only in the beginning church, thereby admitting that at least this one gift was temporary. No one has realistically claimed to be an apostle in the full sense of the New Testament apostle (the Twelve and Paul). Therefore, it is certain that this gift was temporary, which establishes the fact that all gifts are not continually given to the church and that some gifts are in fact temporary. If one gift is temporary, others may be also.

Ephesians 2:20 declares that apostles and prophets are the foundation for the universal church. The context deals with the entire body of Christ and not only with a local church. Therefore, this foundation must have occurred at the beginning of the universal church and was not to be repeated with every new missionary thrust. Since apostles were only in the early church, this is confirmation that Ephesians 2:20 regards the foundation as at the beginning only. The gifts of apostle and prophet are linked together in this verse as foundational. Therefore, prophets were for the beginning of the church as were apostles. This also has been the opinion of the church since its beginning. The claims of those few who have claimed to be a prophet in the full sense of a New Testament prophet have never been validated.

Second Corinthians 12:12 reveals that the apostles performed miraculous signs. These works were signs and were proof of apostleship. We would expect therefore that miraculous works, since they were evidence of apostleship, were also a characteristic of apostleship. It is unlikely that such works extended to any great extent outside the apostolic circle. Our study of miracles shows that the biblical miracles after the crucifixion were performed only by the apostles as well as Stephen and Philip. The miraculous works were linked, therefore, with the foundational gift of apostle. Paul points out explicitly in Romans 15:19 that his evangelistic ministry to unbelieving Gentiles, as the apostle to the Gentiles, was confirmed to the recipients by miraculous signs. This agrees with 2 Corinthians 12:12. Mark 16:15-20, discussed more completely in an earlier chapter, reveals that miraculous signs, which included speaking in tongues, healing, and casting out demons, were given as signs to unbelievers. These statements were addressed to the eleven apostles. Mark 16:20 states that they preached the gospel and that the Lord worked with them, confirming their message with signs. This was past when Mark wrote his Gospel. The signs confirmed the preaching of the eleven. The same concept is apparent in Hebrews 2:3-4, which states that the Lord confirmed the original eyewitness proclamation of the gospel to the Hebrews by miraculous signs. Once again the miraculous works were signs to unbelievers and confirmed the testimony of those who actually "heard the Lord." All of these passages agree in stating that miraculous works, including tongues and healings, were confirmatory signs to unbelievers. This agrees with 1 Corinthians 14:22 where the purpose for the gift of tongues is clearly stated to be a sign to unbelievers. All of these passages agree also in connecting the miraculous works with eyewitness testimony. The testimony is consistent that these signs were to unbelievers, were past, and were closely connected with the original proclamation of the gospel.

Biblical evidence, therefore, demonstrates that apostles and prophets were only for the beginning or foundational stage of the universal church (Eph. 2:20). Biblical evidence also shows that the miracles and signs were only for the first generation of believers and were past by the time some of the New Testament was written (Mark 16:17–20; Heb. 2:3–4). There is biblical evidence that the sign gifts were mainly apostolic and that their purpose was to confirm the original outreach of the church. From the Bible alone we would expect the gifts of apostle, prophet, healings, miracles, and tongues to be temporary.

In addition to the direct biblical evidence, we have also seen that many events described in the book of Acts have not continued in church history such as Pentecost and the blinding of Elymas the sorcerer. This is additional proof that the church is not experiencing all of the phenomena that occurred in the beginning church.

History demonstrates that the gift of tongues ceased about nineteen hundred years ago. No true prophets, healers, or miracle workers fitting the description of those in the New Testament have been seen since that time. The alleged miracles of today do not agree with the miracles in the Bible. The healings of today do not agree with the Bible and often fail, which is contrary to the Bible. Snake handling and the drinking of poison, although seldom practiced, often fail. More decisive than any of these discrepancies is the fact that the alleged gifts of today bear little resemblance to the respective biblical gifts. Church history amplifies this fact, since there are no instances of miracle working, healing, or tongues speaking in all of church history that agree with the biblical descriptions of these gifts. Does the Bible give any information signifying that some gifts were only temporary? Yes, it does, as we have seen in this chapter.

The stated purpose of the sign gifts as confirmatory fits the special need of the initial historical establishment of the beginning church. The Bible implies that some gifts are temporary and states that the gift of apostle is for the beginning church only. The assumption that all gifts are to be present in the church today is entirely gratuitous and is contradictory to the opinion of the church since early times. It is without biblical or historical support. However, the view that some gifts are temporary is a biblical fact and is also supported by the absence of these gifts in history.

✳ ✳ ✳

1. Jack Deere, *Surprised by the Power of the Spirit* (Grand Rapids: Zondervan, 1993), 242.
2. Ibid., 243.
3. Ibid.
4. Ibid., 73.
5. Ibid., 107ff., 278–79. Deere not only totally misrepresents my statements, but seems more than a little confused, since he equates Warfield's arguments against the position that the miracles were necessary for the first three centuries with an argument concerning the miracles in the apostolic age only.
6. 1 Cor. 14:22 uses the anaphoric article to refer to the tongues already under discussion.

CHAPTER 10

Conclusion

An Analysis of the Charismatic Argument

AN ANALYSIS OF THE charismatic position based on their arguments is particularly revealing. In order to better understand their position, let us analyze Deere's argument. His argument is significant primarily because of the nature of his overall approach, but also because of its endorsement and recommendation as a convincing apologetic for the charismatic signs and wonders movement. Although some of the people who endorse Deere's book are considered moderate in their viewpoint, these charismatic leaders and scholars have said that it will "renew your faith and your love for Jesus," "is among the first in the new paradigm in church life," "is narrative theology at its best—at once confessional, testimonial, and biblical," "has all the potential for . . . opening the body of Christ to the full power of God's Holy Spirit," "is a book whose time has come," and is "brilliantly argued, . . . irrefutable."[1] The publisher's catalog says, "This book is for those who are eager to hear what God is saying today."[2] This highly unusual amount of praise makes it certain that these charismatic leaders agree with and highly recommend Deere's book and presentation. Therefore, when we analyze Deere's approach, we are also analyzing an approach that is endorsed and recommended by well-known charismatic scholars and leaders. Thus, we are in effect analyzing the contemporary charismatic approach to this issue, which is why it has been necessary to discuss Deere's book.

The Central Role of Experience

First, there is little question that Deere's book is basically a description of his experience as well as the experiences of others and an exhortation for the reader to seek the same "experience." Fee calls it "narrative theology at its best . . . testimonial," which is simply another way of saying that it describes Deere's "experience."[3] Deere takes up a large portion of his book with a second argument that consists of an unusually strong attack, not on the arguments, but on the honesty and faith of cessationists and any others who do not seek this "experience." He spends a great deal of time and places a great deal of emphasis on these accusations, using almost as much space as he does in describing his "experience." However, the actual argument against the cessationist position receives much less time and emphasis.

Deere issues a plea to avoid insults in the discussion.[4] Thankfully, many charismatic defenders are like Grudem, who has studied the issue and who in my contacts has been gracious and sincere. Despite the plea that we avoid insults, however, Deere's work is filled with attacks against the motives and honesty of noncharismatics. I am not referring to statements that specific cessationist arguments are unscriptural or illogical.[5] Neither am I referring to Deere's use of ridicule when he refers to the cessationist view that miracles helped to establish the church at its beginning as the "rocket launch" theory and to cessationist arguments as equivalent to a "sparrow in a hurricane."[6] Rather I am referring to direct attacks on cessationists themselves rather than attacks on their arguments.

Since many people will only notice his few sentences of disclaimers, I will point out examples. He constantly reiterates the standard charismatic argument that cessationists lack faith. However, his accusations are more extreme. For example, he accuses cessationists of arrogance,[7] of holding their position due to training and tradition rather than due to study of the Scripture,[8] and of knowing that they cannot prove their position from Scripture.[9] He asserts that cessationists rank and teach doctrine as more important than a moral life,[10] make the mind more important than the heart,[11] and foster an intellectual pursuit of doctrinal purity at the expense of personal holiness.[12] He gives the impression that immorality is common in cessationist churches.[13] He states that cessationist churches use God's Word to manipulate and control their members,[14] that they are dishonest in interpreting Scripture,[15] that they are cold, legalistic, self-righteous, and pharisaical,[16] and that they rationalize away biblical commandments.[17] He states that there is more wickedness and sin among "authoritarian" fundamentalist churches than anywhere else in the church and by context gives the impression that he means those churches opposed to charismatic practices.[18] He directly implies that cessationists are deceived, prejudiced, and proud.[19]

He states that no one comes to cessationism simply by studying Scripture.[20] He asserts that the Reformers argued against miracles not for honest reasons but in order to have an argument against the Catholics and to explain a defect in their experience. They "chose" to go with the temporary nature of miracles because they had to come up with a "trick" to prove this. Deere presents the entire approach of the Reformers as basically dishonest.[21] He portrays cessationists as using an antisupernatural hermeneutic and links them with German liberal theologians such as Bultmann. Cessationists are accused of teaching that the Gospels and Acts cannot be used for doctrine, but in actual practice of only using this to apply to certain doctrines, that is, dishonestly.[22] Cessationists are also accused of denying God's ability to heal and of having no real confidence in God's ability to perform difficult healings.[23]

Cessationists are connected with apostasy, legalism, and lukewarm faith,[24] and are accused of trusting their own godliness or tradition rather than Christ's power, wisdom, and goodness.[25] They are afraid to try anything different.[26] They are blind traditionalists, sucking the life out of the church and persecuting any new work of the Holy Spirit.[27] They hold to a defective version of Christianity and love and use cessationism as a convenient way to rationalize their lack of hunger for God.[28] Cessationists are also accused of lacking love, holding to an external obedience to the Bible, justifying lukewarm feelings toward God,[29] and loving the Bible more than God. They are also accused of using cessationism in order to dump whatever they do not like in Scripture into the category of "things that passed out of existence at the end of the first century."[30]

None of the preceding allegations are actually arguments against cessationism; they are merely attacks against cessationists. Unfortunately, much of Deere's book is spent on these attacks rather than argument. Is Deere's plea to avoid insults only to apply to cessationists? When Deere states that we need humility to be right with God, does he mean only cessationists need humility? The great bulk of his book is devoted to his experience and the accusations against cessationists. Not only is it disappointing that Scripture plays a secondary role in his presentation, but it is very disturbing to discover his implication that the Scriptures are insufficient to help believers overcome problems in their lives. He also implies that too much emphasis on Scripture may ruin, and has ruined, the lives of Christians.[31]

Finally, let us look at one specific example of his method of arguing against cessationist statements. I will use one example with which I am very familiar since it is an argument against what I said in my book *Miraculous Gifts*. I have the impression, however, that I am not the only author treated in this fashion. I am taking the time to do this because only someone familiar with the issues and the relevant writings can expose Deere's methodology. Also, I hope that no one will think that I actually believe or wrote the distortions that Deere has attributed to me.

Although the position I presented in my earlier book is probably the most common view and although I had already given scriptural support, Deere introduces his discussion by ridiculing it as the "rocket launch" theory. He asserts that "during his whole discussion Edgar does not cite one verse of Scripture to support his theory."[32] Most of his readers will not be aware of the extremely distorted nature of this statement. I have, previous to this section, cited numerous verses of Scripture specifically supporting the point I am making as well as 260 pages of biblically-based argument. In attempting to lead his readers to believe that I do not rely on Scripture for my arguments, Deere avoids mentioning that I have already established a scriptural foundation. He also fails to mention that I introduce more scriptural evidence directly concerning this subject immediately after this brief section. Even a casual reading of my earlier book and its two sections entitled "Biblical Indications of Change" and "Direct Biblical Evidence That Certain Gifts Are Temporary" should indicate that I do cite Scripture to support my theory.

But an even more glaring distortion is the way in which he attempts to buttress such an accusation. He quotes my book from a section entitled "Logical Considerations." Given this title, I assume that the average reader would expect to find a discussion in this section about logical considerations rather than scriptural ones. However, I make this even clearer when I introduce the section with the words, "Before the direct scriptural evidence is discussed, there are other factors to consider." This section is then followed by the sections, "Biblical Indications of Change" and "Direct Biblical Evidence that Certain Gifts are Temporary." Since I give a great amount of scriptural support both before and after this section, it is not even remotely true that I offer no Scripture to support my position. But it seems particularly misleading to make the accusation that I give no scriptural support when he quotes from a section that I explicitly state covers logical rather than scriptural arguments.

Deere also charges that in my argument I substitute "worldly recognition for God's power." He quotes from me and insinuates that I want to trade God's power for worldly reputation. Then he accuses me of stating that no one could believe the gospel apart from miracles by misusing my rhetorical question, "Who could accept such a message?" However, Deere fails to inform the reader that these statements are from a section where I very specifically state that I am presenting how the original preaching of the gospel would appear from the "human perspective" (i.e., to the unconverted), particularly in evangelistic ministry. At no time do I intimate that this is my view.

Deere also accuses me of stating that miracles were necessary for people to believe in the gospel and that I am, therefore, "dangerously close to demeaning the inherent power of the gospel message." His accusation is patently untrue since nowhere do I state that miracles are or ever were necessary for people to believe in the gospel. This is apparently a distortion of my statement that the need for confirmation was greater at the beginning than it is today, but "need" does not mean "necessary." Even if someone does not know the difference between the words "need" and "necessary," the context alone would make the meaning clear. Why does Deere accuse me of what I did not say?

Deere also takes out of context my rhetorical question, "Who could accept such a message?" Although I specifically said that it was a question from the perspective of an unregenerate human being, he presents it as if it is my belief. Since even the apostle Paul frequently used rhetorical questions in a similar way, Deere should be well aware of how I used this question. In any case, the context in which I used the question should clarify its meaning. Why does Deere present this to his readers as if it is my opinion?

Finally, Deere's accusation that I am demeaning the power of the gospel seems unusually inappropriate for Deere to make. He himself has said that the apostles' miracles were intended to confirm their ministry.[33] He states very clearly that there are situations in the Christian life in which the Word of God and prayer are inadequate. His entire book and position argue that miracles were needed not only at the beginning of the church age but throughout its history, not only for evangelism but for the entire Christian life. In fact he has only words of praise for the leaders of a movement that believes in the necessity of signs and miracles for a full Christian life and that promotes "power evangelism," which also holds to the necessity of signs for an effective evangelistic ministry. In reality, Deere himself and others in the signs and wonders movement are "dangerously close to denying the inherent power" of the gospel message as well as God's Word and prayer. We ask the obvious question, How can all these charismatic leaders and scholars not only condone but so enthusiastically recommend and endorse such an approach? Although many of these scholars are familiar with this issue and should recognize the weakness and improbability of Deere's arguments and biblical interpretations, they still highly praise his work. Personally, I do not believe they are being dishonest. The fact is that they, as well as most charismatics, implicitly believe what Deere says, although they have not stated it explicitly. We must not forget that it is a foundational belief and argument of charismatics that the reason cessationists hold their viewpoint and the reason the miraculous gifts disappeared from history is due to a lack of faith, that is, due to a spiritual defect on the part of noncharismatics. In addition, their main argument has always been based upon their own personal experience. They are so convinced by their experience that it is difficult, if not impossible, for them to believe that anyone open to God could resist and not also seek such an experience. Thus, apparently they believe that only someone resisting God could be against their viewpoint. Since experience is really the determining factor for the charismatic, Scripture is not the final authority on this particular issue.

Since Deere's book is mainly a description of his own experience and it gives only a small place to scriptural argument, it can hardly be called "brilliant, irrefutable." From the charismatic perspective, the spiritual defects of cessationists explain why they do not agree with this experience. Thus, the charismatics can highly recommend such a book because their viewpoint and Deere's are basically the same. However, their experience has no value as evidence to support their view. The same is true of their accusations that cessationists are lacking in faith and spiritually dishonest. Let us now analyze the charismatics' actual argument rather than their assertions about their experience and the defects of cessationists.

The Basic Argument of Charismatics

Charismatics and proponents of the signs and wonders movement insist that their opponents prove by a direct, indisputable statement of Scripture that the New Testament miracles cannot possibly exist today. Otherwise, they claim their experience is the New Testament gift. They reject the evidence that tongues and miracles are highly improbable today. They also reject the suggestion that a logical analysis and deduction of the biblical facts eliminates the possibility of such gifts today.

In another leap of logic, they insist that unless it is specifically stated in Scripture that it is impossible for these gifts to occur today, then their "experiences," no matter how dissimilar to the New Testament gifts, are the genuine gifts. However, even if the miraculous gifts could occur today this still would not prove that the charismatic experiences are, in fact, the gifts.

Let us suppose that someone discovers a farm wagon on an old farm and claims that it is really the chariot of the Ethiopian eunuch described in Acts 8. Some people dispute the claim but are told that unless they can produce evidence to the contrary, namely, a direct biblical statement that the wagon cannot exist in the twentieth century, then they have no reason to doubt the claim. If the skeptics cannot produce a direct biblical statement to the contrary, then the wagon is the chariot. Note that it is not a matter of whether the wagon could theoretically be the chariot, if there were definite evidence to that effect. Rather, unless the Bible directly states that this wagon cannot be the chariot, then apart from any evidence, it is asserted to be the chariot. The assertion, apart from any evidence, is the substance of the claim. Anyone who refuses to accept this and asks for evidence is said to be overly rational and lacking in faith. This is despite the fact that the chariot has not been seen for nineteen hundred years, this wagon is not similar to the chariot, and it is highly improbable that the chariot would reappear at this time. Yet this is the precise manner in which the charismatics argue to support their assertions.

Is It Really Scriptural?

Cessationists provide biblical evidence showing that certain gifts have ceased. They point out verses that demonstrate these miracles are basically apostolic and ceased even by the time that some of the New Testament books were written. Yet charismatics constantly assert that cessationism is not taught in Scripture.

At the same time, charismatics admit that there are no apostles and that no one performs miracles like the apostles. They admit that the gift of apostle ceased and that today's prophets and miracles are not like those in the Bible. In addition, some charismatics teach and admit that infallible prophets or, as Hollenweger says, "biblical prophets" do not exist today. They agree that they did cease, yet argue that the Bible does not teach this. They even invent two theories to explain why the miraculous gifts ceased. Both are an explicit admission that these gifts ceased. While they openly admit that these gifts did cease, nevertheless, they insist that the Bible does not teach this.

If their claim is scriptural, then why do they not interact with cessationist arguments? Why avoid solid arguments by cessationists and mention arguments that most cessationists have never used? Why repeat worn out arguments such as the argument that 1 Corinthians 12:31, 14:1, 39 state that we should seek gifts that we desire? To repeat this time-worn argument without any attempt to mention or answer the solid evidence against it seems unfair to readers who are unaware of the problems.

If Scripture supports charismatic claims, why is it necessary to interpret Ephesians 2:20 in such an unusual way? Do charismatics believe that their position cannot be supported by normal interpretation of passages? Why do they invent an inferior type of prophet for which we have no example in Scripture? Why do they accuse Agabus of mistakes when it can be seen that Agabus's prophecy does not conflict with but reflects what actually happened?

The only way that the present charismatic gifts can be shown to be the scriptural gifts is to show that they are the same thing. If they are scriptural, this should be relatively easy to do. Instead, the charismatics admit they are not the same and attempt to find evidence for substandard gifts in the Bible. While arguing that cessationism is not taught in the Bible, they argue for gifts that do not exist in the Bible. While arguing that cessationism is not taught in the Bible, they admit the basic tenets of cessationism. If the charismatic position is taught in the Scripture, why are they unable to support it by any direct evidence and unable to defend it by normal interpretation?

The Fruit of the Charismatic Movement

What is the fruit of the charismatic movement? As a result of their search for something more, what do the charismatics leave us? Many charismatics claim that their experiences have helped them get their lives on track. However, many who have had the same experiences have come out of the charismatic movement claiming that it was doing just the opposite. Setting aside all of the emotions and experiences, let us examine the true fruit of the charismatic viewpoint. What have they given us? Or another way to approach the situation is to ask, What have they been willing to give up in order to maintain their claims and overcome their feelings of insufficiency?

First, they have given up a sufficient work of Jesus Christ on the cross. Christ's work is reduced to salvation from eternal punishment, but it is not sufficient for living the Christian life. From the perspective of most charismatics, what we have in Christ is not enough. Depending on the particular charismatic perspective, the believer needs a "second work" or "baptism of the Spirit," and repeated "miracles" as evidence that God is working. How many charismatics would be satisfied with one or two "miracles?" According to this perspective the believer cannot live a successful Christian life without repeated evidence that God is working. Thus, to overcome their feeling of insufficiency they give us an insufficient justification.

Second, they leave us with an insufficient Scripture. Deere states that Scripture is helpful, but Scripture and prayer are not enough for some problems. Thus, although the believer is justified and has free access to God and his Word for guidance and motivation, this is insufficient. Not only does Scripture fall short in helping with specific problems, neither it nor the indwelling Spirit are sufficient to give us a passion for God. Instead, we are told, we need signs and miracles. This contrasts with Scripture which supplies us with numerous admonitions and instructions regarding the spiritual life of the believer, yet says nothing about the necessity of miracles or signs for the maintenance of our spiritual lives.

Third, we are now told that Jesus can fail in performing miracles. To defend his charismatic experience, Deere is willing to state that Jesus can and did fail, despite the fact that this contradicts what the Word says about the Son of God and the fact that we have no evidence that he failed. Perhaps Deere's disclaimer that Jesus could not fail in his deity will pacify some, but it is doubtful that most charismatics will be pleased with such an assertion. Scripture, however, gives us a completely different picture of the Son of God. It contains not even the slightest intimation that Jesus could fail. To insinuate that he could do so is pure speculation. The cost of filling up this "feeling" of insufficiency is too high. In fact, it has devalued a proper view of justification, Scripture, and the Lord Jesus Christ.

Fourth, they leave for us a Holy Spirit who presumably distributes defective or deficient gifts to men. The New Testament gift of prophecy, for example, is a lesser gift no matter how much faith or desire the New Testament prophet may have. This seems to be a far less marvelous working of the Holy Spirit than any example described in Scripture.

This is not all. We are also left with a whole order of deficient gifts. The apostles are no more than Old Testament prophets. Their unique office and ability is lost. The New Testament prophets are fallible, cannot be trusted, and are no more than any teacher or counselor, even when speaking by revelation. The miracle workers and healings can often fail but still originate from God. We are confronted with healings of "personality meltdown" as well as "demons" of depression and allergies. Finally, we are left with a "gift" of making unintelligible sounds rather than a miraculous and marvelous ability from the Holy Spirit to speak actual languages for the benefit of others.

The unique nature of the apostolic age is abandoned, and we are informed that the church of that time had all of these weak and inefficient gifts. The gifts rather than being given for a specific ministry for the benefit of others now center in miracles, signs, and other evidences to bolster flagging saints. Ultimately, if we accept all of this, we have paid a terrible price only to justify someone's personal experiences.

Other than enthusiasm, what positive results do we see? Are the charismatics in better physical health than noncharismatics? Unless we count enthusiasm as evidence of spirituality, do we see more spiritual believers? Have the prophecies and visions resulted in any more biblical knowledge? Do charismatics have any new insights on divorce, divine election, or any other difficult questions faced by Bible students?

People within these movements claim to be in direct contact with the Holy Spirit, to have all of the gifts described in the New Testament, and to communicate directly with God, yet they include Roman Catholics, fundamentalists, liberal Protestants, amillennialists, premillennialists, Calvinists, Arminians, noninspirationists, and even those who reject salvation by faith. Ironically, the Spirit with whom they claim to be in direct contact does not seem to be at all concerned to correct these differences, some of which are incorrect and many of which amount to crucial differences. For some inexplicable reason even their alleged direct contact with the supernatural has failed to correct such basic errors. Their experiences have solved no theological issue, produced no advance in biblical knowledge, nor produced more spiritual Christians.

We maintain that we are asked to surrender too much that is important, if not essential. The price we must pay for this experience is entirely too high.

A Proper Response

Should We Be Open to Miraculous Gifts?

Since Matthew 7:22–23 indicates that false workers may perform miracles and exorcisms in Jesus' name, we may potentially open ourselves to false revelations, visions, and signs. First Corinthians 12:1–2 and 1 John 4:1 warn us in regard to the reality of false speakers and prophets. According to 2 Thessalonians and the book of Revelation, there will be false miracle workers. Despite all of these scriptural warnings, charismatics do not appear to have taken them seriously. Instead they emphasize "power" or some other external force. They desire to bypass the rational mind. But the Bible tells believers to verify speakers rather than naively accept them all. To make oneself vulnerable to unknown spirits is spiritually irresponsible, naive, and dangerous. To do this and then be overcome by some spirit is no validation that such is from God. The modern Christian finds it hard to believe that such a spiritual battle is actually going on. However, the Scripture makes it plain that it is and that many believers will be caught in it.

Many noncharismatic pastors and other Christians state that no one should be against the modern charismatic practices unless it can be proved beyond all doubt that they are not genuine. What does the Bible say? It says exactly the opposite. Rather than the attitude that we must *know* something is wrong before we keep it out of our churches and avoid individual practice of it, the Bible says that we should be confident that it is right before we practice it. For example, "Let every man be fully persuaded in his own mind" is commanded in Romans 14:5. In Romans 14:23 we read that "he that doubteth is damned if he eat, because he eateth not of faith: for whatsoever is not of faith is sin." It is sin to eat the food in question unless one is confident it is right. If there is doubt, it cannot be of faith; therefore, it is sin. Pastors and other Christian leaders should not be demanding proof that today's alleged charismatic gifts are wrong. They should be demanding proof that they are right, and until such proof is given, they should not allow such practices in their churches.

Should We Seek Miraculous Gifts?

We are exhorted by those within the charismatic movement to pursue and diligently seek the charismatic experience. If we do so, there is little doubt that we will get the "experience." But this is not the question. The Bible teaches us that we can only exercise biblical faith when we are first confident that we are practicing what God's Word teaches. It is just as clearly taught that when we do something that we are not confident beforehand is pleasing to God, it is not done in faith (Romans 14:5, 23). Thus, to seek the miraculous gifts in order to see what might happen and perhaps receive the "experience" is not exercising biblical faith. It is really just a form of existentialism with a Christian veneer. According to the Bible, faith is belief in what God has said; therefore, the only way one can act in faith is to be confident that God said it. It is not faith to seek the experience and see what happens. No one can seek the miraculous gifts by faith until they are first confident that God gives these gifts today. Even then, they cannot seek the miraculous gifts by faith until they know that God wants believers to seek these particular gifts. However, the Scripture says nothing to indicate that believers should seek any gifts, and it definitely says that Christians should stress the edifying gifts rather than the miraculous gifts. Thus, it seems to be biblically impossible to seek these particular gifts by faith. The question is not whether we can get the experience. Anyone can do this. The question is, Does God's Word clearly teach that we should seek miraculous gifts?

The Seriousness of the Issue

Well-meaning Christians may hold unsound doctrines. For example, both premillennialism and amillennialism cannot be correct; therefore, one of these positions is incorrect. Christians should always be interested in knowing the truth in contrast to error. However, in the case of the charismatic movement, certain physical phenomena occur. Therefore, the issue is more than doctrine. The charismatic is in contact, allegedly, with some spiritual force. These phenomena can only be either from the Holy Spirit, from psychological impulse, from a false spirit, or from a combination of the latter two. If the noncharismatic is wrong, he is missing out on some miraculous events and the experience of tongues. However, these are specifically stated in the Bible to be items of lower priority than the edifying gifts. They are stated to be signs for unbelievers rather than for believers; therefore, the noncharismatic is not missing out on any aspect of the Christian life designed for or necessary for the believer's spirituality. He can still know the correct doctrine and have all the essentials necessary for the fullest Christian life. He can be certain that this noncharismatic emphasis on the edifying gifts instead of the charismatic gifts is scripturally correct. First Corinthians 12:31 says very specifically to be zealous for the greater gifts, the edifying gifts, rather than for the lesser gifts such as tongues. The noncharismatic obviously has all the essentials for spiritual maturity. Charismatics have made no advances in biblical or theological knowledge or any advances in spirituality. Thus, whatever they have is not producing any spiritual qualities that are not also in noncharismatic circles. The noncharismatic is in no way disobedient to the Lord in this matter since believers are never told to seek gifts.

On the other hand, if the charismatic is wrong then he or she is dealing with spiritual forces that are not from God. In addition, there is no way to avoid the fact that this enthusiasm for and seeking of the miraculous is contrary to Scripture. By not seeking the miraculous gifts the noncharismatic places no aspect of the spiritual life in jeopardy. On the contrary, in this he is obeying the biblical instruction. The charismatic is not only disobeying explicit biblical instruction by emphasizing and seeking these gifts but is placing his spiritual life in jeopardy. Thus the noncharismatic loses nothing by being noncharismatic, but the charismatic has nothing to gain by stressing these miraculous gifts.

In Conclusion

Just as there is the concept of what is "politically correct" in the secular realm, so today there is also the concept of what is "correct" in the theological realm. Just as Deere has done, it is common for charismatics to question the faith and sincerity of cessationists. It can safely be said that charismatics are the ones on the attack, and they are persuading many. It is typical today that a book such as Deere's will receive no criticism for this but only glowing reviews. He follows the modern practice of attacking the ability, integrity, and spirituality of his opponents, then occasionally adding a sentence of disclaimer which is supposed to make it all acceptable. I have learned by experience that when a cessationist, on the other hand, merely tries to defend his position without casting any slurs on anyone's faith or integrity, this is not considered "acceptable" and his work is criticized. Of those charismatics referred to in this book, I only know Wayne Grudem personally, whom I consider a friend even though I differ with him on this issue. I certainly would not demean Wayne's character, faith, or spirituality since I know of no flaws in any of them. In fact, from my own experience I would recommend him as a Christian gentleman and scholar. However, I know of cessationists who also fit this description. The issue is not the character of those on each side but which position best fits the Bible. This is a plea to consider these arguments from that perspective.

Do we need to be surprised by an experience from God in order to compensate for feelings of deficiency? No! God has given us everything we need for faith and godliness. We lack nothing. Any feeling of lack is not due to a lack of anything that God has for us. It is due to our own frailty, our own failure to avail ourselves of what God has already done for us. Rather than seeking a surprise, we should be satisfied with what we have in Christ and live the Christian life in conformity to His written Word.

✳ ✳ ✳

1. Comments of Wayne Grudem, Ralph Neighbour, Jr., Gordon D. Fee, C. Peter Wagner, John White, and R. T. Kendall from on the dust jacket and on the introductory page of Jack Deere's, *Surprised by the Power of the Spirit* (Grand Rapids: Zondervan, 1993).
2. Zondervan 1994 catalog of Academic and Professional Books, 18.
3. Fee, on the dust jacket and introductory page to *Surprised*.
4. Deere, *Surprised*, 177.
5. Ibid., 105.
6. Ibid., 102, 107.
7. Ibid., 46.
8. Ibid., 47–53.
9. Ibid., 55–56.
10. Ibid., 81.
11. Ibid., 81–82.
12. Ibid., 82.
13. Ibid., 83.
14. Ibid.
15. Ibid.
16. Ibid., 84.
17. Ibid., 85.
18. Ibid.
19. Ibid., 85–86.
20. Ibid., 99.
21. Ibid., 100–101.
22. Ibid., 112–13.

23. Ibid., 126.
24. Ibid., 147.
25. Ibid., 169.
26. Ibid., 171.
27. Ibid.
28. Ibid., 184.
29. Ibid., 185.
30. Ibid., 190.
31. Ibid., 28–29.
32. Ibid., 108.
33. Ibid., 67.

Bibliography

Abbott-Smith, G. *A Manual Greek Lexicon of the New Testament.* New York: Charles Scribner's Sons, 1921.

Anecdota Graeca.

Aristophanes. *Ranae (The Frogs).* Loeb Classical Library.

Aristotle. *Poetics.* Loeb Classical Library.

———. *Rhetoric.* Loeb Classical Library.

Arndt, William F. and F. Wilbur Gingrich. *A Greek-English Lexicon of the New Testament.* Chicago: University of Chicago Press, 1947.

Augustine. *The Epistle of St. John.* Vol. 7. *The Nicene and Post-Nicene Fathers.* 13 vols. Grand Rapids: Eerdmans, 1956.

Bales, James D. *Pat Boone and the Gift of Tongues.* Searcy, Ark., 1970.

Barrett, C. K. *A Commentary on the Second Epistle to the Corinthians.* London: Adam and Charles Black, 1973.

———. *The First Epistle to the Corinthians.* New York: Harper and Row, 1968.

Beare, F. W. "Speaking With Tongues." *Journal of Biblical Literature* 83 (September 1964): 229–46.

Behm, Johannes. "Glossa." *Theological Dictionary of the New Testament,* edited by Gerhard Kittel, Gerhard Friedrich, and Geoffrey W. Bromiley, and translated by Geoffrey W.

Bromiley, 10 vols. Grand Rapids: Eerdmans, 1964, 1976. 1:719–26.

———. "Kainos." *The Theological Dictionary of the New Testament*, edited by Gerhard Kittel, Gerhard Friedrich, and Geoffrey W. Bromiley, and translated by Geoffrey W. Bromiley, 10 vols. Grand Rapids: Eerdmans, 1964, 1976. 3:447–50.

Blass, F. and A. DeBrunner. *A Greek Grammar of the New Testament and Other Early Christian Literature*. Translated and revised by Robert W. Funk. Chicago: University of Chicago Press, 1961.

Broadbent, E. H. *The Pilgrim Church*. London: Pickering and Inglis, 1963.

Broadus, John. "Style of Mark xvi. 9–20 as bearing upon the question of genuineness." *The Baptist Quarterly* (July 1869).

Brown, Francis, S. R. Driver, and Charles A. Briggs. *A Hebrew and English Lexicon of the Old Testament*. Oxford: Clarendon Press, 1962.

Bruce, F. F. *The Acts of the Apostles*. London: Tyndale, 1951.

Brumback, Carl. *What Meaneth This?* Springfield, Mo.: Gospel Publishing House, 1947.

Bruner, Frederick Dale. *A Theology of the Holy Spirit*. Grand Rapids: Eerdmans, 1970.

Burgon, John William. *The Last Twelve Verses of Mark*. Reprinted. Grand Rapids: Associated Publishers and Authors, n.d.

———. *The Revision Revised*. London: John Murray, 1883.

Carson, D. A. *Showing the Spirit*, Grand Rapids: Baker, 1987.

Cate, B. F. *The Nine Gifts of the Spirit*. Des Plaines, Ill.: Regular Baptist Press, 1965.

Charles, R. H. *The Apocrypha and Pseudepigrapha of the Old Testament*. 2 vols. Oxford: Clarendon Press, 1968.

Chrysostom. *Homilies in First Corinthians*. Vol. 12. *The Nicene and Post-Nicene Fathers*. 13 vols. Grand Rapids: Eerdmans, 1956.

Clement of Rome. *Epistle to the Ephesians*.

Conzelmann, Hans. *First Corinthians.* Hermeneia. Philadelphia: Fortress, 1975.

Cranfield, C. E. B. *The Epistle to the Romans.* ICC. 2 vols. Edinburgh: T. & T. Clark, 1975–79.

Currie, S. D. "Speaking in Tongues." *Interpretation* 19 (July 1965): 274–94.

Cutten, George B. *Speaking With Tongues.* New Haven, Conn.: Yale University Press, 1927.

Dayton, Donald W. "Asa Mahan and the Development of American Holiness Theology." *Wesleyan Theological Journal* 9 (Spring 1974): 60–69.

Deere, Jack. *Surprised by the Power of the Spirit.* Grand Rapids: Zondervan, 1993.

Delitzsch, Franz. *Biblical Commentary on the Prophecies of Isaiah. Biblical Commentary on the Old Testament,* by C. F. Keil and F. Delitzsch. Reprint ed. Grand Rapids: Eerdmans, 1967.

Delling, Gerhard. "Battalogeo." *Theological Dictionary of the New Testament,* edited by Gerhard Kittel, Gerhard Friedrich, and Geoffrey W. Bromiley, and translated by Geoffrey W. Bromiley, 10 vols. Grand Rapids: Eerdmans, 1964, 1976. 1:597.

Demosthenes. *Against Leptines.* Loeb Classical Library.

Dillow, Joseph. *Speaking in Tongues.* Grand Rapids: Zondervan, 1975.

Diodorus Siculus. *Library of History.* Loeb Classical Library.

Dollar, George W. "Church History and the Tongues Movement." *Bibliotheca Sacra* 120 (October 1963): 316–21.

Donnegan, James. *A New Greek and English Lexicon.* Philadelphia: Butler and Williams, 1844.

Durasoff, Steve. *Bright Wind of the Spirit: Pentecostalism Today.* Englewood Cliffs, N.J.: Prentice-Hall, 1972.

Edgar, Thomas R. *Miraculous Gifts.* Neptune, N.J.: Loizeaux, 1983.

Eliade, Mircea. *Shamanism.* New York: Bollinger Foundation, 1964.

Ervin, Howard M. *These Are Not Drunken, As Ye Suppose.* Plainfield, N.J.: Logos, 1968.

Euripides. *Hecuba.* Loeb Classical Library.

Eusebius. *Ecclesiastical History.* Vol. 1. *The Nicene and Post-Nicene Fathers,* 2d series. 14 vols. Grand Rapids: Eerdmans, 1952.

Farmer, W. R. *The Last Twelve Verses of Mark.* Cambridge: The University Press, 1974.

Faupel, David. *The American Pentecostal Movement.* Wilmore, Ky.: Asbury Seminary, 1972.

Ford, Josephine Massyngberde. "The Charismatic Gifts in Worship." *The Charismatic Movement,* edited by Michael Hamilton. Grand Rapids: Eerdmans, 1975.

Gesenius, W. and E. Kautzsch. *Gesenius' Hebrew Grammar.* Translated by A. E. Cowley. 2d ed. Oxford: Clarendon Press, 1963.

Godet, F. L. *The First Epistle to the Corinthians.* 2 vols. Reprint. Grand Rapids: Zondervan, 1971.

Goodman, Felicitas D. *Speaking in Tongues.* Chicago: University of Chicago Press, 1972.

Gromacki, Robert G. *The Modern Tongues Movement.* Philadelphia: Presbyterian and Reformed, 1967.

Grudem, Wayne. *The Gift of Prophecy in the New Testament and Today.* Westchester, Ill.: Crossway, 1988.

Gundry, Robert H. "Ecstatic Utterance (N.E.B.)?" *Journal of Theological Studies* 17 (October 1966): 299–307.

Harnack, Adolf. *History of Dogma.* Translated by Neil Buchanan. 7 vols. New York: Russell and Russell, 1958.

Harrisville, Roy A. "Speaking in Tongues." *Catholic Biblical Quarterly* 38 (January 1976): 35–48.

Hastings, James, ed. *Encyclopedia of Religion and Ethics.* New York: Charles Scribner's Sons, n.d.

Hatch, Edwin and Henry A. Redpath. *A Concordance to the Septuagint and the Other Greek Versions of the Old Testament.* 2 vols. 1897. Reprint. Graz, Austria: Akademische Druck-u Verlagsanstalt, 1954.

Hodge, Charles. *An Exposition of the Second Epistle to the Corinthians.* Grand Rapids: Eerdmans, n.d.

Hodges, Zane C. "The Purpose of Tongues." *Bibliotheca Sacra* 120 (July–September 1963): 226–33.

Hoekema, Anthony. *What About Tongues Speaking?* Grand Rapids: Eerdmans, 1966.

Hollenweger, Walter J. *The Pentecostals.* London: SCM, 1972.

Hughes, Philip E. *Paul's Second Epistle to the Corinthians.* NICNT. Grand Rapids: Eerdmans, 1962.

Ignatius. *To the Philadelphians.*

Irenaeus. *Against Heresies.* Vol. 1. *The Ante-Nicene Fathers.* 8 vols. Buffalo: Christian Literature, 1885.

Jackson, Samuel Macauley, ed. *The New Schaff-Herzog Encyclopedia of Religious Knowledge.* Grand Rapids: Baker, 1969.

Jorstad, Erling. *The Holy Spirit in Today's Church.* New York: Abingdon, 1973.

Josephus. *Against Apion.* Translated by William Whiston. Grand Rapids: Kregel, 1963.

Kydd, Ronald A. *Charismatic Gifts in the Early Church* Peabody, Mass.: Hendrickson, 1984.

———. "Novatian's *De Trinitate,* 29: Evidence of the Charismatic?" *Scottish Journal of Theology* 30 (1977): 313–18.

Lampe, G. W. H. *A Patristic Greek Lexicon.* Oxford: Clarendon Press, 1961.

Lederle, Henry I. *Treasures Old and New: Interpretations of "Spirit-Baptism" in the Charismatic Renewal Movement.* Peabody, Mass.: Hendrickson, 1988.

Liddell, Henry George and Robert Scott. *A Greek-English Lexicon.* Revised by Henry Stuart Jones. Oxford: Clarendon Press, 1968.

Lommel, Andreas. *Shamanism.* New York: McGraw Hill, 1967.

Mackie, Alexander. *The Gift of Tongues.* New York: Doran, 1921.

Mallone, George. *Those Controversial Gifts.* Downers Grove, Ill.: InterVarsity, 1983.

M'Clintoch, John and James Strong, eds. *Cyclopaedia of Biblical, Theological, and Ecclesiastical Literature.* 12 vols. 1887. Reprint. Grand Rapids: Baker, 1970.

McCone, R. Clyde. "The Phenomena of Pentecost." *Journal of the American Scientific Affiliation* 30 (September 1971): 83–88.

McGee, Gary B, ed. *Initial Evidence: Historical and Biblical Perspectives on the Pentecostal Doctrine of Spirit Baptism.* Peabody, Mass.: Hendrickson, 1991.

McGonigle, Herbert. "Pneumatological Nomenclature in Early Methodism." *Wesleyan Theological Journal* 8 (Spring 1973): 61–72.

Marcus Aurelius Antoninus. *The Meditations of Marcus Aurelius Antoninus.* Translated by John Jackson. Oxford: Clarendon Press, 1906.

———. *Thoughts.* Loeb Classical Library.

Menzies, William W. *Anointed to Serve.* Springfield, Mo.: Gospel Publishing House, 1971.

Michel, Otto. "Oikodomeo." *The Theological Dictionary of the New Testament,* edited by Gerhard Kittel, Gerhard Friedrich, and Geoffrey W. Bromiley, and translated by Geoffrey W. Bromiley, 10 vols. Grand Rapids: Eerdmans, 1964, 1976. 5:136–44.

Mitchell, Kurt. "Dispensing with Scofield." *Christianity Today,* 10 January 1994.

Morris, Leon. *The First Epistle of Paul to the Corinthians.* Grand Rapids: Eerdmans, 1958.

Moulton, James Hope and George Milligan. *The Vocabulary of the Greek New Testament.* London: Hodder and Stoughton, 1930.

Moulton, W. F. and A. S. Geden. *A Concordance to the Greek Testament.* Edinburgh: T. & T. Clark, 1963.

Nee, Watchman. *The Normal Christian Church Life.* Washington, D.C.: International Students, rev. ed. 1969.

Nichol, John Thomas. *Pentecostalism.* New York: Harper and Row, 1966.

Novatian. *De Trinitate.* Translated by Robert Ernest Wallis. Vol. 5. *The Ante-Nicene Fathers.* 8 vols. Buffalo: Christian Literature, 1887.

Origen. *Against Celsus.* Vol. 4. *The Ante-Nicene Fathers.* 8 vols. Buffalo: Christian Literature, 1885.

Paulk, Earl P. *Your Pentecostal Neighbor.* Cleveland, Tenn.: Pathway, 1958.

Philo. *De Decalogo (On the Decalogue).* Loeb Classical Library.

———. *De Specialibus Legibus (On the Special Laws).* Loeb Classical Library.

———. *De Vita Mosis (Moses).* Loeb Classical Library.

———. *Quis Rerum Divinarum Heres (Who is the Heir of Divine Things?).* Loeb Classical Library.

Plato. *Timaeus.* Translated by J. Harwood. Vol. 7. *Great Books of the Western World.* 54 vols. Chicago: Encyclopaedia Britannica, 1952.

Plutarch. *Moralia, De Pythiae Oraculus (The Oracles at Delphi).* Loeb Classical Library.

———. *Moralia, Isis and Osiris.* Loeb Classical Library.

Polybius. *The Histories.* Loeb Classical Library.

Quintillian. *Institutio Oratorio.* Loeb Classical Library.

Ramsay, W. M. *A Historical Commentary on St. Paul's Epistle to the Galatians.* London: Hodder and Stoughton, 1899.

Rengstorf, K. H. "Didaktikos." *Theological Dictionary of the New Testament,* edited by Gerhard Kittel, Gerhard Friedrich, and Geoffrey W. Bromiley, and translated by Geoffrey W. Bromiley, 10 vols. Grand Rapids: Eerdmans, 1964, 1976. 2:165.

Robertson, Archibald and Alfred Plummer. *A Critical and Exegetical Commentary on the First Epistle of St. Paul to the Corinthians.* ICC. 2d ed. Edinburgh: T. & T. Clark, 1914.

Robinson, D. W. B. "Charismata Versus Pneumatika." *Reformed Theological Review* 31 (May–August 1972): 49–55.

Robinson, Edward. *Greek-English Lexicon of the New Testament.* Boston: Crocker and Brewster, 1836.

Samarin, William J. *Tongues of Men and Angels.* New York: Macmillan, 1970.

Sarles, Ken. "An Appraisal of the Signs and Wonders Movement." *Bibliotheca Sacra* (January–March 1988).

Schaff, Philip. *History of the Christian Church.* 8 vols. Reprint. Grand Rapids: Eerdmans, 1952.

Sellers, C. Norman. *Biblical Conclusions Concerning Tongues.* n.p., 1970.

Sextus Empiricus. *Against Grammarians.* Loeb Classical Library.

Sharp, Granville. *Remarks on the Uses of the Definitive Article in the Greek Text of the New Testament.* 3d ed. Philadelphia: B. B. Hopkins, 1807.

Smith, Charles R. *Tongues in Biblical Perspective.* Winona Lake, Ind.: BMH Books, 1972.

Sophocles, E. A. *Greek Lexicon of the Roman and Byzantine Periods.* Cambridge: Harvard University Press, 1914.

Stafford, Tim. "Testing the Wine From John Wimber's Vineyard." *Christianity Today,* 8 August 1986.

Stagg, Frank, E. Glenn Hinson, and Wayne E. Oates. *Glossolalia.* Nashville: Abingdon, 1967.

Stauffer, Ethelbert. "Agapao." *Theological Dictionary of the New Testament,* edited by Gerhard Kittel, Gerhard Friedrich, and Geoffrey W. Bromiley, and translated by Geoffrey W. Bromiley, 10 vols. Grand Rapids: Eerdmans, 1964, 1976. 1:49–55.

Strong, James. *The Exhaustive Concordance of the Bible.* Nashville: Abingdon, 1890.

Sweet, W. W. *The Story of Religion in America.* New York: Harper and Brothers, 1930.

Synan, Vinson. *The Holiness Pentecostal Movement in the United States.* Grand Rapids: Eerdmans, 1971.

Tertullian. *Against Marcion.* Vol. 3. *The Ante-Nicene Fathers.* 8 vols. Buffalo: Christian Literature, 1885.

Thayer, Joseph Henry. *Greek-English Lexicon of the New Testament.* Grand Rapids: Zondervan, 1962.

Thistleton, A. C. "The Interpretation of Tongues: A New Suggestion in the Light of Greek Usage in Philo and Josephus." *Journal of Theological Studies* 30 (April 1979): 15–36.

Thucydides. *History of the Peloponnesian War.* Loeb Classical Library.

Toussaint, Stanley D. "A Method of Making a New Testament Word Study." *Bibliotheca Sacra* 120 (January–March 1963): 35–41.

———. "First Corinthians Thirteen and the Tongues Question." *Bibliotheca Sacra.* 120 (October–December 1963): 311–16.

Turner, Nigel. *Syntax.* Vol. 3. *A Grammar of New Testament Greek.* James H. Moulton. 4 vols. Edinburgh: T. & T. Clark, 1963.

Tylor, Sir E. B. *Religion in Primitive Culture.* 2 vols. New York: Harper and Brothers, 1958.

Virgil. *The Aeneid.* Translated by James Rhoades. Vol. 13. *Great Books of the Western World.* 54 vols. Chicago: Encyclopaedia Britannica, 1952.

Wallace, Daniel A. *Exegetical Syntax*, a preliminary draft, 1994.

———. "The Article-Noun-kai-Noun Plural Construction." *Grace Theological Journal* (Spring, 1983).

Warfield, B. B. *Counterfeit Miracles.* 1918. Reprint. London: Banner of Truth, 1972.

Wesley, John. *The Journal of John Wesley.* Chicago: Moody Press, n.d.

White, R. Fowler, "For the Sparrow in the Hurricane: A Review of Jack Deere's *Surprised by the Power of the Spirit.*" A paper presented to the 1994 Annual meeting of the Evangelical Theological Society, Eastern Region, Philadelphia.

Williams, John. *The Holy Spirit: Lord and Life-Giver.* Neptune, N.J.: Loizeaux, 1980.

Windisch, Hans. "Barbaros." *Theological Dictionary of the New Testament,* edited by Gerhard Kittel, Gerhard Friedrich, and Geoffrey W. Bromiley, and translated by Geoffrey W. Bromiley, 10 vols. Grand Rapids: Eerdmans, 1964, 1976. 1:546–53.

Scripture Index

Genesis
15:12 157

Exodus
18:16 .... 80, 88

Numbers
11:25 125

Deuteronomy
18:11 215
18:18 69
18:20–22 ... 65, 203
18:22 ...... 80, 115

1 Samuel
10:5 125
19:20 125
19:24 125

2 Samuel
7 65

1 Kings
3:9 .... 80, 88
14:06 52
18:29 125

2 Kings
9:6–10 133
9:11 132–33

2 Chronicles
15:8 66
32:32 66

Ezra
5:1 66

Psalms
50:4 88
81:1–3 88

Proverbs
31:9 88

Ecclesiastes
3:16–18 88
3:18 88

Isaiah
2:7 172
5:14 167
6:9–10 68
28:10 ..... 125, 141
28:11 ....141, 153, 175, 198, 202–203
29:24 168–69
32:4 168–69

Ezekiel
17:20 88
20:35–36 88
34:20 88
34:22 88
44:24 88

Joel
3:2 88

Zechariah
3:7 .... 80, 88

Matthew
3:7 78
6:7 178
6:7–8 178
7:22–23 .....67, 118, 260
8:28–29 92
8:5–13 91
9:22 92
9:29 92

10:1 106
10:2 53
11:13 66
12:39 186
13:11 144
13:14 68
13:58 104
15:7 66
17:19–20 92
19:28 62
26:53–54 103
26:67–68 67

Mark
1:23–26 91
2:5 92
3:21 147
5:34 92
6:5 92
6:5–6 104
7:6 67
8:12 186
9:17–20 92
9:17–29 91
10:52 92
14:65 67
16:14–20 47
16:15 89
16:15–17 167
16:15–20 . 89–91, 243, 272
16:17 . . . . . 126, 150, 153, 168, 182
16:17–18 134
16:17–20 . . . .
   35–36, 39, 50, 185, 187, 273
16:18 90
16:20 . . . . 46, 91, 182, 264, 272
16:9–20 . . . . 115, 118, 273

Luke
1:14–17 67
1:67 67
2:36 102
5:3 102
5:17 101–2
5:20 92
6:13 53
7:39 69
7:50 92
8:48 92
9:1–10 53
11:7 103
14:20 103
16:2 103
17:11–19 91
17:5 53
18:42 92
22:64 67
24:44–53 47

John
1:38 162
3:16 196
4:19 69
5 102
5:1–16 92
5:19 102–3
5:21 103
6:14 69
7:40 69
7:52 69
9:17 69
11:51 67
12:12 86
14:13–14 179
20:30–31 89
21:16–17 47

Acts
1 85
1–2 63
1:1–14 53
1:2 53
1:2–3 53
1:4–5 47
1:8 . . . . 47, 53
1:21–22 53
1:21–26 53
1:22 53
2 . . . . . . 109, 148–49, 191, 205, 218
2:2 151
2:4 . . . . 126, 128, 131, 132, 134, 142, 148, 150
2:4–11 . . 126–28, 135, 142, 148, 150, 152–53, 168, 175, 182–83, 185, 187, 193, 195
2:5 129
2:6 . . . . 126, 129–130, 158
2:6–11 134
2:7 129
2:8 128–29
2:8–11 126
2:9–11 129
2:11 150
2:12 129
2:13 142
2:14 132
2:16 151
2:17–18 67
2:22 93
2:30–31 . . . . . . 70, 85
2:31 131
2:38 182
2:42 54
2:43 93
3:3–16 93
3:5 93
3:6 93

3:12 104
3:16 93
3:18–25 ..... 70, 85
4:9–10 93
4:14 93
4:16 93
4:18 159
4:29–30 .... 94, 115
4:33 53
4:35–37 54
4:36–37 57
5:1–11 54
5:2 54
5:5 .... 94, 239
5:5–10 98
5:10 .... 94, 239
5:12 .... 54, 114
5:12–16 94
5:17–32 53
5:18 53–54
5:19 95
5:29–32 53
6:2–6 54
6:8 95
7:52 70
8 ..... 114, 119, 256
8:1 54
8:5–40 54
8:06 95
8:13 95
8:18–24 41
8:22 41
9 .... 54, 74
9:1–9 239
9:1–18 95
9:27 54
9:32–34 95
9:36 162
9:36–42 96
10 ......109, 149, 191
10:01–48 187
10:10–15 239
10:34–43 130
10:41–42 53
10:43 70
10:44 130
10:44–46 ... 182–83
10:45 193
10:45–46 182
10:46 ...126, 133–34, 150–51, 153, 168, 180–81, 185, 187, 193
11 74
11:1 .... 54, 187
11:14 187
11:14–18 187
11:15–17 ......134, 164, 187
11:15–18 182
11:17 ..... 134, 182
11:27–28 70
11:28 83
12:7–9 95
12:6–11 239
13:1 .... 70, 109
13:11–12 ....96, 98, 239
14:3 ... 96, 115, 243
14:4 .... 54, 56
14:8–10 96
14:9–10 104
14:14 ...... 54, 56
15:2 .... 54, 78
15:4 78
15:6 78
15:22–23 78
15:32 ... 70, 83, 109
16:4 78
16:26 95
17:14–15 56
17:19 131
18:24 112
19 ....68, 109, 149, 191
19:1–6 188
19:3–6 185
19:06 ......109, 126, 134, 150–51, 153, 168, 182–83, 193
19:11–12 97
19:2 193
19:3 200
19:6 ....67, 150, 193, 238
20:7–12 105
20:9–12 97
20:17–28 99
20:17–38 97
20:32–38 97
21 74
21:4 83–84
21:9 67
21:10 70
21:10–13 84
21:11 81
21:12–13 83
21:27–35 82
22:1–14 92
26:22–23 70
26:25 132
27 97
28 97
28:1–6 97
28:8–9 97
28:17 82
8:5–25 187

Romans
1–11 172
1:1 55
1:5 62
1:7 55
3:19 131
5:5 232

5:10 232	4:6–7 170	12:18 43
6:23 232	4:19–21 ...... 62, 85	12:22 39
8:23 178	5:1–5 113	12:28 ....36, 62,
8:26 ... 178–180, 196	5:3–4 .... 62, 85	182, 191
10:14 109	6:5 80	12:28–29 ..... 71, 98
12 .... 111, 233	7:7 232	12:28–30 36
12–16 47	8:10 170	12:29 68
12:1–2 172	9:1–2 .... 57, 85, 246	12:29–30 191
12:3–8 41	9:14 186	12:30 ...... 150, 166
12:4–5 40	10:1–12 186	12:30–31 36
12:4–8 ...... 47, 191	10:11 186	12:31 ..41–43, 47, 50,
12:6 ....36, 40,	10:12 186	182, 192, 194, 235,
68, 110–11, 115	11 80	257, 262
12:6–8 35–36,	11–14 68	12:39 235
39, 116, 233	11:4–5 67	12:4 182
12:6:8 47	12 ....36, 40,	13 .... 39, 44
12:7 36	43–44, 115, 182,	13:1 ....136–37, 139,
14 167	192, 236	150, 153, 167, 195
14:5 260–61	12–14 ....35, 42,	13:1–3 .. 51, 107, 136
14:22 176	47, 49, 51, 126, 134–	13:1–4 115,
14:23 260–61	35, 139, 153, 162,	166–67
15:16 98	188, 191, 196, 206,	13:2 .... 68, 136
15:18–19 98	223, 237	13:3 137
15:18–20 241–42	12:1 36	13:4–7 167
15:19 ....46, 98,	12:1–2 ..... 206, 260	13:8 .....68, 138–39,
115, 241, 247	12:3 ... 121, 135, 153	180
15:20 55	12:4 ..... 36, 40, 135	13:8–10 167
16 55	12:4–5 233	13:8–13 243–44
16:07 .... 54, 77	12:4–10 182	13:9 .... 67, 136
	12:4–31 191	13:10 19
1 Corinthians	12:7 ..... 38–39, 105	14 ....39, 42, 44,
1:1 55	12:8 40	51, 67, 107, 109,
1:5–7 108	12:8–10 ..... 36, 233	115, 124, 126, 130,
1:7 .... 49, 108	12:9 36	139–40, 143, 146,
1:22–23 186	12:1 36	148–50, 152, 155,
1:26–29 170	12:10 .... 40, 68, 98	163, 165, 169–70,
2:4 98	12:11 .... 38, 41, 43	181, 183, 188, 192,
2:6 131	12:12–30 40–41	194
3:1–3 .... 49, 190	12:14 ... 36, 114, 135	14:1 41–42,
3:3–7 170	12:15 43	44, 47, 50–51, 167,
3:18 170	12:17 40	194, 235, 257
3:21 170	12:17–22 40	14:1–03 174

Scripture Index

14:1–39 67
14:1–40 139
14:2 . . . . 135, 143–44, 150, 162, 174–77
14:3 . . . . 64, 131
14:3–4 169
14:3–5 67
14:4 . . . . 50, 140, 170–71, 173
14:4–6 150
14:5 . . . . 68, 140, 162, 170–71
14:6 . . . . 68, 131, 170
14:7–9 144–45
14:9 . . . . 170, 174
14:11 142
14:12 . . . . 41–42, 140, 192
14:13 . . . . . . 140, 145, 150–51
14:13–14 171
14:14 . . . 39, 145, 171
14:14–17 174
14:15–16 . . . 171, 174
14:16 . . . . 130–31, 135, 170
14:17 170–71
14:18 . . . . . . 111, 150, 162, 191
14:18–19 184
14:19 . . . . . . 131, 140, 145, 150, 181
14:21 . . . 141–42, 184
14:21–22 195
14:21–23 141
14:22 . . . . 39, 68, 106, 141–42, 147, 150, 153, 162, 168, 175, 181–82, 184–86, 195, 197, 248–49
14:23 . . . . 140–42, 145, 150, 222
14:24 . . . . . . 87, 145
14:26 . . . . . . 194, 246
14:26–35 44
14:26–36 106
14:27 150
14:27–28 44
14:27–33 213
14:27–36 151
14:28 . . . . 140, 146, 176–77, 194
14:28–30 233
14:29 . . . . 80, 131
14:29–31 . . . . 45, 143
14:29–32 . . 68, 71, 85
14:30 . . . . 79, 143
14:31 . . . . 67, 103
14:32 . . . 45, 143, 214
14:32–33 143
14:33 . . . . 45, 140, 143, 151, 195
14:34 . . . . . . 131, 140
14:34–35 . . . . 80, 195
14:35 140
14:36 79
14:37 . . . . 62, 68
14:39 . . . . 41–42, 44, 47, 50, 150, 162, 192, 194, 235, 257
14:40 . . 146, 151, 195
15:5–8 57
15:6 57
15:7 234
15:7–8 60
15:8 . . . . 60, 246
15:13 147

2 Corinthians

1:1 55
1:11 232
5:8 102
5:13 147–48
6:7 98
8:23 55
10:1 147
10:10 147
11:13 234
12:1 147
12:1–7 62
12:1–11 85
12:11 57–58
12:11–12 242
12:12 . . . . 57, 85, 98, 241–42, 246–47
13:2–3 . . . . 62, 85
13:10 . . . . 62, 85
15:13 147

Galatians

1–2 62
1:1–2 55
1:7 77
1:17–2:10 54
1:18 54
1:19 56
2:1 54
2:7–9 56
2:8 56
2:9 56
3–5 109
3:1–5 109
3:2 109
3:5 . . . . 99, 109
5:13 196

Ephesians

2:20 19
4:11–12 39
5:3–7 33
1–3 172
1:3–14 48
1:9 144
1:17–19 48
2 60
2:18 179

2:19–22 60
2:20 .... 59–60, 71–72, 76–78, 85, 240, 247–48, 257
3:5 .... 62, 71–72, 76–77, 85
3:12 179
4:1 172
4:7–12 172
4:8 36
4:11 ...... 35–36, 47, 72, 116, 173, 190, 191, 233
4:11–14 46
4:16 .... 38, 198
4:1–5 33
5:15–19 48
5:18 48
5:32 144
6 48
6:18 174

Philippians
1:1 55
2:1–8 196
2:25 .... 56, 77
3:8 137
4:4–6 174

Colossians
1:1 55
1:2 77
2:2 144
4:2 174

1 Thessalonians
1:1 55–56
2 56
2:18 56
2:7 56
3:1–12 56
3:5 56

5:12 77
5:17 174
5:18 109
5:20 68

2 Thessalonians
1:1 55
2:9 .... 98, 241

1 Timothy
1:18 68
1:20 85
2:1, 8 174
2:7 62
3:1 43
3:9 144
4:14 68
5:23 116

2 Timothy
1:6 111

Titus
1:12 72

Philemon
1 77

Hebrews
1:1–2 .... 74, 75
2:3–4 .... 19, 99, 115, 240–41, 243, 247–48
2:5 131
3:1 ...... 74–75, 77
6:5 98

James
1:16–17 114
5:14 ... 106, 115, 225
5:14–15 ..... 99, 116, 118

5:14–16 .... 100, 117
5:16 100

1 Peter
1:1 77
1:10 .... 66, 72
4:10 .. 36, 38–39, 107
4:10–11 ...... 35–36, 47–48, 116, 191

2 Peter
1:4 48
1:20–21 68
2:16 159
2:18 159
1:11 77

1 John
4:1 .... 81, 260

Jude
14 66
17–18 61

Revelation
1 61
1:3 68
2–3 118
2:2 103
4:11–5:14 180
10:11 .... 66, 68
11:06 68
11:3 .... 68, 213
11:6 68
19:10 68
21:14 62
22:10 68
22:18–19 68
22:6 72
22:7 68

Subject Index

Anabaptists, radical 213–14
Andronicus 54–55, 57, 77
Angelic language 123, 136–39, 156, 183, 195
Apollos 112
Apostles
 definition 52–53
 missionary activity 54
 performed miracles 37, 54, 57–59, 62, 93–100, 105, 107–9, 117, 242
 recognition 56
 uniqueness of 62–63
 witnesses of the resurrection 53, 57, 59, 61
Apostleship
 as a gift 63, 85, 112, 232–34
 temporary nature of 61, 232, 240, 246–49
 testimony of church history 63
Augustine 207–8, 223–25, 235

Baptism of the Spirit 12, 14, 182, 186–88, 258
Barnabas 54, 56–57, 234

Casting out demons 36, 67, 89–90, 95, 97, 243, 247
Cessationists
 definition of 13
 logical basis 234
Cessationism 14, 18, 19, 22–23, 25–27, 101, 252, 256, 257
Cevenols 202, 209–11
Charismatic movement
 history of 13–15, 201–18
Chrysostom 202, 206–8, 223, 235

Dialektos 127, 129–30, 132, 149–50
Discerning of spirits 36, 69

Gifts
 as signs 133–34, 247
 cessation of 239–49, 256–57
 control of 44–46
 edifying gifts 42–44, 63, 192, 261
 definition 9–10, 233
 diversity of 40

281

for ministry 46– 49, 100, 105, 166, 181–83, 188–90, 196
inferior gifts 100–107
importance of 46
priority of 191–92
seeking gifts 41–43
temporary nature of some gifts 239–49
to be exercised in love 167, 196
Glossa
classical usage 121–23
in pre–Christian Judaism 123, 126
New Testament usage 126–48
Old Testament usage 125–26
Septuagint usage 124–25
word study 121, 141
Glossolalia 122–24, 126, 130, 133, 145, 154–55, 178, 201–3, 207–11, 213, 215–17, 219–22, 225–26

Healing 36, 90, 91, 99, 104–7, 110, 112, 115–18
heteros 128, 131–32

Irenaeus 202–3, 205–6, 218
Irvingites 201–2, 214

Jansenists 201–2, 209, 211–13

laleo 128–131, 150
Latter–day rain 12–13, 32

Miracles
authenticate the gospel 105
biblical facts 89–100

failure 17–18, 90, 92, 106–7, 114
Montanus 201–5, 210, 223

Neo–Pentecostalism 13, 207, 218

Pagan
oracles 123, 132–33, 145–46, 219,
religions 122–123, 154–55, 162, 180, 219–22, 226
Pentecost
day of 151
Pentecostal movement 12–13, 18, 63–64, 72, 100, 165, 217–18, 222
Prophecy
fallible 30, 100–101
in the assembly 45, 64, 71, 85
women 80, 130–131, 210
Prophet
definition 36, 63–65
direct revelation 45, 65–68, 70, 72, 79, 84
fallible 62, 72, 73, 80, 81, 84, 85, 256, 259
foretelling 63, 65–67, 70, 72, 84–85
test of 66

Quakers 201–2, 215–16

Ranters 202, 215–16

Shakers 201–2, 215–16, 218
Shamans 154, 220
Signs and Wonders

Subject Index

definition 113–114
movement 13–14, 250, 255

Taking up serpents 36, 89
Tertullian 205–6
Tongues
  at Pentecost 133, 135, 142, 148–49, 170, 175, 184, 187, 238
  benefit for the believer 46, 167, 189, 190, 196
  benefit for the unbeliver 39–40, 47, 49, 115–16, 167, 183–185
  biblical restrictions 165
  control 16–18, 23, 42, 44–46, 143, 151, 155, 195, 213–14, 222, 251
  devotional 165–69, 171, 174, 176–78, 181, 183–84, 188–89, 194–96
  definition 121–123, 134–135
  ecstatic 121–36, 140–48, 150–64, 178–79, 189, 195, 203–5, 209, 215, 219–22, 225–26
  in history 201–29, 234, 246, 249
  in the assembly 42–45, 64, 71, 139–40, 145, 148–50, 165, 169–70, 174–77, 181, 183–84, 188, 194–95
  interpretation 67, 139–40, 168, 175, 183, 188–89, 195–96, 206, 219
  ministry to unbelievers 40, 181–184, 187, 241–42
  physical phenomena 151, 195, 261

  praise 165, 168–69, 174–81, 184
  prayer 174–80, 184
  seeking the gift 193–94
  self–edification 138, 166, 169–73
  sign to unbelievers 39, 142, 148–50, 168, 173, 175, 181–86, 188–90, 194–95, 248
  speaking to God 144, 174–75, 178
  spiritual vitality 190, 196
  women 140, 146, 181, 188, 195, 214

Wesley, John 273

Xavier 201–2, 208

Zeloo 42–44, 51
Zeteo 42–43